THE LIBRARY OF DISTINCTIVE SERMONS

❦

VOLUME SIX

GARY W. KLINGSPORN
General Editor

MULTNOMAH PUBLISHERS • SISTERS, OREGON

Executive Editor
Stephen E. Gibson, B.A.

General Editor
Gary W. Klingsporn, Ph.D.

Associate Editor
Mary Ruth Howes, M.A.

THE LIBRARY OF DISTINCTIVE SERMONS, VOLUME 6
published by Questar Publishing Direct
a division of Multnomah Publishers, Inc.
© 1997 by Multnomah Publishers

International Standard Book Number: 1-57673-159-6
Design by David Uttley
Printed in the United States of America

ALL RIGHTS RESERVED
All sermons in this book are used with permission of the individual writers. No part of this publication may be reproduced, stored in a retrieval system, or transmitted, in any form or by any means—electronic, mechanical, photocopying, recording, or otherwise—without written permission from Questar Publishing Direct, except in the case of brief quotations embodied in critical articles and reviews.

Scripture quotations are from:
The King James (Authorized) Verson of the Bible (KJV), 1611
The Holy Bible, New International Version (NIV) © 1973, 1984 by International Bible Society, used by permission of Zondervan Publishing House.

The New Revised Standard Version Bible (NRSV) © 1989 by the Division of Christian Education of the National Council of the Churches of Christ in the United States of America.

The Revised Standard Version (RSV) © 1946, 1952 by the Division of Christian Education of the National Council of the Churches of Christ in the United States of America.

The New Testament in Modern English, Revised Edition (PHILLIPS) © 1972 by J. B. Phillips.

The Message © 1993 by Eugene H. Peterson.

New American Standard Bible (NASB) © 1960, 1977 by the Lockman Foundation.

The New English Bible (NEB), © The Delegates of the Oxford University Press and the Syndics of the Cambridge University Press 1961, 1970; used by permission.

The Revised English Bible (REB) © 1989 by Oxford University Press and Cambridge University Press.
The Good News Bible: The Bible in Today's English Version (TEV) © 1976 by the American Bible Society.
Quotations from Allan Gurganus, "It Had Wings," *White People,* © 1990 by Allan Gurganus, published by Alfred A. Knopf, are used by permission of Random House.

Quotations from John Duckworth, "Angels We Have Heard on High," *Stories That Sneak Up on You,* © 1987 by John Duckworth, are used by permission of Fleming H. Revell/Baker Book House.

For information:
MULTNOMAH PUBLISHERS, INC.•POST OFFICE BOX 1720•SISTERS, OREGON 97759
Library of Congress Cataloging-in-Publication Data

The library of distinctive sermons/Gary W. Klingsporn, general editor. v. <4>:25 cm.
Includes bibliographical references. ISBN 1-57673-159-6 (v. 6) 1. Sermons, American.
2. Preaching. I. Klingsporn, Gary W.
BV4241.L47   1997   96-173243   252—DC20

97 98 99 00 01 02 03 — 10 9 8 7 6 5 4 3 2 1

Table of Contents

Preface 6

Introduction 8

Contributing Editors 12

Jesus' Final Exam
  Rev. Dr. Thomas G. Long 13

How Much More?
  Rev. Dr. Richard L. Eslinger 27

Becoming What We Are
  Rev. William C. Green 39

A Letter to Harold
  Rev. Dr. Kenneth A. Corr 55

The Text You Live By
  Rev. Dr. Mark E. Yurs 67

Angels We Have Heard Nearby
  Rev. Dr. R. Wayne Stacy 79

Jesus the Rabbi?
  Rev. Dr. Mark D. Roberts 95

When the Night Is Darkest
  Rev. Dr. John Killinger 111

Coming Up Short
  Rev. Jeffrey M. Lindsay 123

All That Lives Must Die
  Rev. Dr. John Mark Jones 137

A Crazy, Holy Grace
  Dr. Gary W. Klingsporn 153

A Comfort, Deep and Lasting
  Rev. Dr. F. Dean Lueking 167

FREEDOM!
: *Mary Ruth Howes* 181

THE CHRISTIC JOURNEY
: *Rev. Dr. Gilbert R. Friend-Jones* 189

EASTER FEAR
: *Rev. Dr. David C. Fisher* 209

DEALING WITH NEGATIVE ATTITUDES
: *Rev. Dr. Gary A. Furr* 225

STEPPING OFF THE CURB
: *Rev. Dr. Michael P. Halcomb* 239

RELIGIOUS CLOSED-MINDEDNESS
: *Rev. John G. Hargis* 253

LED BY A LAMB
: *Rev. Dr. C. David Matthews* 267

WHEN THE WINE GIVES OUT
: *Rev. Dr. William J. Ireland, Jr.* 279

TOPICAL INDEX 289

SCRIPTURE INDEX 293

For all who preach

How beautiful upon the mountains
are the feet of the messenger
who announces peace,
who brings good news,
who announces salvation,
who says to Zion, "Your God reigns."

ISAIAH 52:7, NRSV

PREFACE

The idea of *The Library of Distinctive Sermons* originated in painful practical circumstances rather than in an academic context. A pastor friend of mine went through a prolonged ordeal of tension and conflict with a congregation before he was terminated primarily "because his sermons were dry and hard to follow." As a new, young pastor, he was doing the best he could without the benefit of much experience in ministry. By and large, however, he was not connecting with the congregation in his preaching. The congregation became impatient and was less than compassionate in handling the situation. This led to a bitter parting of the ways.

As a layperson sitting in the pew and aware of the tension, I felt the pain on both sides of the issue. I began to ask myself what more might be done to assist ministers in learning and sharing the insights which contribute to effective preaching. *The Library of Distinctive Sermons* originated from that experience. It is a resource designed to promote vital and effective preaching through the sharing of sermons and insights on preaching by working pastors.

The Library of Distinctive Sermons brings together a collection of powerful contemporary sermons of diverse style and content, along with careful reflection as to what makes each sermon effective, and how each sermon relates to biblical, theological, and practical ministry issues facing pastors today.

It is important to note that we have chosen not to engage in an academic critique of each sermon. No sermon is flawless. We have chosen good sermons and have asked some simple questions: What makes each of these sermons good? What can we learn from the creative elements of style and content in each sermon to assist us in the art of preaching?

Discussion of these questions in the Comment section following each sermon makes *The Library of Distinctive Sermons* unique among sermon publications. We have enlisted primarily working pastors for the task of commenting on each sermon. While there are many excellent books on homiletics, we discovered that few are written by pastors for pastors. The Comment sections are a means of sharing practical ideas and insights from pastor to pastor in a way that is helpful to pastors of all backgrounds and levels of experience. Our desire is that *The Library of Distinctive Sermons* will enhance your own process of developing new sermons and contribute to the continual renewal of your preaching ministry.

Many people gave of their talents to this series. First, we are deeply grateful to all of the preachers whose sermons appear in this volume. Their commitment to the proclamation of the gospel and their willingness to share their sermons "out of context" with a wider audience beyond their local congregations, have made this series possible. Special thanks go also to those pastors who shared their wisdom, perspectives, and insights in the Comment sections. Appreciation goes as well to the General Editor, Dr. Gary W. Klingsporn, whose special gifts and talents in communication and publishing are reflected throughout the series. Special thanks to Mary Ruth Howes, who, as Associate Editor, kept us all in line with her wonderful editorial expertise in the written word.

In a rapidly changing consumer culture which is increasingly visually oriented, the sermon "competes" as never before with a multiplicity of media and voices vying for our attention. In a culture where the entertainment world sets the pace and celebrities are often the measure of "success," preaching today is subjected to intense scrutiny and is regarded by many as outmoded, especially if it does not "entertain." And yet, since the beginning of Christianity, followers of Jesus Christ in every age have found preaching the most powerful and effective form of communicating the gospel. Indeed, there is something about the gospel that seems to demand this particular expression, this form of communication, and none other. Through preaching, lives continue to be saved and transformed, liberated, healed, and reconciled. We pray that *The Library of Distinctive Sermons* will encourage you and help you create new and effective ways of proclaiming the gospel of Jesus Christ in today's world.

Stephen E. Gibson
Executive Editor

INTRODUCTION

Welcome to Volume 6 of *The Library of Distinctive Sermons*. As we did in the first five volumes of this series, we are pleased to offer here another twenty outstanding sermons with comment.

Much has been written on the subject of preaching. Seldom, however, do we find good sermons brought together with commentary on why those sermons constitute effective proclamation of the gospel. Among the literature available today, we can read sermons. Or, we can read about preaching. But seldom do we have the opportunity to do both at the same time: to read good sermons, and to reflect on the art of preaching as it is embodied in those sermons.

The Library of Distinctive Sermons is designed to promote the enrichment of preaching through the sharing of good sermons and careful analysis of their style and content. The purpose is to read a sermon and ask, "What makes this sermon effective as the proclamation of God's Word?" The philosophy underlying this series is that, whether we are novices or seasoned preachers, we can always learn from others who preach. One of the best ways to do that is to "listen" to others, to observe how they preach, and pick up on some of the best of what they do in a way that is natural and appropriate in our own preaching.

Each of the sermons in this volume is accompanied by a Comment section. Here working pastors reflect on what makes each sermon distinctive and effective. To some extent, of course, this is a very subjective undertaking. What makes a sermon "good" or "effective" to one person is not always the same in the opinion of others. Given the subjectivity involved, it would be easy to avoid ever undertaking the task of serious reflection about our preaching. However, in the Comment sections in this volume, the writers have taken the risk of opening the dialogue about what constitutes effective preaching. There is much to be gained in this process: new ideas and techniques, new perspectives on texts, creative forms and structures, new stories and illustrations for preaching.

It is one thing to hear or read a good sermon and to have some sense of why we like it. But how often do we give serious analytical reflection, asking what we can learn from a sermon? *The Library of Distinctive Sermons* provides an opportunity for the enrichment of preaching through thoughtful consideration of why each sermon has been done in the way it is done.

In the Comment sections in this series the writers reflect on the style and content of each sermon. They look at such things as the genre and structure of the sermon, its use of biblical texts, illustrations, literary or rhetorical techniques, tone, and language. They also comment on how the content of each sermon proclaims biblical faith; remains true to the biblical text; reflects sound theology; deals with faith questions; addresses ethical and social issues; and shows the relevance of the gospel in today's world.

The Comments are presented in a fairly nontechnical way. The focus of this series is not on an academic analysis or critique of sermons, nor is the focus on theoretical aspects of communication and homiletics. The purpose of this series is to offer practical reflection aimed at stimulating our thoughts and improving our preaching in very practical ways.

The format of this volume is simple. Each sermon is presented as closely as possible to the original form in which it was preached. Obviously, in moving from the original oral medium of preaching to the written form represented here, some editing has been necessary to facilitate literary style, clarity, and comprehension.

The Comment following each sermon assumes that every effective sermon includes at least three basic elements. First, every sermon addresses questions relating to the problems and needs of the human condition. Second, every good sermon has a thesis and makes an assertion. It proclaims truth from the Scriptures using one or more biblical texts. Third, every good sermon invites people to respond or motivates them to think, act, or believe. These preaching elements can be described in many different ways using varieties of language. In their Comments the writers commonly use the terms Text, Problem, Proclamation, and Response (or Invitation) to refer to these elements of sermonic structure and content.

In the Comments, then, you will notice frequent discussion of the following items which are intended as helpful tools of reflection and analysis:

1) Text. How does the preacher interpret and apply the biblical text(s) in the sermon? What techniques are used? What insights into the text(s) are found in the sermon?

2) Problem. What human problem, need, question, or life situation does each sermon address? How is the problem of the human condition understood and presented in the sermon?

3) Proclamation. How does the sermon proclaim the good news of the Christian gospel? What is the truth or "kerygma" drawn from the Scriptures and applied to the human situation?

4) Response. How does the sermon invite us to respond? What does the preacher invite, urge, or encourage us to believe or to do? What motivation is there to act or to change, and how does this flow out of the interpretation of the biblical text(s), the human problem, and the proclamation of the gospel?

5) Suggestions. Each Comment section concludes with some practical suggestions for thought or discussion, for further reading, or for incorporating some of the insights from the sermon into one's own preaching.

The Library of Distinctive Sermons features a wide variety of sermon styles and subjects. This is important in a series designed for the enrichment of preaching. You will undoubtedly like some of the sermons more than others. You will react differently to different sermons. You may agree or disagree with some of the Comments. But all of these reactions can be learning experiences. So as you read, ask yourself: "What do I think about this sermon? Why do I feel as I do?" Interact with the material! Reflect on your own preaching and ministry as you enjoy this volume. Then the sermons and Comments will become a valuable resource for your own ministry.

It is important to remember that each of the sermons in this volume was preached in an original context, most of them in congregations on Sunday mornings. Each was spoken with the presence and guidance of the Holy Spirit to a particular people in a particular time and place. Each sermon had a life of its own as the Word of God in that specific moment.

While the sermons that appear here are removed from those original contexts, there is much we can learn from them. Whenever possible, the attempt has been made to acknowledge significant aspects of the original context. But now these sermons appear in a new context. God can use them in this context to speak home to our hearts and to create new understanding and possibilities for ministry.

The apostle Paul wrote, "So then faith comes from what is heard, and what is heard comes through the word of Christ" (Rom. 10:17, NRSV). It is in and through the preached word of Christ that God directs us to faith in Christ and imparts to us the gift of faith. In preaching, the wonderful work and mystery of God take place: The living Christ becomes present through the preached word. Bonhoeffer said, "The word of Scripture is certain, clear, and plain. The preacher should be assured that Christ enters the congregation through those words which he [or she] proclaims from the Scripture...."[1] Preaching is a holy calling filled with the mystery and promise of God. We do well to give all the careful time and attention we can to this holy task, while always giving ourselves to God. As Augustine said of preaching, "Lord, give me the gifts to make this gift to you."

Gary W. Klingsporn
General Editor

Note
1. Dietrich Bonhoeffer, *Worldly Preaching*, ed. Clyde E. Fant (Nashville and New York: Thomas Nelson, Inc., 1975), p. 130.

CONTRIBUTING EDITORS

Richard A. Davis is Teaching Pastor of Hope Presbyterian Church in Richfield, Minnesota.

Gary W. Downing, D.Min., is Evangelism Pastor of Faith Covenant Church in Burnsville, Minnesota.

Richard L. Eslinger, Ph.D., is Pastor of Trinity United Methodist Church in Niles, Michigan.

Marianna Frost, D.Min., is Professor of Bible and Religion at Athens State College in Athens, Alabama.

Gary A. Furr, Ph.D., is Pastor of Vestavia Hills Baptist Church in Birmingham, Alabama, and adjunct instructor in New Testament at Samford University.

William J. Ireland, Jr., Ph.D., is Pastor of Briarcliff Baptist Church, Atlanta, Georgia.

K. Thomas Greene, D.Min., is Pastor of Greenwich Baptist Church, Greenwich, Connecticut.

Debra K. Klingsporn is a writer, editor, and former public relations and marketing executive.

Paul D. Lowder is a retired United Methodist minister who has served North Carolina churches in Davidson, Greensboro, Eden, and Charlotte.

James J. H. Price, Ph.D., is Professor of Religious Studies at Lynchburg College, Lynchburg, Virginia.

Peter J. Smith is Pastor of First Congregational Church of Thomaston, Connecticut.

Karen F. Younger is Minister to Families and Youth at Faith United Methodist Church, Downers Grove, Illinois.

Jesus' Final Exam

LUKE 20:27–40

REV. DR. THOMAS G. LONG
FRANCIS LANDEY PATTON PROFESSOR OF PREACHING
PRINCETON THEOLOGICAL SEMINARY
PRINCETON, NEW JERSEY

Rev. Dr. Thomas G. Long

Jesus' Final Exam

LUKE 20:27–40

I am not sure that the students who are here this morning would agree with me, but I believe I am right about the following statement. As a teacher I have discovered that the most difficult part of any test or examination is not providing the correct *answers* but asking the right *questions*. The questions on a test can turn out to be tricky when we teachers intended them to be straightforward, vague when we were striving for clarity, or easy-as-pie when we were attempting to create a challenge. It is well known that students are openly terrified they are going to give dumb answers; it is not as well known that we teachers are secretly terrified we are going to ask stupid questions.[1]

I heard recently about a geology professor at another university who was writing a question for his final exam. I am sure he was intending for the students to answer this question with the names of various minerals and rock formations, because the question he asked was: "Name three things which are found on the earth which are not found on the moon." One of the students, knowing a silly question when he saw it, responded, "Roller skates, Bruce Springsteen, and the Republican Party." As I said, the most difficult part of any examination is asking the right questions.

There is a deeper and broader sense in which this statement is true.

Asking the right questions is difficult not only because the questioner might slip up and ask a dumb question, but also because every question we ask reveals something important about ourselves. Questions are not neutral, either morally or intellectually. Every time we ask a question, whether it's teacher to student, police to suspect, parent to child, or friend to friend, we reveal our own assumptions, our convictions about what is important, our notions of truth, our own angles of vision, our biases, our concerns, our limitations. Contained in the question is the assumed world of the questioner.

In his popular book *Between Parent and Child*, Haim Ginott told of Andy, a ten-year-old boy, who asked his father, "What is the number of abandoned children in Harlem?"

His father, a chemist and an intellectual, was pleased by his son's curiosity and responded with a long lecture on the topic. He then looked up the figure.

Andy, however, was not satisfied. "What is the number of abandoned children in New York City?...In the United States?...In Europe?...In the world?"

Finally the father realized that his son was not concerned about a social problem; he was concerned about being abandoned himself. He was not looking for statistics but for reassurance.[2] In the question is the assumed world of the questioner.

You can see this relationship between question and assumption at work in our text today. This is a story about a question some religious leaders, the Sadducees, asked Jesus. In fact, the twentieth chapter of Luke contains a series of questions put to Jesus, each question trickier than the previous one. The twentieth chapter of Luke can be seen as Jesus' final rabbinical exam. And as in all exams, the ones asking the questions are being tested as fully as the one who is questioned.

The last, and most difficult, question they asked Jesus was this: Suppose there was a woman who married a man who had six brothers. The man unfortunately dies before they are able to have any children. Now the Scripture, the law of Moses, is clear about this situation. One of the brothers must take the widow as *his* wife so they can have children for the brother in order to continue the brother's line. So, brother number one steps forward and marries the woman. But, alas, he dies too, before children are born, so brother number two steps forward. He dies too. Then comes brother three, brother four, and on to the sixth. All brothers die. Then the woman dies. There are eight funerals, but no children. Now, here's the question: In the resurrection, whose wife will the woman be?

This is a trick question in multiple choice form. Jesus can choose A or B. If he chooses A, he picks one of the husbands: In the resurrection she will be the wife of, say, her first husband—or of her last husband. It doesn't matter, really. The point is that Jesus, in choosing A selects *one* of them. But the problem with choice A is that it's virtually indefensible. She was equally the wife of all seven brothers. A won't work. So that leaves B. Jesus can choose B, and this is the one the Sadducee questioners secretly hope he will be forced to choose. B is: You got me there, fellows; she can't be the wife of all of them in the resurrection; she can't be the wife of only one of them in the resurrection, so *reductio ad absurdum*, there must be no resurrection.

As I said, this is a trick question. Jesus is given two equally unacceptable choices—A or B. But Jesus surprises his questioners: He chooses...C! Which is to say, he doesn't *answer* the question; he *challenges* it. In the question is the assumed world of the questioner, and Jesus calls that world into question.

What is the world assumed in the question? To begin with, there is the assumption that if there is a resurrection, the woman will belong to somebody in it. A first-century husband had something like property rights over a wife, and this woman had belonged to seven men in her life. So the only question is, Which one will she belong to in the resurrection? In the question is the assumed world of the questioner, and in that world the woman is some man's possession. As Justo and Catherine Gonzalez point out, "For all intents and purposes, the story could have been about seven brothers who successively inherited a cow from each other."[3]

In her book *Jesus According to a Woman*, Rachel Wahlberg observes that, by challenging this assumed world, Jesus' response creates a new and gracious world for the woman. She writes,

> A woman hears Jesus declaring that she is not someone's property, that she has equal status in the resurrection, that she has a position not relative to anyone else.... At least in heaven she will not achieve her identity through someone else.[4]

In a larger sense the question Jesus was asked assumes that God's future is simply an extension of what we can see, do, and understand in the present. God's future is merely "more of the same." The woman was somebody's wife in the present, and it follows logically that she will be somebody's wife in the future. In short, the assumed world of the question is closed to the possibility that God's future might be radically new, radically different from the present constraints on human life. But Jesus does not answer the question; he goes behind the question to challenge the assumption. "In this age people marry; but in that age, the age to come, they do not. In this age people die; in the age to come there is no death. In this age people are children of pain and suffering; in the age to come they are children of the resurrection—children of God. The age to come is radically new; it is not more of the same."

I know of a church which several years ago formed a committee on hunger. When the committee got together to discuss the issue of hunger, the members were struck by the sheer size of the hunger problem in their city. Many in the city were hungry, and the committee was forced to ask the question, "What can we possibly do about a hunger problem of such magnitude?" Now notice, the assumed world of the questioner is in the question: What can *we* do about the problem of hunger?

Nonetheless, several projects were launched, including a special hunger offering to be taken on the last Sunday of every month. People were to march forward during the singing of the final hymn to place their gifts in baskets, and the money would be spent to alleviate hunger in the city. This program was a great success; thousands and thousands of dollars were given—more than anyone had dreamed. But as the months wore on, there was discouragement. Some of the money was misused by the agencies to which it was given. Some was unaccounted for, and, most of all, it was difficult to see any real impact from the program. People were being fed, to be sure, but the lines of hungry people only got longer. In short, for all of their efforts to make a dent in the problem of hunger, every tomorrow looked just like another today—more of the same.

One Sunday, however, during the time for the hunger offering, something unusual happened. People were coming forward bringing dollar bills, envelopes with checks; children marched down with dimes and quarters. Suddenly a woman whom no one recognized got up from her pew and moved toward the basket in the front. She was not very well dressed and she carried no offering in her hand. When she got to the basket, she paused for a moment, folded her hands, and prayed. That was it; she had no money to place in the basket. She had only a prayer. The prayer was her offering, but it was something else as well. It was a visible reminder to all who saw her that their gifts were not solutions to the problem of hunger in the city; they were, in their own way, prayers for God to bring in a new age. The woman's action challenged the assumption that gifts to feed the hungry are wasted unless they somehow "solve" the problem of hunger. The offerings were, rather, signs of the new age, the age which will arrive not because we make it come, but because God is bringing it to be.

Most of the religious questions we know how to ask are too small and too narrow:

> In the resurrection, whose wife will she be? A or B?
> How can we put an end to hunger? What are the solutions?
> Why do bad things happen to good people? Give me some reasons.
> What is God's will for me today? This or that?

These are not evil questions; they are simply shortsighted questions. In such questions there are the assumptions of the questioners, namely that our questions have answers which can be woven out of the possibilities we can see, responses forged from the circumstances we can touch. Choose one—either A or B.

The hard news is that neither A nor B is correct. The good news is that on the other side of our questions there is, not an answer, but God—who makes all things new, who brings a future more redemptive than we can imagine.

Much about the life of Charles de Gaulle is well known. What is not so widely known is that Charles and Evonne de Gaulle were the parents of a Down's syndrome child. She was a treasure to them; she was a concern for them. Regardless of what was occurring in the affairs of state, Charles arranged his life so that he and Evonne would have some time almost every day with their infant daughter. After they had put her to bed, and the child had fallen asleep, Evonne would often ask, "Oh, Charles, why couldn't she have been like the others?"

As had been predicted by the physicians, the de Gaulle's daughter died in her youth. There was a private, graveside Mass. After the priest had pronounced the benediction, all present began to leave the grave—except for Evonne. In her grief, she could not pull herself away. Charles went back to her, gently touched her on the arm, and said, "Come, Evonne. Did you not hear the blessing of the priest? Now she is like the others."

"In this age," Jesus said, "people marry, are given in marriage, and die." In this age people shiver through the night with no place to call home, find themselves deprived of human dignity, and perish from loneliness. That is the way it is in this age. In this age people have to make answers for their questions out of the material at hand—either A or B. "But in that age…" Jesus goes on to say, and so points toward an age not governed by the limitations or presumptions of this age. The promise of the gospel is that the possibilities for human life are not contained in the assumptions of "this age." Because, by the grace of God, there is "that age"—the age to come—this present age loses its power to condemn. Even now God's new age is gathering us into its embrace, setting us free, and claiming us as God's own sons and daughters.

Notes
 1. This sermon was preached at the Duke University Chapel and originally published in *The Princeton Seminary Bulletin,* New Series, Vol. 8 (February 1987), pp. 47–52.
 2. Haim G. Ginott, *Between Parent and Child* (New York: Avon Books, 1965), pp. 21–22.
 3. Justo L. Gonzalez and Catherine G. Gonzalez, *Liberation Preaching* (Nashville: Abingdon Press, 1980), p. 65.
 4. Rachel Conrad Wahlberg, *Jesus According to a Woman* (New York: Paulist Press, 1975), p. 65.

Comment

Thomas Long would probably not appreciate hearing his message described as a "New Age" sermon. However, if the biblical "new age" is that time in the future when God has promised he will restore creation and resolve the problems of the human condition, then this sermon is worthy of the label "new age" in the appropriate biblical sense. The sermon is laudable for its success in lifting us out of the mire of our troubled age and showing us the way to God's future age.

Long's message is both inspirational and practical. It connects the past, present, and future by presenting an ancient teaching of Jesus, addressing our present assumptions, and directing us toward a coming age. This message is for both the head and the heart. Delivered in a style which makes it accessible to all kinds of listeners, the sermon never once sacrifices the core of its biblical and theological content. Long makes easy listening of a hard teaching and then wraps it all up with a happy (read: hopeful) ending. Perhaps this explains why he is well suited to be a preaching professor at a seminary the likes of Princeton. The guy is good!

What Human Problem Is Addressed?

Long recognizes a problem all of us face in life. We want the right answers, but we don't ask the right questions. According to Long, the problem lies in our assumptions. They can be all wrong. If we come to the Bible expecting pat answers to perplexing questions, we'd best beware. Our perceptions of reality may be out of whack. If our frame of thinking is incompatible with God's, we're in for some frustrations. In fact, there is even a risk in our posing the questions. As Long says, "The ones asking the questions are being tested as fully as the one who is questioned." We may think we are putting God to the test, but in doing so, we are actually exposing our own presuppositions to divine scrutiny. The result? We often discover that our presuppositions are wrong.

The root of our problem is pride. We tend to run God through the wringer whenever we come up against a problem we can't solve, a crisis we can't resolve, or a pain we can't soothe. Long reminds us how risky it is to put God to the test. We who "see through a glass darkly" are in no position to examine the Almighty. We are the ones with clouded notions and warped perceptions, not God. Before we give up on God, we need to reassess our own assumptions.

How Does the Preacher Use Scripture?

The sermon is rooted in a single text, the Sadducees' interrogation of Jesus in Luke 20:27–40. Long calls it "Jesus' final rabbinical exam," and he skillfully dissects it to reveal its many layers. On one level, this text is a study of the mind of Jesus and his methods for handling confrontation. On another level, the text reveals the Saducean mind-set and the tendency to maintain control by confining theology to carefully constructed boxes. On still another level, the text is a glimpse into the mysterious realm of the Divine, where worldly laws no longer apply and human judgments are rendered meaningless. On top of all this, Long shows this text to be a corrective for our own narrow-mindedness. It reveals the Sadducee within each of us.

Long's method is to walk us through the entire text, paraphrasing each verse by spicing it up with modern parlance. All the while, he remains faithful to the original context without burdening his listeners with too much higher textual criticism or peripheral minutiae. Via the text, Long focuses on our tendency to think wrongly and to ask the wrong questions. The Sadducees were inclined to do just that. This discourages us from looking down our noses at those who dare to question or oppose Jesus. It isn't an "us/them" thing. In this text, "they" (the Sadducees) are "us." Like them, we approach Jesus with errant assumptions.

It is helpful to have Long delineate the options presented to Jesus by the Sadducees. A brief explanation of the role of women in the ancient world gives a fuller appreciation of the challenge put to Jesus in their question. Interestingly enough, Long decides not to spend time on the fact that the Sadducees did not believe in the reality of resurrection. Although he implies they may have been trying to maneuver Jesus into a denial of the resurrection, this is, apparently, of secondary interest to Long. Many commentators would view this as the primary emphasis of this text, but Long points us to something more basic underlying the story: presuppositions about God. Long's treatment of Luke's text is less about the party politics and theologies in ancient Judaism and more about the limitations each of us brings to our evaluation of Jesus.

How Is the Good News Proclaimed?

The final lines of the sermon capture the theme that runs throughout the message. The promise of the gospel is that the possibilities for human life are not contained in the assumptions of "this age." Because, by the grace of God, there is "that age"—the age to come—this present age loses its power to condemn. "Even now God's new age is gathering us into its embrace, setting us free, and claiming us as God's own sons and daughters." Here is the declaration of a "new age" awaiting all who believe. It is an age of clarity and justice, where the burdens of this world are lifted off our shoulders and placed squarely on God's.

What will the coming new age mean for each of us? For women and others who have been relegated to second-class status in this life, it will mean full equality. For those who suffer from physical and/or mental impairment (such as the de Gaulles' Down's syndrome daughter), it will mean health and wholeness. For those who fear, it will mean trust and security. For each of us, the promise of the coming age will mean something different. But for all of us, one thing will be the same. When we feel ourselves trapped between two unacceptable options—what Long calls "either A or B"—God's grace will reveal a liberating option that has never occurred to us. And why hasn't it occurred to us? Because we are prisoners of our own false assumptions, just as the Sadducees were. We have blinders on.

How May We Respond?

Long gives us several courses of action. First, we would do well to reexamine our assumptions about God and about other people. We may be less than satisfied with the answers we're currently finding in life because we've been asking the wrong questions. Second, we need to put on new glasses to see things from a clearer and more Christlike perspective. To illustrate, Long tells the story of the woman who prays over the hunger offering, showing that sincere effort of any kind on behalf of others is never wasted. Even when a final solution is not reached, there is merit in every act, every prayer, every gesture of charity.

Third, we who grope for intellectual satisfaction from God should sift through our unsatisfactory attitudes and adopt a new humility regarding the things we cannot know in this life. Instead of assessing blame and losing faith, we might want to accept our limitations and turn the rest over to God. In the end, our best response may be to stop assuming we're responsible for knowing it all and doing it all in this life. God is in control, and God will tie up the loose ends in the age to come. The sermon is thus a powerful theological statement of the sovereignty of God.

What Can We Learn from This Sermon?

- There is a refreshing lightness of spirit about this message. It is neither heavy-handed nor pedagogical, though the preacher is a professional teacher and handles sophisticated theology on a regular basis. The sermon is accessible to everyone because Long throws in a dash of humor ("Three things not found on the moon...Roller skates, Bruce Springsteen, and the Republican Party"). He also tells three poignant real-life stories (the child who fears abandonment, the hunger committee, and the death of the de Gaulle child) to draw us in and engage our emotions. In the end, the message seamlessly weaves these elements into the scriptural text and gives us the sense that each piece supports the whole.
- The rule for every writer is to "write what you know." The rule for

every speaker is to "know your audience." Long obeys both rules. As a seminary professor, he works and lives in an environment of questions and answers, and he draws from this context in building the framework of his message. The sermon was originally delivered in a chapel service at Duke University to students and faculty who share in the academic enterprise. It's obvious Long has taken good advantage of their mutual environment for the enrichment of his message.

- This sermon has a rare combination of left brain and right brain appeal. For the left-brainers (rational and linear thinkers), Long methodically delineates the theological bind in which Jesus finds himself in Luke 20. He lays it out like a math problem or a judicial argument. Clear and logical. Then, refreshingly, he tells several evocative stories to draw in the right-brainers (creative and non-linear thinkers). Consider evaluating your own presentations using the right brain/left brain measure, to see if you are weighted too heavily on one side or the other. Be aware that any given audience is made up of some who respond best to logic and others who look for imagination. The preacher who can appeal to both sides of the brain will be most effective.

Richard A. Davis

How Much More?

2 KINGS 5:1–14

REV. DR. RICHARD L. ESLINGER
TRINITY UNITED METHODIST CHRUCH
NILES, MICHIGAN

Rev. Dr. Richard L. Eslinger

How Much More?

2 KINGS 5:1–14, NRSV

There was a commander from the land of Aram by the name of Naaman. He was a great warrior, brave and strong against the country's foes. A great warrior, Naaman. He had only one problem, but a huge one—he was a leper. He had contracted that terrible disease. Leper Commander Naaman.

Now there was in his household a young girl, a captive of the land of Israel. There in the place of her captivity, she served Naaman's wife. What makes the story happen is her attitude and her convictions. She had every right to despise Naaman, to regard him as an oppressor to be resented and destroyed. This servant girl did come up with a liberation theology, but it focused more on her captor than herself. Instead of judgment against Naaman, she spoke good news to him. "If only my lord were with the prophet who is in Samaria!" she says to her mistress. "He would cure him of his leprosy" (v. 3). That word from the girl sets some mighty things in motion. The king of Aram writes a letter to be given to the king of Israel. It is sent on ahead by diplomatic pouch and Naaman sets off for Israel. Actually, he goes off in a procession with wagon after wagon of stuff, including ten talents of silver, six thousand gold shekels, and ten sets of festal garments, along with his staff and guards.

An odd thing happens. When the king of Israel receives the letter about Naaman's impending arrival, he becomes paranoid. He rends his royal garments, tears them in shreds, muttering about trickery. Clearly this is a trick by Aram's king! "Am I God," he cries, "to give death or life?... Just look...how he is trying to pick a quarrel with me" (v. 7). So look at the poor king of Israel, kneeling there in shreds, seeing plots and trickery everywhere. Sound familiar?

But events do not halt with paranoia. Elisha, the man of God, hears about the king's reaction and sends him a message by prophetic pouch. "Let him come to me," Elisha announces, "that he may learn that there is a prophet in Israel" (v. 8). By the way, notice that in this welcome is the same insistence on hospitality that is always characteristic of God's people. Foreign commander, smitten with leprosy? "Let him come." In fact, what the king forgets is that he is, by God, the chief officer of Israel's hospitality. At least that was what he was supposed to be.

All of these events now lead to this scene at Elisha's little house in Samaria. Around the bend in the road comes Naaman's entourage. At first, only a column of dust on the horizon; but now as it lumbers up the road, Naaman gives the signal to halt. There in the noontime sun is the squeal of axles on the carts, the shouts of the drivers pulling in the reins on those treasure wagons, the clinking of the armor and swords of the guards. Then all the noise dies down. The dust slowly blows away and a silence settles in on the column, broken only by the occasional snort of a horse or the cough of a soldier clearing his throat. Otherwise nothing happens. Nothing at Elisha's little house or in Naaman's long convoy. Nothing, out in the bright sun.

Finally, though, there is movement. A messenger comes out of Elisha's house, comes over to Commander Naaman and speaks: "Go, wash in the Jordan seven times, and your flesh shall be restored and you shall be clean" (v. 10). A simple prescription from Doctor Elisha, "Wash in Jordan times seven." Elisha's signature at the bottom. Oh, and he's checked the box that says, "May not be substituted by a generic."

Naaman's response: He "became angry." He became self-righteously indignant and insufferably defensive. Naaman blurts out for all to hear,

"I thought that for me he would surely come out, and stand and call on the name of the Lord his God, and would wave his hand over the spot, and cure the leprosy" (v. 11). What ensues is a geography lesson about the rivers of Damascus compared to all the waters of Israel. Which may be translated, "I want my money's worth! A fair exchange with God." Naaman sounds like a kid arguing with his mother. "Unfair," he shouts. Just listen to his argument: "On my side, I've brought all the wagons crammed with talents and shekels, not to mention the ten festal garments." Then comes Naaman's demand of God: "In exchange for all this stuff, I want some bona fide and dramatic ceremony!" As to the prophet's prescription, "Wash times seven," Naaman sputters, "Unfair!" (Which, of course, we might add it is.)

We, too, come with all our wagons. Oh, not filled with Naaman's loot. But filled nonetheless. What's in our wagons—for our fair exchange with God? Maybe a wagonload of promises to serve God if we are healed. Or a cart full of gifts for ministry and service if God will only put us in the right place. Maybe just some funds of substance if a memorial plaque is properly installed when we die. Who knows—only we ourselves—what we've brought to trade fair and square with God.

Naaman is enraged. No prophetic gestures or incantations. No drama at high noon in Samaria. Only that word about the Jordan. Naaman stomps off hurt and angry in full sight of his servants—which is a good thing, because they care for him as much as that Hebrew girl back in Aram. Naaman is standing off on a little rise, his back to the bunch of them, hands on his hips, staring off into the distance. "Father," they begin, "if the prophet had commanded you to do something difficult, would you not have done it?" Knowing the answer of this brave and proud commander, they add, "How much more, when all he said to you was, 'Wash, and be clean'?" (v. 13). How much more? Yes, Naaman, how much more? Especially when this puzzling God sweeps aside all our bargains and offers us a simple gift of grace, free of charge. This simple thing. How much more, indeed?

Look at Naaman now, going down to the Jordan. This simple thing.

Seven times immersed there, plunged beneath the waters of healing. Cleansing fountain, living waters. Amazing grace. Look now, coming up out of the Jordan, his skin like that of a child. Clean, whole and born again really. To God be the glory, Naaman. Yes, Naaman, to God be the glory.

Comment

The Best Questions Are Not Always the Ones We Want to Ask

A few generations ago, theologian Paul Tillich popularized the idea that the culture frames the questions which the church seeks to answer. Every good apologetic theology, he contended, tries to understand what it is that society is asking. This interplay of cultural questions and answering theology, Tillich said, is how theology should work. Unfortunately, the church too often answers questions that no one is asking.

While Tillich's idea is important, it is also crucial that we not concede all the asking to the side of the culture. Sometimes the questions that Christian faith puts to culture can awaken new possibilities. They are questions that the culture would not even think to ask unless we asked them.

"How can I be healed?" is Naaman's question. It is straightforward and honest. He comes seeking religion, but more than that, he comes seeking help for a desperate plight. He is uninterested in theology or in theological questions.

Many people today dismiss theology as an abstract, useless body of speculation. Nothing could be further from the truth. Naaman's question is pushed aside and replaced by Elisha's actions that pose larger questions: "Who is the God with whom we are dealing? What is God's way of dealing with us?"

Richard Eslinger's sermon, "How Much More?" allows these important questions to arise from the biblical text itself. He does not begin with an illustration from current culture or *Time* magazine, but his questions are indeed timely.

Relevance can be one of the most overblown virtues in the Christian church. Being relevant is important, but not in an ultimate sense. To put it another way, sometimes what is urgent is not necessarily important.

Our culture is consumed with what seems important but is really only of passing urgency. We are like Naaman, obsessed with a debilitating problem that we want solved.

Have you ever watched those "time capsule" reports on TV that go back ten, twenty, or thirty years? Often the "news" of another time seems brittle and antiquated, not asking or not even seeing the questions that are eternally relevant. The biblical tradition helps us to ask these questions of eternal relevance at every point and in every age. One of the great virtues of Eslinger's sermon is that he lets the biblical story itself raise the question: "What sort of God is this with whom we are dealing?"

TEXT

There are of course many ways to approach a biblical text in preaching. We can explore a text in the light of the rest of the Bible. We can delve into its historical background and language. We might elucidate the difficult issues involved in a passage, or contrast it with another passage highlighting an apparently contrary interest. But we can also simply and faithfully retell the biblical story, and that is what Eslinger does in this sermon. He retells it artfully, inviting us to hear the questions it asks and to make connections in our own lives.

In today's congregation, we cannot assume that people know the biblical stories at all. So this retelling can be an important task. It is also subject to great misuse. We can "import" our own pet causes into a text which has nothing to do with those issues. To Eslinger's credit, he permits "main things" to be main things.

Now a few words in praise of brevity and concreteness! In this sermon Eslinger does not use long, abstract sentences. Thirty-five times he uses sentences of seven words or less. The effect of these short sentences is unconsciously to convey simplicity and forcefulness to the congregation in the telling.

Eslinger's retelling is also very effective in its use of visual, descriptive words. Expansion and amplification are not always negative in preaching. Notice, for example, the way he expands verse 9:

At first, only a column of dust on the horizon; but now as it lumbers up the road, Naaman gives the signal to halt. There in the noontime sun is the squeal of axles on the carts, the shouts of the drivers pulling in the reins on those treasure wagons, the clinking of the armor and swords of the guards. Then all the noise dies down. The dust slowly blows away and a silence settles in on the column, broken only by the occasional snort of a horse or the cough of a soldier clearing his throat. Otherwise nothing happens. Nothing at Elisha's little house or in Naaman's long convoy. Nothing, out in the bright sun.

The biblical text simply says, "So Naaman came with his horses and chariots, and halted at the entrance of Elisha's house" (2 Kings 5:9). Elsinger's retelling of the story does not add anything to the biblical story in a factual sense, but it powerfully conveys mental pictures to the hearer. The more visually we preach (using concrete visual images and picture words), the more we invite our television-soaked hearers to experience the biblical story rather than merely to hear a sermon.

Eslinger's vivid description also slows down our hearing to enable us to enter into the story more effectively. We are able to consider it, to mull it over, to ponder it. Often we hurry past Scripture like we race through our lives. I suspect that many Christians roar through their quiet times and Scripture reading like Indy racers in a pit stop.

Haste is not conducive to hearing God. This attitude of haste enters into the sanctuaries of our churches with the petulance of a hungry infant whining in a highchair. People often complain to pastors that they don't want "all that theology and stuff." Instead, they demand, "Give me something practical for my life." It is a fatal mistake—eternally fatal—for preachers to acquiesce to those demands.

Application is important, but it is not the same thing as adapting the gospel to modern problems. Modern living *is* the problem. If we are to find the answers, we must call modern life into question.

Good preaching "slows us down." It leads us to roads less traveled. It is part of our task to invite our hearers into quiet, meditative rhythms where they might hear the voice of God.

THE BEST ANSWERS ARE THE ONES WE DIDN'T SEEK

The proclamation in Eslinger's sermon is about grace. We wouldn't think grace to be a source of confusion in the Protestant culture of America. But it is! Naaman's story can easily be subverted into a legalistic diatribe about obedience. It is true that Naaman must respond in faith, but first his misunderstanding of the God with whom he is dealing must be subverted and destroyed. God is no Canaanite deity who jumps when magicians or generals snap their fingers! No deals, no bargains—only a simple gift. That is the gospel, however imperfectly it is spoken in this peculiar story.

Forget all your claims on God. God graces us only because it is the nature of love to give to those in need. Too much religion is a calculation, another column of figures added onto our spreadsheet. Eslinger invites us really to hear what is being said: God cannot be bought, sold, intimidated or controlled. If God is to love us, it will only be because God wants to love us.

It is indeed a frightening place to stand when we depend on grace. We have nothing to claim and no guarantees. The image Eslinger uses of the wagons is a powerful one to convey this truth. "What's in our 'wagons'?" he asks. In other words, what makes us think that we have a claim on God?

These sorts of deals go on all the time. People go into the ministry to deal with guilty pasts. Church members may not pay indulgences any longer, but they still make contributions in the misguided notion that they are accruing some sort of credit for themselves.

Notice also that while Eslinger confronts us, he does not try to spell out every way in which we may be guilty of loading up our wagons to cut a deal with God. The preacher leaves room for the Holy Spirit and the hearer's mind and heart to have further conversation about this matter. If a person goes off on her own reflection or resumes thinking about this later that day or that week, the sermon has accomplished one of its purposes.

RESPONSE

This sermon is a powerful reminder that grace cuts through our deals, does away with them, and offers us only trust as a response. We understand this verbally, but to grasp it with the heart is to experience an inward transformation. Eslinger effectively helps us identify with Naaman and to consider: What proud claim must we relinquish if we are to enter the waters of grace? What simple response must we make to say to God, "I believe, Lord"?

This would be a powerful sermon to use in connection with baptism. How do we respond to grace? We can flee it. Or we can receive it like a child. Because he has used a story to proclaim this grace to us, Eslinger does not manipulate us. He does not tell us what we must do, or ask us to raise our hands or "walk the aisle." This sermon, however, does ask for a response.

As our minds and hearts turn to our own lives with the question, "What's in our wagons?" we are invited to reflect upon our deepest self-perceptions. Some clearing away is necessary before we can get to the larger question.

It is likely that every person sitting in a congregation wants what Naaman wanted—healing, wholeness, and new life. It is also likely that most of us will not like the price of that wholeness—that we surrender control and trust in One whom we know by faith alone. The instruction to go and wash in the muddy Jordan is the great question each of us face. Will we put away our angry expectations, personal agendas, pride and position, in order to receive the treasure of the kingdom?

SUGGESTIONS

- Look at some biblical stories that "tell themselves." Try retelling them, as Eslinger has done, in a way that uses imagination and visual description. Pick out a crucial verse and practice imaginative reconstruction, helping the hearer "see" what is happening. For starters, try one of the following: Genesis 32:22–32; 1 Kings 19:1–18; John 18:12–27; or Acts 8:25–40. Look particularly at some of the visual images. How can you convey what you "see" when you imagine the scene?

- Try taking your most recent (or next) sermon and practice conciseness! Look at your sentences. Can you shorten some of them to say the same thing with half as many words?
- Today we hear a great deal about the revived interest in spirituality. Look at some popular magazines and books, or engage some laypersons in a conversation focusing on the questions, "What are people in your world seeking spiritually? What questions do they seem to be asking about God?" How do these questions square with our understanding of the gospel?

Gary A. Furr

BECOMING WHAT WE ARE

PSALM 103:1–14;
2 CORINTHIANS 4:6–12; 5:17–18

REV. WILLIAM C. GREEN
ASSOCIATE CONFERENCE MINISTER,
PENN NORTHEAST CONFERENCE
UNITED CHURCH OF CHRIST
PALMERTON, PENNSYLVANIA

REV. WILLIAM C. GREEN

BECOMING WHAT WE ARE

PSALM 103:1–14;
2 CORINTHIANS 4:6–12; 5:17–18

We've only just begun." Remember that wedding song? Those words will forever haunt me after all the weddings I've done. Of course I've had to negotiate many a perilous nuptial moment, when world history seemed to hang in the balance. Where was Madeleine Albright when I needed her, amid delicate mediation with the mother of the bride—who probably had the service planned and flowers ordered before her daughter was born? And surely the United Nations has not faced a crisis more severe than that involving the father who insists on "giving away" his daughter who decides that her marriage is *her* business and that she doesn't want to be "given away," but knows this will also upset her grandmother who already has heart trouble. I did have one moment of true diplomatic success. I once was able to get deferred until *after* the service the loud blasts right outside the sanctuary that were to finish inflating a hot air balloon in which the young couple expected to fly away.

But never have I succeeded in suggesting alternatives to the song that begins, "We've only just begun." It's a lovely song, I guess, and its selection is probably none of my business. But after the ten-thousandth time, it's been known to lull the officiating pastor into something of a trance.

It's then hard to remember which couple it is this time that is being joined together in holy matrimony.

Today, this gathering isn't a wedding, although it is a celebration of another new beginning. We are not singing that song! Yet, here I am recalling the words: "We've only just begun." But I want to change those words to say something else—something that sounds truly strange. On this occasion of installation, at the beginning of this turning point, as you welcome a new Conference Minister, I want to say, "We've already ended!"[1]

To say this sounds depressing—almost as though I've just said, "There's no hope." We are accustomed to thinking of the future as the promised land, the goal of our dreams, the end product of our vision. "The best is yet to be."[2] By contrast, the present is all those things that remain unresolved, and all the things we must do to make a good future possible.

But today I want us to consider how what lies ahead is *already* present this very moment, here at what we call the beginning. What the future holds for Tim Downs and for you as you work together in the years ahead, what lies ahead for me and my colleagues up in Penn Northeast, what lies ahead for us all—all of that is already part of the present moment. "The best" already is. It awaits our recognition.

If we can understand this, and allow it to shape our life together, we can live even now with clarity, confidence, and joy, witnessing the love of God in all its glory.

Where we are going is already here. That is what Paul means when he declares, "I tell you, now is the time of God's favor, now is the day of salvation" (2 Cor. 6:2, NIV). We are already reconciled, says Paul. (See also Rom. 5:10; Col. 1:20.) While he was thinking in his day primarily of Jew and Greek, he speaks as well of male and female (Gal. 3:26–28). Following Paul's logic, we can speak today of conservative and liberal, gay and straight, friend and stranger, young and old; European-American, Native American, African-American, and Asian-American; Georgia and Alabama, South Carolina and Tennessee, Mississippi and the panhandle of Florida!

We are already reconciled! "From first to last this has been the work of God," Paul writes (2 Cor. 5:18, NEB). Not next month or next year or ten years from now...or after we die. Now. Right now! *Today* is the day of salvation: the day to be and to decide and to love.

Salvation—what Paul also calls "reconciliation," which is nothing but salvation in action—does not await the outcome of all our hard work. It does not depend on the planning and fulfillment of our programs. It does not depend on the charisma and diplomacy of your new Conference Minister (although you will find Tim has those qualities).

Of course, all these things are important. But what has ended once and for all on the cross of Jesus Christ is the presumption that it all depends on us. No longer is the future a matter of our dreams and schemes. No longer is what lies ahead a matter of our worrisome work, as though, with a little help from God, "just maybe" we'll make it. "Just maybe?" No. No longer is the past just prologue to a present that is prelude to a future we pray will turn out all right. It's over already. "Just maybe" is ended.

As the great Easter hymn puts it, "The strife is o'er, the battle done; The victory of life is won; The song of triumph has begun: Alleluia!" The future as well as the past are fulfilled in the present, right now.

Remember all that God has done so powerfully, so lovingly, so often throughout the past. Then, let us also remember what Lewis Carroll has the Queen say to Alice in *Through the Looking Glass:* "It's a poor sort of memory that only works backward." To which we might add, "And it's a poor sort of hope that only looks forward."

As Archbishop Desmond Tutu has always put it—even amid the most stunning revelations of atrocity the human spirit could possibly witness: "I am simply living out the victory God has already won."

How in the world can this be when all around us we continue to see so much sin and evil, suffering and injustice? How can the strife be "o'er" when we are still in the thick of the battle? How dare we speak of *victory* when God knows how many young children in this rich land are going to bed tonight in tears, hungry, if not also starving for some kind of simple affection? Good Lord, are we engaged here in some sort of massive denial?

Yes. The answer is yes, we are engaged in massive denial! Thank God for exceptions where they exist in the Southeast Conference too. But what far too many of us North American Christians are denying is the reality of God: God present in the middle of all that trouble. What increasing numbers of church people these days cannot see is that those children going to bed tonight scared and hungry are not far from lovely sanctuaries like this one. Those children are what God is all about and where God is found. Indeed, amid all suffering and injustice, there is the Lord. There is the cross.

What almost guarantees our denial is something just as deep, but far closer to us right now—as near as our next breath, as close as our last heartbeat. And that is the reality of our own hurt, the presence of our own pain, the anguish of tears not always shed. For there, *here*, hidden in our own hearts, God is also present: "Just as I am"…just as we are…"without one plea."

It is not just on the other side of trouble that the Lord is found. It is *amid* challenge and difficulty, even our own, when with the psalmist we walk through the dark valley (Ps. 23:4). *Through* the valley, not just around it, or before it, or beyond it: through the shadow of hurt all too often hidden, regularly denied. That is also where God is found. Just where we are when we are honest about our own pain.

It's hard to care much about the hurt of others when we fail to confront our own. But it is hard really to know, much less name, our own pain when feeling negative about anything is regarded as spiritual weakness or a moral failing. So we clam up and get on with the business of being positive. Sometimes we Christians are a lot like Stimpy in the *Ren and Stimpy* show on television. Our faith can be so restrictive that it's a lot like being made to wear that electronic helmet designed by cheery Stimpy for his gloomy friend Ren. The helmet forces the wearer to grin inanely and sing the "Happy, Happy, Joy, Joy" song.

Perhaps we are more like the young father in the supermarket, seen pushing the shopping cart carrying the screaming baby. The father could be heard muttering gently under his breath, "Easy, Freddy, calm down now. Everything's all right, boy. Come on, Freddy, don't get upset."

A woman customer commented approvingly to him, saying, "You are very patient with little Freddy."

The young father looked up glumly and said, "Lady, I'm Freddy."

We are all something like Freddy and Ren, and yes, Stimpy too. Perhaps we are most like the little girl who was asked what color she would be if all the good people in the world were red and all the bad people green. Replied the girl, "I'd be streaky."

The point is not that the truest thing about us is what we deny. It's that there is much more to us than what we commonly affirm. God made us a mixture of dust and deity. And as with us, so with our churches and with society at large—we're all "streaky." Which is to say that, in becoming flesh, God's Word got mixed in with everything else: the good, the bad, the ugly; the beautiful and the terrible; the agony and the ecstasy; the boredom and the excitement.

In reducing our understanding and experience of God to what seems positive, we make it seem that God is absent in all the rest. What is not good then becomes "our problem" to fix or deny or just stay frustrated about. Daily life becomes a burden, faith a chore—and the love of God more a source of pain and guilt than joy. We need to listen again to the words of the psalmist, when he sings: "Bless the Lord, O my soul, and *all* that is within me, bless his holy name" (Psalm 103:1, NRSV, italics added). "All" means *everything*.

Like Freddy, the psalmist is talking to himself, practicing the assurance he too needs. But in his case, he's really *got* the assurance because he understands that everything, every last truth about himself, must be referred to God's goodness.[3] That means pain as well as pleasure, anger as well as joy; tears, laughter, hunger, contentment, yearning, satisfaction, uncertainty, fulfillment. All these things have their place, in the life of the psalmist, in the life of the worshiping community, in the church at large, indeed in our whole experience of life. Nothing about us is simply canceled out, much less covered up. Everything about us is redeemed from denial. What would otherwise be the energy of sin and guilt is transformed by faith into the power of hope, mercy, justice, and reconciliation.

What we Christians are given to believe is that the goodness of God does not exclude things we don't like. Dare I say that God's goodness does not exclude people we don't like, or problems we don't like, or challenges we would rather not face? The love of God, as we learn in Jesus Christ, incorporates it all. In his tears we weep; in his laughter we rejoice; in his hope we hope; in his anger we cry out; in his God-forsakenness we too are like a fatherless, a motherless child. On Christ's cross, we experience death. And "Made like him, like him we rise, Ours the cross, the grave, the skies, Alleluia!"[4]

So it is that Paul need not mince words. Rather, in the complete honesty of faith, he can acknowledge the worst and affirm the best, denying neither, asserting both. He declares straight-out his affliction, his perplexity, his persecution. He says he's been struck down. But Paul knows he hasn't struck out. Instead of limiting God to the best, he discovers the love of God through the worst and affirms God's goodness in words of unmistakable praise (2 Cor. 4:8–12).

Like the psalmist, Paul's range of vision starts with what he has learned about himself and then extends to the whole of creation. And so it is that in short order Paul speaks of the reconciliation of the whole world in what he calls a new creation (2 Cor. 5:17).

Reconciliation overcomes our tendency to try to be holy without being human first. It overcomes our tendency to deny what is human for the sake of what is divine. And Christ is the "overcomer." In and through him, and for our sake, God healed the breach between the holy and the human, dust and deity, sacred and secular, church and world.

This is not to say the human is divine. It is to say that what is human is glorified by the divine—as is the rest of creation. It's to say what Samuel Rutherford, that great Scottish Presbyterian, said some three hundred and fifty years ago: "When I realized last night that Jesus Christ was in my prison cell, every stone flashed like a ruby." It's to say what Irenaeus of Lyon, one of the earliest saints of the church, said some eighteen hundred years ago: "The glory of God is a human being who is fully alive." It's to say what the poet Elizabeth Barrett Browning said one hundred and fifty years ago: "Earth's crammed with heaven, / And every common bush afire with God; / But only he who sees takes off his shoes; / The rest sit round it and pluck blackberries."[5]

Imagine that! Every thought, feeling, and pain, every pleasure, failure, and success, every problem, challenge, and circumstance, every joy and sorrow—all "crammed with heaven," all made for glory and meant to "flash like a ruby!"

The tragedy is not that the world is bereft of holiness, but that it is bereft of humanity! Our job is not to bring God to the world. God has taken care of that. Our job is to bring ourselves to the world. Our job is to become what we are and to help the world become what it is: the habitation of the holy, the home of the Most High, the place where God loves us and welcomes us all, just as we are, "without one plea." Denying this is the only sin left…all we have to fear.

Jesus is tenderly calling us home, calling today. So why from the sunshine of love will you roam, farther and farther away?

Come home. Come home.

Come to those motherless children, and in their tears find your own.

Come to the hovels of your cities and the steps of city hall. Come to the shelters of the homeless and the refuge of the wealthy. Come to the exercise of citizenship and the practice of piety.

Come to serve God. Come to church. Come home.

"In my end is my beginning," says the poet.[6] And so I guess, somewhat reluctantly, I have to say after all: "We've only just begun." For Tim, and for all of you in the Southeast Conference, you have only begun to explore your life together. Just remember, as the poet goes on to say, "The end of all [our] exploring / Will be to arrive where [we] started / And know the place for the first time."[7]

"We've already ended." All that is left for me to say is, "Welcome home."

But not knowing when to leave well enough alone, I can't resist saying one more thing: "Flash like a ruby!" For the Lord is with you, the future is now, and today *is* the day of salvation: the day to be and to decide and to love. In Jesus' name. Amen.

Notes

1. This sermon was preached on the occasion of the installation of Rev. Tim Downs as Conference Minister of the Southeast Conference, United Church of Christ.
2. Robert Browning, "Rabbi Ben Ezra."
3. Walter Brueggemann, *The Message of the Psalms: A Theological Commentary* (Minneapolis: Augsburg Publishing House, 1984), p. 160.
4. Charles Wesley, "Christ the Lord Is Risen Today."
5. Elizabeth Barrett Browning, *Aurora Leigh*, VII, l. 820–21.
6. T. S. Eliot, *Four Quartets*, "East Coker," V, *The Complete Poems and Plays, 1901–1950* (New York: Harcourt, Brace, 1952), p. 123.
7. Ibid., "Little Gidding," V, p. 145.

COMMENT

William Green's sermon, "Becoming What We Are," was preached at the installation of Tim Downs as new Conference Minister of the Southeast Conference of the United Churches of Christ. It was a new time in the life of that association of churches. Appropriate to the day was a sermon exploring the Christian perspective on new beginnings. Green's style and content convey both clarity and creativity. He challenges us to explore our misguided assumptions and our erroneous understandings of God and God's place in the world.

We live in a time when there are many attempts to erase God's activity from the world. We live in a culture that proclaims humanity's endless potential while tolerating or despairing over unspeakable human tragedies and problems. In this context Green asserts that God is actively involved in the world and in our lives. To a church that sometimes limits God's involvement to what seems positive, Green says, "The goodness of God does not exclude things we don't like.... The love of God...incorporates it all." This is a message to a specific audience, but its meaning is relevant to all. There are no new beginnings. The best already is. Our challenge is to be aware of God's presence in all of life. A timely message. A never-failing truth.

PROBLEM & TEXT

"We've only just begun." They are the opening words of a powerful sermon that combines poetry and prose, question and answer, statement and illustration. The sermon is characterized by harmony and rhythm, movement and direction. It is the kind of sermon that effects change and affects hearts.

After a well-conceived introduction, Green quickly comes to his point: "Today I want us to consider how what lies ahead is *already* present this very moment, here at what we call the beginning.... If we can understand this...we can live even now with clarity, confidence, and joy, witnessing the love of God in all its glory." Green then spends the rest of the sermon explaining, proving, and applying this truth.

Interestingly, Green is nearly halfway through the sermon before he even addresses a problem or question. Typical inductive sermons use the element of surprise and climactic endings to capture the listener's attention. The desire for resolution is the driving force behind such sermons. But we know Green's main idea up front. This is not typical inductive preaching. It is much more deductive. Green spends the first half of the sermon explaining and restating his proposition, namely, that the future is already part of the present. The implications of that proposition follow later in the sermon.

Green builds his case through the exposition of portions of 2 Corinthians 4 and 5, focusing on what it means to be reconciled. "Today is the day of salvation"—a salvation that is not dependent on our work but on the work of Jesus Christ. Hence, where we are going is already here. The future of any person, any church, any denomination does not depend entirely upon us. The victory is God's. It is real. It is now. There follows a crescendo of emotion and feeling as Green illustrates this truth quoting a powerful Easter hymn and two thoughtful quotes, one from a fictional book character, the other from Archbishop Desmond Tutu. Finally, Green brings us down, asking the question which has lain dormant in the back of our minds: "How can this be?" How, in the face of reality, can we believe in victory? How can Christians believe God is present in bad times and tragedy?

Green has subtly led his listeners right to where he wants them. From here the sermon takes an unexpected turn. We discover it is not so much about new beginnings as about Christian denial. To answer the question of how we are to believe in victory when we live in the midst of sin and evil, Green asks another question: "Are we engaged here in some sort of massive denial?" "Yes," he answers, "we are engaged in massive denial," but not in the denial we think. Our denial is far worse. We are denying the reality of God.

In our efforts to fit God into our self-made boxes and to mold him after our own image, Green asserts, we limit God to the good and positive. And it is our own reduction of God that limits our awareness of God's presence: "Everything...must be referred to God's goodness.... What Christians are given to believe is that the goodness of God does not exclude things we don't like."

In an effort to prove this point, Green refers back to his texts (Ps. 103:1; 2 Cor. 4:6–12, 5:17–18). The psalmist praises God with *all* his soul. The apostle Paul says that reconciliation—"salvation in action"— allows us to be human and to overcome denial.

In his final movement, Green uses several well-placed quotations to heighten our awareness and our emotions. Back-to-back quotes lead into a moving, celebratory conclusion. "Imagine that! Every thought, feeling and pain, every pleasure, failure, and success, every problem, challenge, and circumstance, every joy and sorrow—'all crammed with heaven'...."

Green ends where he began: "'We've only just begun'...You have only begun to explore your life together...'We've already ended.' All that is left for me to say is, 'Welcome home.'"

STYLE & STRUCTURE

There are three essentials to a well-planned, effective sermon: unity, order, and progression. One reason this sermon is so compelling is its adherence to all three.

Listeners need unity. They need to see the relationship of the parts to the whole. One way Green does this is by tying his introduction to the conclusion. We've been taken on a journey that has stopped in several places. In the conclusion, Green helps us come full circle, back home.

It is obvious that Green knew where he was going in this sermon. There is a sense of order and direction. Order is integral to good preaching and communication. This is because the preacher must do the thinking for the audience, relating the parts of the sermon to the whole. Good communicators must always be aware of the total unity in order to know where to go and what to emphasize. Green understands what needs to be explained, proved, and applied. He explains what needs clarification.

He anticipates the congregation's questions and asks the right questions at the right time. In short, Green knows his text, his audience, his context.

If the task of preaching is to change lives, then preachers must do everything within their power to maintain the congregation's attention in order to communicate truth. Having a sense of progression is the best way to do this. There must be a sense of movement within the unity and order. There must be a destination. Progression must incorporate tension. Lose the tension in a sermon, and you lose the sermon. Green does an excellent job of maintaining tension. The sermon is more deductive than inductive, making it more difficult to create and maintain tension. Yet Green has no trouble building tension and heightening the listener's awareness.

Green advances this sermon's proposition through restatement. In order to get the point across, Green often restates in different words what has gone before. For example, twice Green uses hymns, poets, or preachers in back-to-back quotations, emphasizing and restating what he has already said.

Green also uses explanation to show in greater detail the meaning of certain terms. For example: "Reconciliation is nothing but salvation in action." "Where we are going is already here. That is what Paul means...." In this way, Green helps make clear what may be fuzzy in the minds of his listeners.

Unlike so many modern sermons, this sermon is not illustration driven. Instead, Green uses short illustrations and quotes to make his sermon's proposition understandable, convincing and believable. His illustrations advance his sermon without becoming the sermon.

Response

At the beginning of a new chapter in its church life, Green's message to his audience is clear. It is easy as Christians to believe that we are the ones controlling our destiny. If we work harder, do more, sin less, then God will bless our energies and enterprises. Ministry becomes our business, not God's. Green urges his audience to rethink this assumption, to remember that this is God's business and not ours. In fact, Green says, new beginnings are nonexistent. The present is the future. The victory is ours.

The truth is a reassuring and comforting promise for all of us. Perhaps it is an especially important message for preachers and pastors. As we dissect and scrutinize sermons and our own ministries, when we are depressed or elated, let us remember that God is with us. We are home.

SUGGESTIONS

- Are your sermons cohesive? Do you carefully build the relationship of the parts to the whole? Do your sermons have order and direction? Are you always cognizant of where you are going?
- Do you attempt to explain concepts and terms? Or do you assume your audience knows what you take for granted?
- Ask yourself concerning your text, "What keeps me from believing this?" Next apply the question to your congregation, "What will my audience ask? Do they believe this?" In this way, you can anticipate the questions and concerns of the congregation.

Karen F. Younger

A Letter to Harold

1 JOHN 5:1–5

Rev. Dr. Kenneth A. Corr
First Baptist Church
Memphis, Tennessee

Rev. Dr. Kenneth A. Corr

A Letter to Harold

1 JOHN 5:1–5, NAS

Last week, our church staff went to lunch together at a local restaurant. Our waiter was Harold, an attractive, articulate, young adult. He joked with us for a few minutes and asked if we worked together. We told him that we worked at the First Baptist Church and gave him the location. He said that he might have seen it, but it was clear that he did not have a clue where First Baptist Church was. He asked if we were on TV, and we told him the time and the channel. He said that he might have seen us when he was channel surfing for a ball game. We invited him to attend our church, but he was clearly uncomfortable with us and even apologized for joking earlier.

Harold is typical of many young adults today. He is the kind of person we are trying to reach with the gospel. I think Harold is representative of this group, and I'd like to give you a profile that describes them.

Many young adults like Harold have a minimal Christian background. They probably attended church as children and know something of Christianity.

I think we can assume that Harold and those like him have a materialistic world-view and goals but are looking for something more to give meaning to their lives.

I think we can assume that Harold is interested in spirituality and has probably dabbled in some form of New Age spirituality.

I think we can also assume that Harold is not interested in the church. He has bad memories of church from his childhood; he feels uncomfortable around Christians who, he thinks, are judgmental of his lifestyle and share very few of his values. He doesn't want to be preached at or asked for money. He can't imagine church being enjoyable or meaningful for him.

Does this description fit someone you know? Maybe a friend at school, one of your children or grandchildren, maybe a neighbor or young adult who works with you?

I want to talk to Harold this morning and all those just like him. Since Harold will not come to hear me preach, I have written my sermon in the form of a letter. As you listen this morning, pray for all the Harolds whom you know and whom we are trying to reach.

Dear Harold (and others just like him),

I am writing this letter to you because I know that it will be difficult to get you to come to hear me preach. Somehow the church has lost most of your generation. But I have watched you search for meaning and purpose and a genuine encounter with God, and I want to make an appeal to you to consider the Christian faith again. Are you open-minded enough to set aside your prejudices and stereotypes about Christians for just a few minutes and give me one more hearing? Even though our rituals may seem meaningless to you, our hymns out-of-date, and our values old-fashioned, the message of the gospel is as relevant today as it was two thousand years ago.

I will use the words of the apostle John found in the New Testament and organize my thoughts around two themes.

First, John reminds us of *who Christians are*. He writes, "Whoever believes that Jesus is the Christ is born of God."

Christians are people who believe that Jesus is the Christ, the Son of God, and so they have experienced a spiritual rebirth.

Our faith is not just an intellectual belief. It is a belief that Jesus Christ is God, who died on the cross to save us from our sin. That belief results in a life-transforming spiritual encounter with God, something so radical that it is like being born all over again.

Harold, Christianity has become so confused with politics, school-board elections, moral debates about homosexuality and abortion, legal battles over prayer in public schools and courtrooms, arguments about creation and evolution, and so many other things, that the real issues of belief and rebirth are sometimes completely lost. The moral, social, and political issues are important, but they don't define Christianity. Don't listen when someone says that unless you vote or live or act or believe like they do, you can't be a Christian. Being a Christian is not defined by a person's political views or lifestyle choices or moral opinions. The family of God is large enough for diversity of opinions on these issues. Instead, a Christian is one who believes that Jesus is the Son of God and who has been born of God. Harold, if you are looking for a genuine spiritual encounter, look here first.

I know that in your search for God you may have experimented with different spiritualities. I do not condemn you for that. There is much that Christians can learn from other faith traditions. We can learn about the sanctity of the earth from Native American spirituality. We can learn about the value of nurturing and the maternal qualities of God from feminist spirituality. We can learn about the interior life from oriental spiritualities. But as good as those things are, none of them are our pathway to God. The message of Christianity is that the pathway to spiritual life is through Jesus Christ who promised, "I am the way, and the truth, and the life; no one comes to the Father, but through me" (John 14:6). Don't give up too soon on this way to truth about God, Harold.

Regardless of what you may have assumed or heard or

believed about Christians, this is who we are: people who have believed that Jesus is the Christ, the Son of God, and, as a result, have been born of God.

The second point I want to make, is that the apostle John also reminds us of *what we are about*. He writes, "Whoever believes that Jesus is the Christ is born of God; and whoever loves the Father loves the child born of Him."

Don't misunderstand what I have said. Moral values, ethical decisions, doctrinal beliefs, political views, and a Christian lifestyle are important, but Christians are called first and foremost to love God and each other. Jesus said that this is the greatest commandment. The apostle James said that it is the royal law (James 2:8). The apostle Paul said that love is the fulfillment of the whole law (Rom. 13:10).

But Christians are the first to admit that in this high calling of love we have failed miserably. For this failure, you have good reason to turn us off and tune us out. I sadly agree with the preacher who said, "I think it's awful that the word 'Christian' is now so greasy...that it has become slippery and slimy until one hesitates to pick it up."[1]

In recent years, the Christian church has been better known for denominational battles, church splits, clergy sexual scandals, name-calling and a downright mean spirit, than for our love. But don't judge us only by our obvious failures. The church has also sheltered the homeless, befriended the lost, provided disaster relief, counseled with the distressed, fed the hungry, prayed for our nation's leaders, and helped in countless ways that will never be known. Don't underestimate the loving influence of millions of Christians. Without them, it is hard to imagine what our world would be like.

Even though we admit that we have fallen short of our calling to love God and our neighbors as we should, at least we know what our purposes and calling are, and we work to fulfill them. Our goal is the upward call of God in Jesus Christ. I am as disappointed as you with the church's failures, but I am not willing to reject the church because of its failures. Instead, I want to work with and through the church to make positive changes. Harold, if you are looking for a place in which to serve, something to give meaning and purpose to your existence, something more to work toward than your material goals, you can find all this in the Christian faith.

Harold, this is who we are and what we are about. Simply put, we are people with the same hopes, dreams, and struggles as you. But we have believed that Jesus is the Son of God, we have been born of God, and we are called to love God and our neighbors.

So, I extend an invitation to you. Join with us. Believe that Jesus Christ is the Son of God and be born of God. Don't settle for anything less.

Harold, thank you for listening. We will keep a seat open for you just in case, one day, you decide to visit. You may find that the rituals aren't quite as meaningless as you thought, the hymns aren't quite as out-of-date as you remembered, our values aren't quite as old-fashioned as you have wanted to believe. Believe it or not, a few of your peers have already found their place here.

Your spiritual friend,
Ken Corr

Note
1. Quoted in Leonard Sweet, *Homiletics* (April–June, 1997), p. 43.

Comment

A cartoon in *The New Yorker* once showed a psychologist reporting on some tests to a counselee. He said, "Our findings show that your problem is not an inferiority complex. You simply *are* inferior." In another cartoon a young boy on his way out of church was asked by the minister what he thought about the worship service. To his parents' chagrin, he replied, "It wasn't a bad show for a quarter."

Many find it easy to succumb to the negative press given the church today and conclude that the church is inferior, that it has lost its effectiveness and has no hope for itself and none to give the world. But it can't give in, for its task is to show that there are answers we have to live out—not just spell out.

Despite the negative press traditional Christianity has received in our culture, the search is on for the spiritual. People hunger for meaning and purpose that goes beyond the material. They are no longer convinced that only the visible, tangible things matter in life. The inner caverns of their spiritual lives remain empty as they go through their day-to-day existence maintaining only a distant view of God.

As I read Kenneth Corr's sermon, I found myself nodding agreeably and thinking of William Willimon's book, *What's Right with the Church?* I thought of how often we dwell on what is wrong with the church rather than what is right. To be sure, it is easy for anyone to see the faults, the shortcomings, and the failures of the church. Most people who attend church know that the church doesn't measure up to what it is called to be. As someone once said, Jesus has many admirers who feel he married below his station. This does not, however, lessen the church's obligations to the Harolds of the world. What is right about the church can provide a light to the world. The church can offer an imaginative alternative to the seeking Harolds.

Although preaching is often considered a stuffy, stilted form of communication, this sermon challenges that stereotype. Corr takes a fresh, creative approach in style, structure, and delivery. In Corr's sermon one can see the awesome responsibility entrusted to the church. We benefit immeasurably when we are willing to reassess and rework our programs and practices—particularly if the church is ever to reach the Harolds of this world. After all, people *are* what mattered most to Jesus. We are, by grace, given the privilege of offering a sense of the holy that satisfies the longings of people's hearts. To people whose relationship with God lacks something vital, the church can point the way to a sensitive and sincere response to the love of God that meets us in Jesus.

Text & Proclamation

The first thing that one notices is Corr's experimental style. Experimental sermons are good opportunities for the preacher to hear and see in new ways. A willingness to experiment maintains an edge of creativity in the preacher's art, sharpens one's perceptions, and opens one to new discoveries. At the same time, experimental sermons give the congregation a wake-up call, providing a challenge to hear and understand the gospel in new ways. The fairly high degree of predictability in most sermons and the dead air of familiarity are removed by an occasional experimental sermon or change of style.

Corr's introduction is to the point—personal yet intriguing. He sets up a situation that easily leads the listener into the sermon. Corr allows us to "overhear" the reading of a personal letter to Harold, the young man he and his staff met at lunch. The assumptions he makes about Harold in the introduction form the foundation for the letter itself and prepare the listener for the rest of the sermon. Corr rattles off a number of demographic realities that create a profile of this young man, while reminding us of the research findings from church-growth specialists. But the real question is what we do once we know the results of the research. How we reach out to the "Harolds" we meet is the challenge of this sermon.

Corr uses a casual encounter in a restaurant to relate the gospel to the human situation. The restaurant scene, so true to life, involves us as listeners. Soon the story becomes our story, because it speaks to our own experiences. We all know some Harolds—or we ourselves have been Harold!

Although he centers the sermon around a personal story, Corr doesn't allow this story to put himself in a favorable light. Rather, he is willing to be seen as fully human with the same questions, disappointments, and doubts as Harold. This strengthens the sermon by enabling people to see the good news of Jesus Christ applied by a very human preacher to a very human situation with which they can identify.

"How many points should a good sermon have?" my friend, Gardner Taylor, was once asked. "At least one," he replied. Corr makes his point through the two themes drawn from 1 John 5:1–5: (1) The word of God is relevant to Harold's search, and (2) Christians are to make love their first priority. He joins, and asks us to join, with Harold in a new exploration of what the Christian faith is all about. This sermon is designed to cut through all the encrusted "human" layers that distort Christianity, in order to return to the basics. The heart of Christianity, Corr proclaims, is the simple good news of Jesus Christ, God's Son. As a community of faith—the church—we are a people called to love God and each other.

One story begins the sermon. One letter is the focal point. It might seem that the sermon lacks strong illustrative material, since the letter in its entirety is an illustration. Yet, this style of sermon does not easily lend itself to abundant illustrations. In fact, multiple illustrations could easily distract. But even in a letter one can give brief illustrations to drive home a point.

Another strong element of this sermon is the way in which Corr begins and ends his letter. He answers his own statements to Harold about the church's seemingly meaningless rituals, the church's hymns that seem out-of-date, the church's values that seem old-fashioned, by saying at the end that they aren't as Harold may think. Corr neatly uses these statements and responses as bookends to hold the sermon together.

There are several high moments in Corr's sermon. One comes when he warns Harold against confusing Christianity with politics and social issues. Another comes after he admits the church's failure, when he assures Harold of his unwillingness to reject the church and commits to the need to make some positive changes.

Response

If a sermon exists to point people to Christ, and I think it does, then Corr has done it beautifully. He invites participation in his story and in the letter, not to illustrate the way things are, but to point to what they can become. This sermon is not only for the Harolds outside the church, but also for the Harolds inside the church. Corr uses the Scripture to address the problem and hopefully allow it to transform the situation. The sermon acknowledges what is wrong with the church and lifts up the possibility of change. At the same time, it points out what is right with the church. But most importantly, it points away from human beings as the church, to Jesus Christ, the center of the church.

Corr knows that this focus on the person of Christ is finally the only compelling and transforming reality the church has to offer Harold or anyone else in the world. And Christ alone is sufficient.

Corr's sermon offers a warmth and a kind of intimacy helpful in dealing with Harold's needs and questions. The sermon's style and content show sensitivity to the basic needs and desires of the Harolds inside and outside the church.

Corr demonstrates here that a sermon need not be tedious and colorless. This sermon is fresh and full of color. It has the potential to stir people to action. One can almost hear the "ahas" arising from the congregation as listeners recall the Harolds in their own lives. Some may even identify themselves as Harold. But now, together they can join in lifting the sail of faith to catch the breeze, the breeze of the Spirit, and be sent out with renewed vigor.

One comes away from Corr's sermon-letter with the hope that Harold might someday accept this open-ended invitation. Just as important, one comes away from the sermon with a renewed vision of what it means to be the church. That is critical for those who worship and serve both in the church and in the everyday world.

SUGGESTIONS

- Preach an experimental style sermon. It can be a monologue, a shared sermon, or the telling of a story. Accept the challenge to try something fresh and different from the style you use weekly.
- Choose a local or national issue and write an epistolary-style sermon. Some examples are: John Killinger's "An Open Letter to TV Evangelists," Ernest Campbell's, "An Open Letter to Billy Graham."
- Preach an epistolary sermon from the New Testament (see, for instance, Jude, Philemon, 1 John, etc.).

K. Thomas Greene

The Text You Live By

ROMANS 8:28–30

Rev. Dr. Mark E. Yurs
Salem United Church of Christ
Verona, Wisconsin

Rev. Dr. Mark E. Yurs

The Text You Live By

ROMANS 8:28–30, NRSV

There are texts that shape our lives. For example, in a current John Updike novel, one of the characters, Teddy Wilmont, searches for his life's work with the help of his family. Updike describes the issue for the character and the family: "He needed something respectable, because he was a Wilmont, and yet not too demanding because he was Teddy."[1] That sentence reveals there were two texts shaping Teddy Wilmont's life in his own family's estimation. One read, "Wilmonts work only in noble professions"; the other stated, "Less is expected of Teddy because he is less capable than other Wilmonts."

All of us have texts we live by, visions that keep us going. They may or may not be written down. They may or may not be spoken in so many words. But they are part of us. They may come from a grandmother or a parent, a teacher or a friend. Whatever their origin, these texts we live by factor into our feelings about ourselves, our perspectives on the world, and our attitudes about the future. Before we take any step forward in life, large or small, we consult the texts we live by to determine if that step is one we could and should take.

What is the vision that keeps you going? What is the text you live by?

I hope the text you live by says that you are loved. You are, you know.

This may not be a message that comes through loud and clear on the job or the playground, or even in church or at home. But you are loved; loved by the God who made you and claims you and is proud of you.

God loves you immeasurably. Whenever the Bible talks about how much God loves, it runs out of words. The holiest of writers in the holiest of books cannot describe what is the height and depth and length and breadth of the love of God. God's love for you is so wide and deep and full that it cannot be measured. (See Eph. 3:18–19.) Not only are the hairs of your head all numbered by God, but God gave his only Son for your sake. You've seen those figurines depicting a person with outstretched arms that says, "I love you this much." There is no set of arms long enough to show how much God loves you. God loves you immeasurably.

God loves you unconditionally. This means that God's love for you goes back farther than you can remember. It is God's gift to you. You did not do anything to get it started. God loved you before you were baptized. God loved you before you decided to believe in Jesus and to love God. The Bible says that God loved you before the foundation of the world. There has never been a point in your life when God did not love you; there may have been actions and attitudes God did not approve of, but God has never fallen out of love with you. "God proves his love for us," says Paul, "in that while we still were sinners Christ died for us" (Rom. 5:8). That is unconditional love. God loves you that way. God loves you unconditionally.

God loves you unceasingly. This unconditional love which goes back before the foundation of the world and which cannot be measured will go on forever. One of the few vocabulary words I remember with ease from my study of Hebrew, the language of the Old Testament, is *hesed*. It means steadfast loving-kindness. When the psalmist said of God, "Your steadfast love endures forever," he used the word *hesed*. The apostle Paul reflected on this *hesed*, the steadfast loving-kindness of the Lord, particularly as God has shown it to us in Jesus, and declared, "I am convinced that neither death, nor life, nor angels, nor rulers, nor things present, nor things to come, nor powers, nor height, nor depth, nor anything else in all creation, will be able to separate us from the love of God in Christ Jesus our Lord" (Rom. 8:38–39). God's love for you is here to stay. God loves you unceasingly.

Write these words into the text you live by: "I am loved—loved immeasurably, unconditionally, unceasingly."

I hope the text you live by says you are loved and I hope it says you are called. Again we turn to Paul, who wrote, "We know that all things work together for good for those who love God, who are called according to his purpose. For those whom he foreknew he also predestined to be conformed to the image of his Son" (Rom. 8:28–29). Words like *called* and *foreknew* and *predestined* carry us out into some deep theological waters, but they are not meant to make us drown. They are meant to be lifejackets around our shoulders to buoy us up with hope when we fear we are about to drown spiritually.

God has a plan for your life. Every day may not be marked out. The calendar of your days may not even be penciled in, to say nothing of being etched in stone. Your every activity is not a foregone conclusion, as if you had no say in the matter. But God does have a plan for your life. There is some purpose God wants to work out in and through you. You are upon this earth for a reason, not haphazardly. Your life is not like any other; you are unique. God has made you an individual. Everything about your body declares that. What is true physically is also true spiritually. You have a purpose in life that is different from anyone else's. God has a plan for you.

God's plan is not always easy to see. That statement may go down as this pulpit's understatement of the year! God's plan is seldom easy to see—for many reasons. Barriers like disappointment, failure, suffering, fatigue, and what at times appears to be the bane of other people, all work to block your vision of what God wants to do with your life. God asks you to believe you are called even when you cannot see what you are called to. Faith means, in part, trusting that God indeed has a plan even when no plan seems to be in sight.

God's plan for you is created by God's love. Some may believe that God has a plan for them, but that it relates more to what God wants to do *to* them than to what God wants to do *with* them and *through* them. To those and to all I say, remember God's plan is always in the service of God's love. Whatever plan God has for you is a good one—better than you can dream up for yourself—because God is both wisdom and love.

When our family was on vacation recently, we took a hike along a path in Mount Rainier National Park recommended by my wife, Sherrol's, parents. The walk was long and at times tiring and difficult. At the end of the trail, we weren't back where we started, nor were we at a place to turn around. We were at the scene of a breathtakingly beautiful waterfall—so beautiful I don't have words to describe it. *That* was why we were sent on the difficult hike. Much the same is true of the plan of God for your life. Though the way between here and the end of the path may be arduous, the purpose to be revealed at the end is more glorious than you can imagine. You are called to something wonderful.

Write that into the text you live by. You are called. It may not be easy to see, but God has a plan for your life that is in the service of his love.

I hope the text you live by says that you are loved, that you are called, and I hope it says that you are glory bound. You are, you know. God did not bring you this far to leave you. Paul says you are on the way to glory: Those whom God "predestined he also called; and those whom he called he also justified; and those whom he justified he also glorified" (v. 30).

I pity those who believe in reincarnation. What a long, lonely path through the cosmos! What an endless source of frustration to believe that once you get through this vale of tears, another awaits, and then another after that—with no guarantee of improvement. No wonder reincarnation does not appear in the gospel; it is not good news.

I am happy to be among those who believe in resurrection as opposed to reincarnation. It is glorification that awaits, not another season of humiliation and limitation. The mortal body shall take on immortality. Imperfection shall take on perfection. Tears, pain, disappointment, and confusion will all be gone. Safety will be unchallenged, and peace will be uncompromised by any risk or threat or evil. Death will be transformed into life—life eternal, bright and fair.

Write that into the text you live by. You are glory bound!

"He needed something respectable because he was a Wilmont, and yet not too demanding because he was Teddy." So, prior decisions about what it meant to be a Wilmont and what could be expected of him as an individual shaped Teddy Wilmont's life, becoming texts he lived by.

What is the text you live by? There is some text written deep inside your soul. Maybe Grandma put it there, or Dad or a teacher at school—one you either liked or not. You may not know its exact words, but you know the gist of it and it dictates what you think about yourself, the world around you, and the stuff of which you are capable.

I hope the text you live by says you are loved, called, and glory bound. If it does, I thank God, because that means you have peace and happiness at the core of your being—at the place where your plot gets written.

If the text you live by does not say you are loved, called, and glory bound, it can. If the text you live by says you are unloved, ignored, and doomed to be mired in the muck of misery, whoever wrote that text was wrong. Don't let that person or those people have that kind of power over you. Believe instead the promise of God: "All things work together for good for those who love God, who are called according to his purpose" (v. 28). Jesus went to the cross and rose from the dead to prove that you are included in that promise. You are not left behind. You are not left out. You are loved. You are called. You are glory bound.

Note
1. John Updike, *In the Beauty of the Lilies* (New York: Alfred A. Knopf, 1996), p. 203.

COMMENT

A business deal falls through. A divorce is finalized. An aging parent is placed in a nursing home. A teenage son or daughter admits drug use. A tumor is discovered.

These are the events that punctuate the week before a congregation gathers on a Sunday morning. Week after week. Sunday after Sunday. Among the weddings and baptisms, the graduations and promotions, the joy and laughter, are the disappointments, anxieties, fear, and heartaches.

Within any given week are moments of great joy and great sorrow. Into that variety of human experience comes the task of proclaiming the Word. For those whose life's work brings them into the pulpit week after week, there is a time and place for teaching, for exposition, for exhortation, even for a prophetic voice. Equally important, but often overlooked, is the value of a pastoral care sermon. Yet it's a challenge to preach a sermon that touches the heart and soul of those at both ends of the spectrum of joy and sorrow. What can be said that has meaning and relevance to both the joyful and the sorrowful?

One writer has said that when you don't know where to begin, just start with the basics. Mark Yurs does just that. "The Text You Live By" is pastoral care from the pulpit at its purest. Simple. Direct. Reassuring. This is a sermon for every individual whose week has been long, whose heart is heavy, and who needs to hear that God is loving, present, and ultimately in control. This is a good news sermon. But the appeal of the sermon doesn't stop there. The three points Yurs makes are equally meaningful for the individual whose heart is full of joy and for whom life's roller coaster is still riding easy.

Style & Structure

Mention a three-point sermon and three words come to my mind: long, old-fashioned—and too often—uninteresting. Not so with "The Text You Live By." Yurs has crafted a three-point sermon with warmth, clarity, and brevity. A primary strength of this sermon is its simplicity. No doubt remains about what the message is: "You are loved. You are called. You are glory bound."

In the tradition of centuries of great rhetoric, Yurs has developed this sermon with nice symmetry: a three-point sermon, with each of the three primary points supported by subpoints. The first two points clearly have three subpoints each. The third point has one to three subpoints, depending on how you view the structure. Into this pattern, Yurs brings symmetrical repetition. As he moves from one major point to the next, he repeats the previous one:

> "I hope the text you live by says you are loved. You are, you know...."
>
> "I hope the text you live by says you are loved and I hope it says you are called...."
>
> "I hope the text that you live by says you are loved, that you are called, and I hope it says that you are glory bound. You are, you know...."

Accompanying this structured approach is the warmth of a very personal tone. Juxtaposing the two—structure and warmth—makes this sermon both memorable and pastoral. Yurs doesn't allow his knowledge of theology or biblical exegesis to set him apart from his congregation. He clearly puts himself on the same level as his listeners when he says, "One of the few vocabulary words I remember with ease from my study of Hebrew...." He may have studied a biblical language in the past, but that isn't an area of academic expertise he claims for himself at the present. He does the same thing again when he says, "Words like *called* and *foreknew* and *predestined* carry us out into some deep theological waters, but..." He consistently keeps the tone of this sermon personal and caring, as if he were sitting across the table from the listener, sharing a cup of coffee and offering a few insights he's learned along the way.

Use of the Text

This sermon gets to the point and makes a point with the opening line creating a subtle double entendre: "There are texts that shape our lives." Is he talking about biblical texts? Preachers always do! If so, in what way? The Updike quote about Teddy Wilmont carries us quickly into a larger world of meaning for the term "text." Now we're listening. Texts are "visions that keep us going." But what does this have to do with biblical texts?

Whether our frame of reference is the corporate world or the helping professions, the language may vary but the concept is the same. Call them mission statements, core beliefs, or inner convictions. Each of us lives by an internal voice that guides the way we believe the world works—beliefs that impact everything from our simplest decisions to our most overwhelming dilemmas. This inner voice—that automatically comes to mind unbidden—can be either positive or negative. It can grow us or destroy us.

Pop psychology has termed this running dialogue in our heads "self talk," and countless books in the self-help section of bookstores advocate self-actualization through rescripting that inner dialogue. But Yurs takes the idea of "texts" out of the realm of pop psychology and self-actualization. He turns to the biblical "text" and the traditions of biblical faith to offer us a text we can live by.

By using the word "text," Yurs accomplishes two things. First, he takes a familiar word out of its typical context and gives it a new twist. He creates a verbal hook on which to hang the sermon. Second, he makes it clear that this "text" is not something we determine. Rather, the text of our lives is determined by God. The orientation isn't what we bring to God. It's what God has already brought to us. The biblical text on which the sermon is based, Paul's words in Romans 8:28–30, underscores a primary theological theme: the transcendent sovereignty of God. "There is some purpose God wants to work out in and through you." It's not about self-actualization. It's about God at work in us. For the person sitting in the pew, Yurs makes these texts as valid for the skeptic, the wounded, the unloved, or the unsure, as he does for the faithful. He addresses a universal problem and offers a universal solution.

Yurs's style is crisp and clean. He writes with short sentences and selective repetition of key phrases. He keeps the language straightforward and uncluttered. He avoids the use of religious or psychological jargon. By couching the sermon in the "I hope," Yurs comes across as loving, affirming, freeing. "The Text You Live By" is a defining sermon: defining God's vision for each of us and a pastor's vision for the spiritual life of his congregation.

SUGGESTIONS

- With so much attention given to narrative preaching in some circles in the last few years, the three-point sermon is less common among preachers. The effectiveness of this particular sermon is the combination of the classic structure with warmth and brevity. If you haven't done any three-point sermons recently, approach the texts for the next few weeks' sermons with the question, "Is a three-point structure appropriate to this text?"
- If you were to write down the three things you would most want your congregation to know, what would those three things be? Is there a sermon or series in those three phrases?
- What are the biblical texts that have shaped *your* life personally? Congregations want and need to know the person behind the profession. If your congregation doesn't know which book of the Bible (or which text) is your favorite and why, there's a sermon in that simple question.

Debra K. Klingsporn

Angels We Have Heard Nearby

LUKE 1:26–38

Rev. Dr. R. Wayne Stacy
Dean, School of Divinity
Gardner-Webb University
Boiling Springs, North Carolina

Rev. Dr. R. Wayne Stacy

Angels We Have Heard Nearby

LUKE 1:26-38

In Allan Gurganus's amazing book of short stories entitled *White People*, he tells the story of an old woman, a widow, whose sons now live far away. She is standing at the sink early one morning dressed in a tatty robe, doing the dishes she left from the night before, and gazing out the window, looking everywhere and nowhere. Out of the corner of her eye she happens to notice something fall to the ground in her backyard. There out near the picnic table lies something white, with wings, shivering as though it were cold, but it wasn't a cold day.

"No way," she says. But when she looks again, there it is, plain as day, resting on its side on a bright air mattress of its own wings. It looks hurt.

Though her arthritis slows her a bit, she hurries—if you can call it that—outside to investigate. She stoops, creaky, over what can only be a young angel, unconscious.

Quick, she checks overhead, ready for what?—some TV news crew in a helicopter? She sees only a sky of the usual size, a Tuesday sky stretched between weekends. She allows herself to touch this thing's white forehead. She gets a mild electric shock. Then, odd, her tickled finger joints stop aching. They've hurt so long. A practical person, she quickly cures her other hand. The angel grunts but sounds pleased. His temperature's a hundred and fifty, easy—but for him, this seems somehow normal. "Poor thing," she says, and carefully pulls his heavy curly head into her lap. The head hums like a phone knocked off its cradle. She scans for neighbors, hoping they'll come out, wishing they wouldn't, both.

As her courage grows, she touches his skin. Feels hard and rough, like a frozen ice tray that clings to everything it touches. But she also notices that with every touch thirty-year-old pains leave her. Emboldened, she whispers to him her private woes: the Medicare cuts, the sons too busy to come by, the daughters-in-law not bad, but not so great either. They, too, seem lifted from her just by the telling. And with every pain healed, with every heartache canceled, the angel seems rejuvenated too. "Her griefs seem to fatten him like vitamins," Gurganus writes.

Regaining consciousness, he whispers to her, "We're just another army. We all look alike—we didn't before. It's not what you expect. We miss the other. Don't count so much on the next. Notice things here. We're just another army."

"Oh," she says, like she understands. She doesn't.

Then, struggling to his feet and stretching his wings, with one solemn grunt, he heaves himself upward, just missing the phone lines.

"Go, go," the old woman, grinning, points the way. He signals back at her, open-mouthed and left behind. First a glinting man-shaped kite, then an oblong of aluminum in the sun, a new moon shrunk to the size of a decent sized star, a final fleck of light, and then a memory, Tuesday memory.

What does she do? Who does she tell? Who'll believe her? She can't tell her neighbor, Lydia. She'll phone her missing sons, "Come right home. Your Mom's inventing company!"

She hears the neighbor's collie barking in the distance. (It saw!)

Maybe other angels have dropped into other backyards, she wonders. Behind fences, did neighbors help earlier ones? Folks keep so much of the best stuff quiet, don't they?

Regaining her aplomb, she bounces back inside to finish her dishes. Slowly, she notices, her joints start to ache again. The age spots that had totally vanished only moments before start to darken again. Everything is as it was before. Well, not everything.

Standing there at the sink, she seems to be expecting something. Look at her, crazy old woman, staring out at the backyard, nowhere, everywhere. She plunges her aching hands into the warm, soapy water and whispers, "I'm right here, ready. Ready for more."[1]

An old woman, who seems to be washing dishes, but she's not. She's guarding the world. Only, nobody knows.

Seen any angels lately? I have. Well, let me rephrase that. I've seen a lot about angels lately, and in the strangest places. Not long ago NBC television did a two-hour special, hosted by Patty Duke, called *Angels: Those Mysterious Messengers*. Two hours! Imagine, a commercial television network devoting two hours of prime time to angels! Apparently due to the current interest (and marketability) in the whole subject of spirituality in general and angels in particular, NBC has launched a series titled, *Touched by an Angel*.

Then there was the feature article in *USA Today* recently about guardian angels. The story was about the current practice, popular among many, of wearing little guardian angel pins on their lapels. You've seen them too. Apparently many still believe that there's more to life than meets the eye.

Time magazine devoted the cover of a recent issue to angels. Inside, the feature article, "Angels among Us," trumpeted (sorry about that) the statistic that 69 percent of Americans polled said they believed in angels.

In a recent issue of *Ladies Home Journal* there was another article about guardian angels, stories about people who, they believed, were miraculously delivered from all kinds of difficulties, people who sincerely believe it was angels who made the difference.

In 1990 there were only five books in print on the subject of angels, according to Gannett News Service. Today there are over two hundred, many of which have become bestsellers!

Unless you're hiding under a rock, you'll hardly make it through the Christmas season without seeing yet again the marvelous, if not altogether competent, angel, Clarence, in Frank Capra's classic movie *It's a Wonderful Life*.

Frederick Buechner says of angels,

> Sleight-of-hand magic is based on the demonstrable fact that as a rule people see only what they expect to see. Angels are powerful spirits whom God sends into the world to wish us well. Since we don't expect to see them, we don't. An angel spreads his glittering wings over us, and we say things like "It was one of those days that made you feed good just to be alive" or "I had a hunch everything was going to turn out all right" or "I don't know where I ever found the courage."[2]

Seen any angels lately? Well, the Bible has. Apparently without even the decency to be embarrassed, the Bible speaks of a world populated with angels. Abraham and his aging wife, Sarah, entertain three visitors among the oaks of Mamre who reveal to them that they will have a son. When the bewildered old couple protests that this sounds too good to be true, the "visitors," angels unawares, say, "Is anything too hard for the Lord?" (Gen. 18:14, RSV). Jacob wrestles by the brook Jabbok with an angel in human disguise. Samson's father, Manoah, carried on a conversation with a messenger completely unaware that he was talking to an angel, until after the messenger had disappeared.

In the New Testament, angels accompany critical events in the life of Jesus. They announce his birth, minister to him after his temptation, announce his resurrection, and attend his ascension. They assist the fledgling church at crucial times, aiding the apostles under persecution, assisting the spread of the gospel to the Gentiles, rescuing Paul and Silas from a Philippian jail.

The word *angel* means "messenger." It translates *malach* in Hebrew, *angelos* in Greek. More often than not, that's how angels function in the Bible, as messengers of God. Angels were not a part of Jewish theology in its earliest development. Israel had thought of its God as being a very immanent, personal, even anthropomorphic God, walking and chatting with Adam in the garden in the cool of the day.

Later on, this immanent concept of God gave way to a more transcendent idea of God, a God who was distant, unapproachable, removed from his creation. Probably under the influence of her neighbors, Israel's theologians posited angels as intermediary beings between God and his creation, facilitating communication between the Almighty and his creatures. They were conceived of as having special assignments as guides, messengers, or caretakers, and certain ones had names, such as Michael or Gabriel. In some ancient texts, angels were thought to be the personification of stars, the heavenly hosts of God, the "army of God" who accompanied him in battle against all the cosmic forces arrayed against the Almighty. In the Book of Judges the Song of Deborah celebrates Israel's victory over Sisera, the commander of King Jabin's Canaanite army, as a victory of Israel's God YHWH over the cosmic forces arrayed against him.

> From heaven fought the stars,
> from their courses they fought against Sisera (Judges 5:20, RSV).[3]

Coming out of late Judaism, Christianity was from the start influenced by the widespread belief in angels and demons. So, it's not at all surprising that when Luke gets to the part of his story where the birth of the Messiah is to be announced to his unsuspecting mother, the "messenger" is an angel.

Across the galactic emptiness the angel flew to a particular province named Galilee, to a particular city named Nazareth, and then in that city to one particular house, to one particular woman in that house. Her name was Mary.[4]

"Hail!" he said. He whispered it actually. But angels aren't very good at whispering. Try though they may, their voices sound like thunder. Scared poor Mary nearly to death! I mean when an angel appears in the middle of the night in your bedroom and says "Hail!" it gets your heart going!

Realizing that Mary was frightened, Gabriel said what all angels say, "Fear not." It's sort of basic training for angels, you know. Before they're sent out "into the field," they always receive from the D.I. (Divine Instructor) these instructions, "Now look, don't just land and start in with the 'Thus saith the Lord' stuff! Remember what we taught you here; it's *very* important that you always begin with the words, 'Fear not!'"

One of the angels who slept through that lecture raised his wing and asked, "Well, why?"

"Never mind why! You'll understand when you get there! Just do it!"

With Mary somewhat composed, Gabriel did his job. He delivered his message. "Mary, you've been graced by God, and though you're a virgin, you shall bear a son, and you shall call his name Jesus; and he will be great, and will be called the Son of the Most High; and the Lord God will give to him the throne of his father David, and of his kingdom there shall be no end!"

Still confused, however, Mary asked, "How can this be?"

The angel, just as he had said to Abraham and Sarah long ago, looked at Mary, smiled, and said, "With God nothing is impossible!"

Seen any angels lately? Don't be too disappointed if you haven't. Not everyone believes in angels.

Some biblical scholars disbelieve in angels, at least as spiritual beings. They find it hard to buy into any mumbo jumbo about ghosts and spirits, which is where they put angels. I have to admit that there was a time when I disbelieved in a spiritual world. I thought it was an anachronistic residue of a more primitive age in which the world was populated with spiritual, incorporeal beings who could pass through solid objects and suddenly appear and disappear, as angels do throughout Scripture. I thought such a world belonged to fairy tales and children's books with their trolls and enchanted creatures. But having read C. S. Lewis's marvelous book *The Great Divorce,* I'm not so sure anymore. You see, he suggests that perhaps we've got it backwards. Rather than angels being insubstantial and translucent, able to pass through solid objects because they have no substance, what if it's the reverse? What if it is we who are insubstantial and incorporeal relative to their world, and it is they, not we, who are so solid, so dense in fact that they pass through what we regard as solid objects as though they were merely a mist or a fog? "Earth," he says, "is the gray town with its continual hope of morning."[5]

I don't know.

The word *angel* simply means "messenger." Some scholars believe that angels may not be spiritual beings at all, but anybody who brings a message from God. There is some precedence for this view. The Old Testament book of Malachi takes its title from the Hebrew word *malachi,* which can also be translated as *angel.* Was Malachi a prophet or an angel?

I don't know. And I don't know who knows.

I know this. Sometimes God sends his messages to us in some pretty unusual packaging, and if we're not attentive, if we're not looking, if we're not listening, we can miss it!

A friend of mine was preaching a revival sometime ago, and because of some pressing business back at his office, he was traveling back and forth from his office to the church every evening for the services. By the end of the week he was tired.

One night as he was traveling home, he stopped at a convenience store to get a cup of coffee to steel him against the long drive ahead. It was late, and he was tired as he came out of the store. As he walked to his car, an old man came up to him and asked if he had any spare change he could give him. Well…it was late and my friend was tired and wanted to get home. Besides, you can't be too careful, can you? Can you? My friend said, "No," with his hand on some quarters in his pocket.

The next night at the church, a lady came up to him and told him that as a result of his moving sermon on grace which he had preached the night before, she had been moved to give a homeless man some spare change from her purse. She said, "You never know…maybe God sent him my way!"

Do you think…maybe…he was…? Nah.

Even so, I can't help remembering what the writer of Hebrews says, "Do not neglect to show hospitality to strangers, for thereby some have entertained angels unawares" (Heb. 13:2, RSV).

Have you seen any angels lately?

John Duckworth did. He tells a story about Pastor Torgenson who stood before his congregation as they gathered one cold Christmas Eve for a testimony service.[6] It was their custom in that little church every

Christmas Eve to share with each other how God had blessed them during the previous year.

As the people gathered, Pastor Torgenson began, "Before the choir sings our anthem, 'Angels We Have Heard on High,' let me remind you of a Scripture passage about angels. Turn with me to Hebrews 13:2."

A tissue-thin shuffle of Bible pages went through the sanctuary and then was rudely interrupted as a haggard couple entered the back. The man had a bushy beard and old, faded clothes. She was pregnant and wore a tattered dress.

"Wonder if they're even married?" someone murmured.

"Well, I never…" said another.

Old Mizzie Everett just squinted, apparently as confused as ever. Pastor Torgenson smiled and invited them to find a seat. It wasn't easy. The church was full, it being Christmas Eve. They had to make their way all the way down front.

Then, Pastor Torgenson read those verses, you know, about entertaining angels unawares. He was surprised himself at the timing of it all, this young couple showing up unexpectedly like that.

After the choir sang, he invited people to give their testimonies.

"Anyone want to share a *brief* word of testimony?" He had emphasized "brief" on account of Old Mizzie. My, the way she could carry on about nothing! Trying to remember dates, singing with an awful squeal. Folks just kind of shook their heads, chuckled under their breath, and said, "Well, you know Old Mizzie."

Sure enough, Mizzie was the first to the microphone. You could almost hear an audible "ahhhh." True to form, she went on and on, with Pastor Torgenson politely interjecting from time to time, "Thank you very much, Mizzie," as though that would stop her. It didn't. Finally, she was through.

Then, the haggard young man rose. "I don't know nothin' 'bout talkin' in church," he began, "but me and my old lady, uh…my wife, we really need a place to stay. I ain't got no job."

When he finished, Pastor Torgenson commented, "We appreciate your sharing with us. I think we can help. By the way, what's your name?"

"I'm Joe. She's Mary."

You could see the wheels turning—Joseph and Mary? C'mon now!

Yeah, I know how it sounds. Really, though.

In the fellowship time later, a good number of folks talked with the young couple while nibbling on cookies. Several offered places to stay, and one of the men talked to Joe about a job. Old Mizzie stood in the corner, ignored, sipping coffee and nibbling on a cookie.

Suddenly, she looked at her watch, put down her coffee cup and started for the door. She mounted her three-wheel bike and began pedaling slowly back outside of town. The night air was cold and her old body was so worn. When she reached the edge of town, she stopped near an empty field. The highway was deserted. Only the stars and heaven watched as she climbed the sloping hill. A dog barked in the distance.

"Christmas Eve," she said to herself. "Just like that first Christmas Eve when we sang of His birth. That was easy compared to this assignment! Well, time to go home now."

She smiled, closed her eyes, and reached heavenward. "Goin' home," she whispered, "goin' home."

How's that go again? "Angels We Have Heard *Nearby?*" Who knows? Is there *anything* too hard for God?

Seen any angels lately? Are you...are you sure?

Notes
1. Allan Gurganus, "It Had Wings," in *White People: Stories and Novellas* (New York: Ballantine Books, 1992), pp. 162–66.
2. Frederick Buechner, *Wishful Thinking: A Theological ABC* (New York: Harper Collins, Publishers, 1973), pp. 1–2.
3. For a brief, but excellent treatment of the function of angels in the Bible, see Dale C. Allison, Jr., "What Was the Star that Guided the Magi?" *Bible Review,* vol. IX, no. 6 (December 1993), pp. 20–24, 64.
4. Adapted from Walter Wangerin, Jr., "The Christmas Story," in *The Manger is Empty: Stories in Time* (San Francisco: Harper & Row, Publishers, 1989), pp. 29–32.
5. C. S. Lewis, *The Great Divorce,* reprint edition (New York: Macmillan, 1979), p. 38.
6. John Duckworth, "Angels We Have Heard on High," *Stories That Sneak Up on You* (Grand Rapids: Fleming H. Revell, 1987), pp. 154–58.

Comment

Some years ago I served a church in an outlying parish near the city of New Orleans. While I was there, a local TV station aired an investigative report on some incidents of what appeared to be the ritual slaughter of animals. The reporter speculated that these incidents might be linked to Satan worship, and he interviewed a number of specialists on the subject, including priests and law enforcement officers. Needless to say, the program generated tremendous ratings and a great deal of discussion. As a result, a rumor swept through the local high school that some Satan worshipers in our area were intent on kidnapping a blond, blue-eyed girl for ritual sacrifice. This caused panic among the youth and their parents. These happenings gave me an unprecedented opportunity to speak on evil and the demonic.

Sometimes the culture in which we live presents an opportunity to proclaim the gospel. Wayne Stacy has taken note of the renewed interest in angels in our culture and has used that as an occasion to preach the gospel.

Question

"Seen any angels lately?" That question sets up Stacy's sermon. Beginning with the retelling of a short story in which an angel figures prominently, Stacy catalogs the number of recent news stories, TV shows, and books on the subject of angels. His review reveals that angels are a hot topic in today's world. An upsurge in spirituality has generated an unprecedented interest in angels. Stacy uses his sermon to speak to that widespread curiosity and to define briefly the role of angels in the Bible.

Text

The text of this sermon from Luke 1:26–38 provides a backdrop against which the entire subject is explored. The biblical text is not the primary focus of the sermon, and Stacy does not attempt to work through it in detail.

Instead, he treats it broadly, using the story of the angel's announcement to Mary to illustrate how angels most often functioned as recorded in the Bible.

PROCLAMATION

This sermon affords us a good example of form married to function. "Seen any angels lately?" Stacy asks. He repeats that question, or some form of it, throughout the sermon and uses it to give the sermon its structure and convey its message. The mere suggestion that angels dance in and out of our lives invites us to look at our world differently and to acknowledge that more is going on than we know. The possibility that angels move among us calls for us to acknowledge that reality itself is not flat; there's a lot we don't understand and can't explain.

Stacy's use of biblical texts lends much to his presentation. He provides numerous examples from Scripture of how angels have gone about their work in the past. Even those examples, however, don't tell us everything. The biblical stories point to a reality they refuse to explain. Consequently, much of the sermon relies on stories about encounters in our own time with angels. Even then, the characters involved can't say for sure what happened.

Interestingly, Stacy effects a tone of uncertainty throughout this sermon, and that tone reinforces his message. "Seen any angels lately?" he asks. "Are you sure?" he adds. The questioning, searching tone of the sermon complements his purpose. He wants his listeners to take a second look at the world. What about our encounters with strangers? Have we entertained angels unawares?

The uncertain tone is not just a matter of style; it is also one of honesty. Stacy himself leaves open the question of angels. Tracing the development of his own thought, he acknowledges that he has moved from outright dismissal to a sort of cautious openness. He doesn't know what to make of angels and doesn't know anyone who can offer a definitive word. In this light, he provides some solid background material on angels along with some scholars' perspectives. He includes this material in a way that does not detract from the sermon, but gives his listeners something more to chew on than the stuff offered up by the peddlers of popular spirituality.

Although most people show up at church hoping for a robust pronouncement of an eternal certainty by their minister, here Stacy's questioning tone and candor make his sermon work. By confessing what he does not know, Stacy is able to proclaim what he does know: "Sometimes God sends his messages to us in some pretty unusual packaging, and if we're not attentive, if we're not looking, if we're not listening, we can miss them!"

The gospel proclaimed by this sermon is not obvious at first glance. It shows up like an encounter with an angel. Stacy's good news is that God is nearer every day than we can imagine. Whenever we have been reminded of that or have found ourselves renewed in courage, chances are we have been touched by an angel.

Response

We live in a wonder-killing world. We want to explain everything, reduce it to a formula, and manipulate it. We're also in a hurry about everything. Speed is the name of the game. In this kind of world, there's just not much mystery. Stacy invites his listeners to think otherwise. His sermon reminds us that ours is a wonder-filled world. There's more going on than we know. Open your eyes. Expect something. You may find an angel nearby.

Suggestions

- Open your eyes to your own world. What is happening where you live? What topics have captured the interest of your people? Where does God fit in? Is there an opportunity for you to address those concerns with a word from Scripture?
- As I read this sermon, I realized that no one attitude toward the prevailing culture suffices. Sometimes we have to confront the culture, naming its evils and calling for repentance. Sometimes the

culture invites us to build a bridge. This sermon is a good example of the latter. Again, listen to the concerns of your congregation. Do those concerns give you an opportunity to define what Christianity is and is not?
- How honest can you be with your congregation? Can you openly acknowledge what you know and what you do not know? At heart, the most powerful realities of our faith are mystery, and words fail us. By admitting the limits of our own knowledge, we may prompt others to worship.

William J. Ireland, Jr.

JESUS THE RABBI?

MARK 1:16–22

REV. DR. MARK D. ROBERTS
IRVINE PRESBYTERIAN CHURCH
IRVINE, CALIFORNIA

REV. DR. MARK D. ROBERTS

JESUS THE RABBI?

MARK 1:16–22, NRSV

A rabbi and a minister were at a neighborhood picnic. As they rode in one of the boats on the lake, the rabbi stood up, stepped out of the boat, and walked over the water to the nearest stretch of land. Astonished, the minister decided to see if he could duplicate this miraculous feat. He stepped out of the boat and sank. But he managed to swim to shore. As he started to dry himself off, the rabbi walked over and said, "If you're a nice guy, next time I'll show you where the rocks are!"[1]

This is not a sermon about walking on water. But it is about a rabbi.

Today we are focusing on the title for Jesus, "Rabbi." Fifteen times in the Greek New Testament Jesus is addressed by the Hebrew word *Rabbî* (for example, Mark 9:5, where Peter calls Jesus "Rabbi").[2] What did it mean when people spoke to Jesus in this way? To what extent did Jesus play the role of a Jewish rabbi? How do we, as twentieth-century gentiles (for the most part), relate to Jesus as our "Rabbi"?

JESUS, THE JEWISH RABBI, IN CONTEXT

That Jesus was called "Rabbi" emphasizes one crucial fact that we must remember if we are to understand him truly: *Jesus was Jewish*. I know this is obvious to you, but more than once in my life I have encountered someone who insisted that Jesus was not Jewish, but Christian. Let there be no mistake about it, Jesus was Jewish. He was born to a Jewish mother, spoke the languages of Jews in the first century (Aramaic and probably Hebrew), was raised in the Jewish culture, prayed in the Jewish synagogue, worshiped in the Jewish temple, read the Jewish scriptures, and saw his mission as essentially connected to the Jewish people.

Judaism in the time of Jesus was a religious and cultural phenomenon of considerable diversity. Even within Palestine, there were many conceptions and expressions of Jewish faith. In the Gospels we see Jesus interacting with different groups, including the scribes, Pharisees, Sadducees, priests, Herodians, and the common people. If we want to understand what it meant for Jesus to be called "Rabbi," then we should know something about the scribes and the Pharisees.

The scribes were religious scholars, students of the Jewish scriptures. Before the advent of the printing press, scribes were the ones who made handwritten copies of the Hebrew scriptures. As the ones with primary access to these sacred documents, they became learned in the Law, the Prophets, and the Writings of the Jews (the traditional Jewish division of the Hebrew scriptures). Many scribes became teachers of what they had learned. Some set up schools or taught in their homes; many taught in the synagogues or in the Jerusalem temple. Students would come to them for religious education, and would enter into long-term relationships with their teachers, whom they might then address as "Rabbi," a Hebrew term meaning "great one" or "master." A student who learned completely the teaching of his master scribe could become a scribe himself. A close modern analogy to the scribes would be seminary professors, more than pastors or even Jewish rabbis today. Scribes in the first century were scholars and teachers, not priests or anything like modern-day clergy.

The Pharisees were members of a reform movement that arose within Judaism around the time of Jesus. Although their history is not completely clear, the movement appears to have begun as a well-organized political group that was committed to national renewal through exceptional faithfulness to the law of Moses.

As the Pharisaic movement developed and as the power of Rome dominated Judea, the Pharisees came to focus less on political aspirations and more on matters of personal piety. Yet their theology had political implications, since they believed that obedience to the law would hasten the coming of the Messiah, who would overthrow the Romans and bring complete renewal to the nation of Israel.

A modern analogy for the early Pharisees would be the politically active Christian Coalition. In both cases we observe a lay movement that crosses theological lines and that blends religious conservatism with a dominant political agenda. The later Pharisees would resemble something like Faith at Work or Promise Keepers, groups with a primary concern for spiritual renewal. A Pharisee could be a professional scholar—a scribe—but most were neither scribes nor priests. They were simply laypeople committed to national and religious renewal.[3]

The Pharisees intended to obey the law of Moses as they found it both in the written Torah and as passed on through oral tradition. The individual Pharisee was not free to interpret the written law for himself, but rather received the meaning of the law from his teachers, who traced their authority through other teachers back to Moses himself. Every teaching Pharisee would make specific references to those whose authority he claimed. His own authority lay not in his personal inspiration, not in the authority of the written text, but in the tradition behind him. It would be as if, when I preached, I always cited my mentor, Lloyd Ogilvie, who cited his mentor, James Stewart, who cited his mentor, who cited his mentor—and so on back to Jesus himself!

Pharisees in the time of Jesus were particularly concerned about maintaining ritual purity. They were not priests, but applied priestly regulations to their lives as laypeople. Their name, "Pharisee," probably comes from the Hebrew word that means "separatist." They separated themselves from the common people who followed only the general law of Moses but not the laws of purity. The separated Pharisees maintained close fellowship with each other, especially through sharing meals and religious education together.

After the destruction of Jerusalem in A.D. 70, the Pharisees were instrumental in redefining Judaism, now without a temple and its priesthood. Rabbinic Judaism, the synagogue-based Judaism we know today with professional clergy known as rabbis, grew from Pharisaic roots. Prior to A.D. 70, however, while the term *rabbi* could be used for religious teachers, it was a general term of respect for all persons worthy of honor.

THE DISTINCTIVENESS OF JESUS AS RABBI

To a casual observer, Jesus would have appeared as a "scribe." He demonstrated a knowledge of the Hebrew scriptures and taught the things of God. Around him were gathered a group of students who followed him and were committed to him as their sole teacher. It should come as no surprise, therefore, that his followers and others addressed him as "Rabbi." This was a gesture of respect that acknowledged his role as a teacher.

Jesus also had much in common with the Pharisees. He and his followers were laypeople, not priests or professional scholars. Their vision for national renewal focused upon faithfulness to God and the coming of the Messiah.

But Jesus the Rabbi also distinguished himself from the scribes and the Pharisees in crucial ways. In the passage we read from Mark 1, notice that *Jesus calls people* to follow him as his disciples. Jesus chooses his own students, not the other way around. No scribe or Pharisee in the time of Jesus would have done this. Nor would a potential student expect to be drafted as a disciple of a rabbi. One of the early rabbinic teachers said specifically, "Procure for yourself a teacher [in Hebrew, *rab,* the basis for *rabbi*]."[4] The one who wanted to learn would go find his own rabbi. The opposite was true for Jesus and his disciples.

By calling his disciples, rather than waiting until they came to him, Jesus projects his unique authority. He is in charge. His word to his potential disciples is clear and unapologetic: "Follow me" (Mark 1:17). Not, "Follow me if that's convenient for you," or "Follow me if it fits into your five-year plan," but simply "Follow me—now—just do it!" Notice, too, that the word of Jesus is not something to which one can merely assent, "Oh, that's true. What a nice idea, Rabbi." Rather, it demands a full response, a change in life, a new direction.

Like the scribes and the Pharisees, Jesus begins teaching in a synagogue (Mark 1:21). Those gathered for instruction would expect to hear from a lay Pharisee, or if they were particularly blessed, from a professional scribe. In either case the teacher would expound the law of God, with specific reference to the oral traditions that interpreted that law. No teacher of stature would simply proclaim God's will but would instead derive God's will through the intricacies of Jewish tradition.

Not so with Jesus. Those gathered in Capernaum for his synagogue message "were astounded at his teaching, for he taught them as one having authority, and not as the scribes" (Mark 1:22). In other words, Jesus didn't defend his teaching with lengthy citations from the law or with lists of human authorities. He spoke simply, with the conviction that he spoke the very truth of God.

At times Jesus actually contradicted the Jewish traditions so beloved by the Pharisees and revered by the scribes. Once when they asked him why his disciples didn't wash their hands before they ate, as demanded by "the tradition of the elders" (Mark 7:5), Jesus accused the scribes and Pharisees of abandoning the commandment of God and holding to human tradition (Mark 7:8).

Jesus' bold authority as a teacher caused people to marvel at his teaching. In some quarters his fame spread rapidly (Mark 1:28). Though many were astounded, some were offended and tried to kill Jesus (Luke 4:28–29). This was not simply a new teacher to be addressed as Rabbi. This was a man whose word demanded a vigorous response—either positive or negative.

Was Jesus a rabbi? Well, yes and no. As a Jewish teacher he certainly was addressed with the deferential title "Rabbi." He taught God's truth to his disciples and others. But, unlike other teaching rabbis in his day, Jesus selected his own inner core of students. He was in control; his authoritative call set the stage for his teaching. And when he taught, he assumed an authority that was unheard of among his contemporaries. He spoke as if conveying the very words of God. So Jesus, who was known as "Rabbi," nevertheless stood alone among the teachers of his day in his method of recruitment and in the authority of his teaching. Jesus the Rabbi? Yes, but in a uniquely authoritative way.

Responding to Jesus the Rabbi Today

How should we respond to Jesus the Rabbi today? How should we respond to one who speaks with unique authority—as if conveying the very words of God?

Have you ever had someone speak to you with authority? While in high school, a friend of mine was speeding along a residential street of my hometown when he saw the lights of a police car in his rearview mirror. For some crazy reason Bill decided to evade the police. He whipped around the corner, pulled quickly into someone's driveway, turned off his motor and lights, and crouched down in the front seat so that no one could see him. Thirty seconds later he heard the stern order from behind his car, "Put your hands up and get out of the car!" Raising his head, Bill saw a policeman glaring at him. Continuing in his folly, Bill did not do as he was told, but started to fiddle around in his pockets to find his driver's license. "I mean now!" the officer yelled. Bill turned to see the barrel of a revolver glaring at him. Finally he got the message, put his hands up, and got out of the car. Sometimes it's dangerous to disregard one who speaks with authority!

Yet that's exactly how many of us respond to Jesus. We hear his teaching and say, "Oh, that's nice. Jesus is such a fine moral example and teacher." We take Jesus as simply one authority among many. To be sure, we have no shortage of experts for living today. Spend five minutes in your local bookstore and you can find dozens of self-help books from self-ordained gurus. They'll tell you how to manage your time, improve your marriage, heal your inner child, and discover your spiritual self.

But in the midst of so many authorities today—our modern-day rabbis—Jesus stands out just as he did twenty centuries ago. He speaks with an uncompromising authority that demands obedience. He is unwilling to share with others his role as our principal teacher. His word comes to us, not as one more piece of good advice, but as the word of God that calls forth a response. When we accept Jesus' call to follow him, we give him a unique place in our life. He becomes, not one rabbi among many, but our great teacher, faithful guide, and unparalleled authority. We commit ourselves to learning from him how to live—and then to living in his ways.

So may I ask you: Are you learning from Jesus? Does his word function as the unique authority in your life? Have you committed yourself to learning from Jesus—and does this commitment show in your daily life?

If we respond appropriately to Jesus our Rabbi, then we will indeed devote our lives to being his students, his disciples. We will seek his truth—through personal Bible study, through studying the Scriptures with other Christians, through praying for guidance from Jesus, through meditating upon the truth of God, through living actively in the community of his disciples. Does this describe your life? How much of your time and energy do you devote to learning about Jesus?

Moreover, if we respond appropriately to Jesus our Rabbi, then we will seek to live out his truth each and every day—no matter how difficult or countercultural.

I know that it isn't always easy to live as a faithful disciple of Rabbi Jesus. Last week I spent time with a man in this church who faces extremely difficult and complex challenges in his professional life. He is being tempted to do what he feels is wrong. Many "authorities" would urge him to do what is "practical," to do what "makes the most sense," to do "what is best for the company." But as a Christian he wants to do what is right—what Jesus would have him do—no matter what the cost or the consequences for his personal advancement. As we talked, I couldn't begin to sort out all the confusing details of his situation, but I could work with him to find what is really quite simple: the call of Jesus to seek first the kingdom of God and God's righteousness, to be truthful, to forgive, to be a peacemaker. After first seeking to learn from Jesus, this man then chose to act as Jesus' disciple, to obey the teaching of his master even in the face of ambiguity or "expert" opinion to the contrary. That's what it means to respond to Jesus the Rabbi!

How will you respond to Jesus the Rabbi in the nitty-gritty realities of your life? When you're figuring out your income tax? When you're falling in love with someone who is not your spouse? When you're tempted to cheat at school?

How will you respond to Jesus the Rabbi? His unique authority calls you to follow him, to hear his word above all others, to hear his word and then to do it (Luke 8:21).

Hear how some men responded to Jesus the Rabbi almost two thousand years ago:

> As Jesus passed along the Sea of Galilee, he saw Simon and his brother Andrew casting a net into the sea—for they were fishermen. And Jesus said to them, "Follow me and I will make you fish for people." And immediately they left their nets and followed him. As he went a little farther, he saw James son of Zebedee and his brother John, who were in their boat mending the nets. Immediately he called them, and they left their father Zebedee in the boat with the hired men, and followed him. (Mark 1:16–20)

So how will you respond to Jesus the Rabbi?

Notes
1. Joke inspired by Milton Berle, *More of the Best of Milton Berle's Private Joke File* (New York: Avon Books, 1993), p. 417.
2. Twice *"Rabbouni"* appears instead of "Rabbi" (Mark 10:51 and John 20:16).
3. By comparing the Pharisees with the Christian Coalition, Faith at Work, and Promise Keepers, I am pointing to structural and missional similarities. I do not mean to disparage any of these organizations. Too often Christians look down upon the Pharisees without understanding who they were or what they intended. In many ways we Christians have much in common with the ancient Pharisees, though we differ in key respects.
4. *Mishnah*, Aboth 1:6.

COMMENT

Mark Roberts's sermon presents us with an opportunity to investigate the difference between preaching and teaching. In a sense, what we have here are two sermons packed into one. It is debatable how well they work together as compared to how they might work being divided into two separate messages. As Roberts has chosen to craft the sermon, we find an introductory minicourse on the parties of early Judaism followed by a traditional homily on following Jesus. In short, we have here the marriage of pedagogy and homiletics. It is our task to evaluate whether the marriage works.

STYLES IN THE SERMON

Roberts begins with the time-tested device of humor, telling a Milton Berle joke touching on the relationship between Jews and Christians. Laughter can serve as an icebreaker by lightening the atmosphere of stuffiness that seems to surround most pulpits. Has this somberness been created by us preachers? Or is it imposed upon us by our listeners? You decide. Either way, assuming our jokes are funny and elicit the desired results, they can clear the cobwebs and rid us of pulpit-pomp.

Somewhere back in my homiletical training, I recall being warned that telling a joke in the midst of a message will ensure that everything said before it will be wiped from the listener's memory. Whether this is true or not, we need to be aware that humor should be used in such a way that it won't derail the message. Perhaps wisely, Roberts places his joke at the beginning.

All joking aside, we soon discover not only that there are two messages here, but there are also two distinct styles. Roberts puts on his pedagogical cap to describe the religious world in which Jesus ministered. In the style of a lecture he becomes the teacher who delivers a treatise on the parties within first-century Judaism. It's rich in content, but I wonder how well this portion of the sermon would hold the attention of someone who rarely goes to church. Is it too technical for the seeker or for those only marginally involved in the church? Roberts is conscientious in giving his audience a comprehensive background on scribal, Pharisaic, and rabbinic tradition—devoting nearly 40 percent of his time to it. But, in the process, does he risk losing his listener's attention?

It strikes me that Roberts could have more efficiently captured the essence of each group or party by going straight to his good analogies, showing the scribes to be like today's "seminar professors...scholars and teachers, not priests or anything like modern-day clergy." The early Pharisees are "the politically active Christian Coalition...a lay movement... that blends religious conservatism with a dominant political agenda." And, as for the title Rabbi? This was "a general term of respect for all persons worthy of honor." Reducing the longer explanations to these few analogies would have streamlined the message. Does Roberts, who is clearly an able scholar himself, give more information than is necessary to make his point? You make the call.

The second of the preacher's two messages begins with the section entitled: "Responding to Jesus the Rabbi Today." Suddenly the teacher lets down his hair, loosens his tie, and reveals the storyteller in him. The academics are finished and now the real-life application begins. You can almost see those whose attention may have strayed during the Jewish lesson cock their heads to reengage with the speaker. From here on through the end of the sermon, the teacher converts to the preacher, and his chalkboard gives way to his challenge to live for Christ. In this section of the message, all the head-level stuff comes down to the heart-level. To his credit, Roberts knows this is the ultimate goal of every effective sermon.

USE OF SCRIPTURE

Since we have two messages, as you might expect, we have two different ways of using Scripture. The first half of the sermon is not expository preaching, in the truest sense, even though it is firmly grounded in a scriptural context. Roberts uses the Markan passage as a springboard to describe the religious and social milieu in first-century Israel. This is the environment in which Jesus' rabbinical role is defined. Roberts shows us how much baggage is attached to the simple title Rabbi. By the time we're halfway through the message, we have been exposed to a primer on first-century Judaism and culture.

Based on what we see here, it's a good guess Roberts's congregants possess an unusually high level of biblical literacy. The message reminds us that every preacher establishes a certain standard of biblical sophistication (or lack thereof!) among his or her parishioners. And this will be the standard on which all future messages are built. It's evident that this sermon was delivered to a congregation either possessing a firm grasp of the Scriptures or desirous of learning more about the Bible.

In the second half of the sermon, Roberts switches to a more traditional expository style, citing specific words and phrases from the Gospel text, culminating with a direct quote from Mark 1:16–20 which is used as a call to action. Scripture is woven into the message in a natural manner, punctuating the main points with brief quotes and peppering the preacher's own thoughts with biblical images. Never are we left feeling that Mark's words are misrepresented, or, worse yet, that they are cast aside in favor of another agenda. Roberts's genuine and gentle exegesis undergirds his message throughout.

PROBLEMS & SOLUTIONS

What is the problem Roberts addresses in this sermon? To answer, we must return to his two tracks. Each half of the message addresses a different problem. In the first section, Roberts speaks to the misconception that Jesus was not Jewish. He argues that by ignoring the Jewishness and the rabbinic stature of Jesus we will overlook his authority. In order to submit to Jesus as our Lord, we have to know him as our rabbi, one who is uniquely equipped to enlighten us regarding the will of his Father.

The second section of the sermon addresses the problem of Christians who acknowledge Jesus as their rabbi (or teacher) but fail to integrate his teachings into their daily lives. The anecdote about the young man caught by the police effectively hammers the problem home.

Like the boy in the car, are we among those who ignore the call of one in authority in hopes he will go away? If so, Roberts warns us, we're in danger of disregarding the gospel. He presents the problem to us using three consecutive questions:

1) "Are you learning from Jesus?"
2) "Does his word function as the unique authority in your life?"
3) "Have you committed yourself to learning from Jesus—and does this commitment show in your daily life?"

How are we to respond? Roberts answers directly: "If we respond appropriately to Jesus our Rabbi, then we will indeed devote our lives to being his students, his disciples." He goes on to list how such devotion manifests itself: through Bible study, regular prayer, meditation upon the truth, and living in community with others. More specifically, our devotion should lead to integrating the teachings of Rabbi Jesus into our daily decision making. In this case, the story of a fellow parishioner struggling with ethical challenges in the workplace serves as an illustration. As with the man in the story, the measure of our responsiveness will be found in "the nitty-gritty realities" of our lives—in how we handle our income taxes, our relationships, and our temptations. In the end, how serious are we about following in the steps of Jesus the Rabbi?

Is the Gospel Proclaimed?

The gospel proclaims that Jesus is not a dead mentor; he is a living influence on all who choose to follow him and apply his teachings to their lives. To follow Jesus is to do so not in some vaguely ideological sense, but in a real and practical way. Roberts shows us a Jesus who is our "faithful guide," one who gives us the strength and courage to stand up against the culture, one who sustains us amid the temptations to make moral compromises. The decision to obey Jesus is not an easy one. Far from it. It calls us to a full allegiance to him in all that we say and do. And what's in it for us? This sermon doesn't answer that question specifically, but Roberts makes it clear that refusing to obey is not an option for the

Christian. To remain faithful to Christ is an uncomfortable task. It means living in obedience to the truth of God all the time. Going halfway is unacceptable.

SUGGESTIONS

- Analyze this message from the perspective of its effectiveness for different audiences. Are there some who might get snowed under by the heavy teaching in the first half of the sermon? Or is it engaging enough to bring enlightenment to even the most occasional churchgoer? It is important to learn how to teach effectively in our preaching. It's also important to be aware of when we are in danger of becoming too instructional for our congregation's own good.
- Notice how each of Roberts's major illustrations provides an oasis within a message loaded with content. This is not the "sermon-lite" fare being served up by many pulpits today. It's not for the neophytes among us, nor is it for the fainthearted regulars. This is industrial-grade preaching. If conveying this much content feels cumbersome to you, stay away from it. The teaching style of preaching is not for everyone. Be true to your own style and personality, and don't overestimate your own reach.
- Take this opportunity to evaluate how well your own preaching balances the call to obedience with the word of comfort and encouragement. Our culture's preoccupation with individualism and self-absorption has made many people today overly sensitive about being told what they "should" or "ought" to do. It's amazing how little it takes to make people feel beaten down these days. Consider giving your congregation regular doses of pure grace to balance the burden of true discipleship.

Richard A. Davis

When the Night Is Darkest

ACTS 16:16–26

Rev. Dr. John Killinger
Williamsburg, Virginia

Rev. Dr. John Killinger

When the Night is Darkest

ACTS 16:16–26

Do you think you have trouble? Consider the case of LeRoy Masche, a farmer five miles north of the small town of Fertile, Minnesota. Mr. Masche farms one hundred and eighty acres, tends nineteen head of cattle, repairs his own farm machinery and is totally blind. He avoids objects in his path by snapping his fingers and listening to the sound, a kind of human radar. The wind, he says, plays havoc with his hearing and causes him to stumble over things.

Antonia DeLattre, a sixteen-year-old in Harlem, fell down the stairs at school one morning and broke her leg. On the way to the hospital, the ambulance she was riding in was involved in an accident, and her collarbone and three ribs were broken. When she got out of the hospital several days later, the car she was riding in broke an axle when it hit a pothole and she had to be taken home in a police car. When the police car arrived at her home, one of the officers recognized her brother as a fugitive and arrested him. Later that day the house caught fire and the family had to move in with relatives on another block.

William Ramirez, a respected real-estate man in a southwestern city, married for the second time. His new wife was beautiful, talented, and charming. He was extremely happy. Six months after they were married, however, the FBI arrested his wife for trafficking in narcotics and prostitution. She was using his listed properties as assignation places, and he was charged as an accessory in crime. An investigation revealed that she had been married three times before and had not bothered to secure a divorce from any of her previous husbands.

Human beings have a talent for getting into unbelievable predicaments. What does the Book of Job say? "Man is born to trouble as the sparks fly upward" (5:7, RSV). Maybe we shouldn't be surprised when disaster strikes us. As my wife is fond of saying, "Every silver lining has a black cloud." Whether you step on the cracks of the sidewalk or not, you are going to have trouble.

Perhaps we ought to condition our children not to expect otherwise. We like to shield them, to protect them from the unhappy endings of life, to place a pillow under them when they fall. If their feelings are hurt, we sympathize. If they scrape their knees, we kiss them to make them well. If they fail in school, we set them up in business and tell them schools are not a measure of success. But maybe they should learn early what a hard, tough world it is.

We cannot take the falls out of life for our children. The world is a vale of tears, a valley of shadows, a canyon where the best must hurt before they can soar. We are "born to trouble, as the sparks fly upward."

How do we deal with trouble? That's something else—that's another matter.

I am always impressed by people who manage to experience hardship after hardship and still come through with smiles and determination. Like Tiny Tim, a four-year-old boy I met in the Denver airport. Tiny Tim, whose real name is Roger, has been crippled since birth. He wears leg braces and uses little crutches to walk. When I first noticed him, he came flying past me at incredible speed, stopped at an ash stand he pretended was a telephone, and called the police to see if there were any strange characters in his neighborhood. His mother said he rarely seems to notice that he is different from other children. If anything, she said, he feels sorry for them that they don't have handy crutches like his.

The Trans, one of our Vietnamese families, came to see us last Sunday afternoon to tell us they are moving to San Diego. Mr. Tran doesn't speak English. He earns only five dollars an hour as a TV repairman, and his wife, when she can get work as a seamstress, earns minimum wage. They are not making enough to support their family of nine. They do not want to leave our city. The girls are especially reluctant to leave their high school, where one would be a senior this fall. But they came to our home with a plate full of egg rolls, which Mrs. Tran makes with an expertise few can match. They smiled and talked bravely of selling all their belongings and making the trip by bus to a new life in California. They have done it before, under even more adverse circumstances, and now they are ready to do it again.

In our text this morning, Paul and Silas were summarily arrested, brutally beaten, and imprisoned in the city of Philippi. They had cast an unclean spirit out of a slave girl. So her owners, who had earned money by her sorcery, stirred up a mob against them. The beating they received was severe, according to Luke, and that was by the barbaric standards of ancient times. Yet at midnight, when many prisoners would have been sleeping, Paul and Silas were wide awake singing praises to God. I don't expect they were singing loudly, to disturb anyone; but in the solitariness of the night they were softly intoning Jewish psalms and Christian hymns.

Why, after a beating that would have left most people sniveling and whining and feeling sorry for themselves, perhaps even railing against God, would those men have been expressing praise? We don't know what gave Tiny Tim his extraordinary courage and exuberance. We aren't even sure what has kept the Trans going with such faith and determination. But we do know what motivated Paul and Silas. They knew the Savior of the world, who had endured much worse than they and then was glorified beyond death. They had heard the stories, how Jesus was beaten, then made to carry his cross out to the hill called Golgotha, where he was stripped and nailed to the wood and hung up to die like a malefactor. They knew what he had suffered for his goodness, honesty, and love, and they were under no illusions about the nature of the world we live in. They knew it is a hard world where the innocent as well as the tough get hurt. But they also knew that God, who was present with Christ in all of it and in the end raised him up as the sign of all life and resurrection, was present with them there in that Philippian prison and would be with them in even worse, if worse was possible.

Knowing all of this, Paul and Silas saw their imprisonment and beating as a means of glorifying Christ. By bearing their hardships and suffering with courage and enthusiasm, they could render praise to the Redeemer of the world. Of course the world was a difficult place where the good were persecuted and the innocent were broken. But, said Paul, "to me to live is Christ" (Phil. 1:21, RSV). By singing hymns when the night was darkest, when their pains were greatest, Paul and Silas testified to God's faithfulness and his eventual victory over all the forces of darkness and evil. They were thus able to transform their suffering into an offering.

Think of that the next time your burdens are getting the best of you and you think your heart will break. You can turn your suffering into an offering to God. It isn't hard to do. First, you remember the terrible suffering of Jesus, the agony of the cross. Then you think, "My suffering is certainly no worse than that." Even if you are grieving the loss of a loved one, you can think of Mary, the mother of Jesus, standing near the cross and watching her son being tortured to death and not being able to do anything about it. You realize that your suffering is not worse than that. Then you remember, "God was in all of that, working for our salvation. God knows what a hard place the world is. God has borne it too. And now God is here with me in my suffering, as God was there with Jesus. I'll be all right, whatever happens."

Finally, you say a little prayer of surrender, or maybe you sing a verse of a hymn, the way Paul and Silas did, and your suffering has become an offering to God. You use it to say to God, "I am yours, whatever happens to me." You will find that it's perfectly amazing what this does to transform the situation you are in.

When the night is darkest
And your soul is sorely tried,
Merely breathe the name of Jesus,
Who for you was crucified.
Remember how he suffered,
How he drank the bitter cup;
Then recall his resurrection
And the power that raised him up.
Say a prayer or sing a hymn
And make an offering of your soul.
God will hear and give you peace;
God will touch and make you whole.[1]

The pastor of a large church in the Midwest told me about Tom, a young man from Ethiopia who joined his church. Tom had to leave his home after the Communists became strong in Ethiopia. He had participated in a protest march and was put in prison for a while. When he got out of prison, his father urged him to leave the country, for many young men who had been sent to prison were later disappearing, and some were known to have been shot by the Communists. So Tom fled to the Sudan, walking through the desert for seven days. Eventually he made his way to Paris and then to the United States. He had been living in the midwestern city for three years and was very lonely until he met the pastor and joined the church. One day he came to the pastor with tears in his eyes. He had received word that his father had died, and of course he was unable to return home for the funeral. He deeply regretted that he could not care for his seven brothers and sisters, as he was the oldest child in the family, and this was a duty that ordinarily fell to the oldest.

A few weeks later Tom came back to the pastor and told him he was going to Kenya. He had received a letter from his girlfriend in Ethiopia, and she was planning to visit an aunt in Kenya. Tom said he would meet her there and they would be married. Then in nine months she could come to this country as his wife and he would not be alone anymore.

"But, Tom," the pastor said, "you can't go to Kenya. You don't have a visa."

"Ah," said Tom, "but I know Africa. With God as my friend, I shall do it."

Weeks passed and the pastor did not see Tom. Then one day Tom appeared in his study. He had been caught at the border of Kenya, he said, and was imprisoned for several days. Then he was allowed to spend enough time in the country to meet his girlfriend and be married. "Soon," he said, "she will be joining me here. I will not be alone anymore."

"It doesn't sound to me as if you've been alone at all," said the pastor. "God must have been with you."

"Oh, yes, he was," Tom said. "God is always with me. That is how I have been able to bear these years in exile."

As I listened to the story, I wondered how many Christians there are around the world who feel that way. "God is always with me." Christians in Ethiopia, Kenya, Bulgaria, Taiwan, Australia, Nicaragua, Haiti—and wherever the word of hope has gone. Maybe it will give us courage to remember that in this hard world, God is with all of us, working for peace and justice and love. God is with us. If we will only remember that, we too can sing when the night is darkest.

Note
1. Source unknown.

Comment

Problem

Telling the Story

Every preacher faces the challenging task of making the Scripture come alive for people in the pew. One of the most effective ways to do this is by telling a contemporary story that parallels a biblical story. John Killinger is a master of telling powerful stories that have specific applications both to the Scripture and to the individual listener. In this sermon the stories are about human pain and adversity.

There is something in the human condition that makes us want to hear about the troubles of other people. We tune in to the daily newscast and are intrigued by the human-interest stories about people facing great adversity. We buy the daily newspaper and are captivated by stories about death, disaster and dreadful events. We want to know what's happening in our world. We want to hear how other people survive the difficulties of life, how they overcome adversity. Somehow hearing about the troubles of other people helps make our own troubles seem more tolerable.

Killinger's sermon addresses the subject of trouble in our lives. He announces the sermon subject in the opening sentence: "Do you think you have trouble?" Then with rapid-fire efficiency, he tells three stories of people who are confronted with troubles of such magnitude that the listener is moved to sympathy. These stories of human suffering stir our emotions. We become involved with these strangers in the sermon and we listen with rapt attention. There is an ache in our hearts for LeRoy Masche, Antonia DeLattre, and William Ramirez. The sermon works because we are drawn into these people's lives. The troubles of our own lives seem to shrink in comparison. Surely, if these people have overcome such terrible troubles, we, too, can endure and overcome our problems. We want to hear more.

Killinger reminds us we are "born to trouble as the sparks fly upward" (Job 5:7, RSV). Here he plants a subtle suggestion in our minds. Perhaps we should help prepare our children to survive the difficulties of life rather than pretend that life is always happy and trouble-free. Killinger's words about preparing our children for suffering constitute a minisermon within the larger sermon. This section speaks to the needs of parents faced with tough decisions regarding the care and keeping of adult children. It's a very common problem in contemporary America.

Killinger then tells us two stories. These are from his own personal experience. Up until now he has been telling us about other people somewhere else. Now he brings the story home to the listening congregation. The Trans, "one of our Vietnamese families," appear to be a part of the church where he is preaching. These people are known. Their troubles are here and now. They will be giving up everything and moving to another part of the country. Trouble is no longer a distant word. It is personal. It is about people we know.

Notice the movement of this sermon. It begins in another time and place, moving smoothly from story to story (Minnesota to Harlem to the Southwest) until it becomes "our story," the story of people known in the listening congregation. The transitions are flawless. The storyteller has condensed and clarified each of the individual stories, then joined them with a clearly identifiable theme. Each story flows easily into the next story until we arrive at the primary story—the biblical story—the story of Paul and Silas in prison in Philippi.

Offering Adversity to God as Praise

Killinger has a gift for storytelling. When he tells the story of Paul and Silas—prisoners praising God at midnight in a Roman jail, singing hymns despite their suffering, overcoming the pain, the injustice of it all—the story comes alive and becomes our story. The point? Life isn't fair. Love God anyway. Life is sometimes lonely and dark. But Christ, the Light of God, is our constant companion.

But wait. Yes, we are to love God despite all the troubles of this world.

Yes, we are to allow Jesus Christ to be our constant companion in pain and suffering. But there's more. The preacher moves well beyond our common thinking when he gently suggests that we can offer our heartache to God-in-Christ as *our gift*. Then he tells us how to do just that.

PROCLAMATION

Offering God Our Troubles

The good news of the gospel of Jesus Christ is that God cares about us. God is in our world overcoming our trials and tribulations through the victory of the cross of Jesus Christ. Good preaching always proclaims Christ as Lord and Savior. Killinger's sermon is an example of the best of that kind of proclamation.

After retelling the story from the text in Acts 16 in such a way that it takes on new life and meaning for the person in the pew, the preacher asks us to remember the suffering of Jesus and to offer our own suffering as a gift to God. What an amazing transformation is possible in our lives as we choose to hear and to respond to the gospel of Jesus Christ.

RESPONSE

Good preaching should elicit a response from the person in the pew or from a congregation as an agent of God-in-Christ. The sermon should not leave one floundering, wondering where to go from here. Good sermons provide direction for a possible course of action. That action may be mental, physical, spiritual, or emotional.

The response in this sermon is directed to the individual. The course of action is mental and spiritual. We are called to make our suffering an offering to God. That is very different from asking God to remove the suffering (or the source of the suffering). Paul endured all kinds of suffering in service to Christ. Jesus himself endured the cruel agony of the cross. Our own suffering or loss, no matter how great, pales in comparison. We cannot always control the events of our lives, but we can control our reactions to them. We can offer our troubles, our very lives, as a gift to God.

Killinger's sermon closes with one more poignant story of a young man from Ethiopia who overcomes unbelievable obstacles. It is a story to remind us that God is always with us. That is what we most need to remember. As Tom said, "God is always with me. That is how I have been able to bear these years in exile." Killinger concludes by reemphasizing just that point: "God is with us. If we will only remember that, we too can sing when the night is darkest." Enough said!

SUGGESTIONS

- Condense your illustrations to the bare bones. Make them short and memorable. Eliminate excess verbiage. A good story does not require elaborate description.
- Tell your stories into a tape recorder and listen to them several times before using them in a sermon. For that matter, tape your sermon and listen to it with a critical ear before you preach it. Is this a sermon you would want to hear again? How could it be improved?
- Practice storytelling in front of a mirror. The best stories improve with practice.
- Read. Read. Read. Read widely. Good illustrative stories come from a diversity of reading material. Killinger is a prolific writer, a favorite of this commentator. Read his books. Listen to his tapes, "How to Enrich Your Preaching" (Abingdon Audio-Graphics).
- Use personal experiences where appropriate in your preaching. Just be careful not to make yourself the hero or heroine of the story.

Marianna Frost

Coming Up Short

LUKE 19:1–10; ROMANS 3:23–24

REV. JEFFREY M. LINDSAY
COLONIAL CHURCH
EDINA, MINNESOTA

Rev. Jeffrey M. Lindsay

Coming Up Short

LUKE 19:1–10; ROMANS 3:23–24

You may remember from previous times I've shared with you, that I grew up in Seattle, Washington. Our house was in a new development. At the end of our road was a big field, and beyond the field were some woods. On the other side of those woods was the grocery store. One of the things I feared the most was when my mother called out my full name. When she called, "Jeffrey Morrison Lindsay," I knew I was in trouble! But if she simply called, "Jeff," I would think, "Aw, she wants me to do something…go somewhere…it's an errand of some sort, I'm sure." So I'd say, "What, Mom?"

She'd say, "Come here for a second. I want you to do something for me. I want you to run to the store."

"The grocery store?"

"Yes, I just need a few things. Will you go for me?"

"Sure, Mom."

One day when she sent me to the store she said, "There are just three things for you to remember today: milk, bread, and SOS pads. OK? Milk, bread, and SOS pads. Can you remember that? Now tell me what you're going to get."

"Milk, bread, and SOS pads," I told her. "I can remember that!"

So she gave me three dollars and sent me on my way—which meant all the way to the end of the block, across the field, through the woods, out to the street on the other side, down another block, and around the corner to the grocery store. As I left with the three dollars clenched in my hand, I was muttering all the way down the block, "Milk, bread, SOS pads." (I didn't even know what SOS pads were!) "Milk, bread, SOS pads. Milk, bread, SOS pads." I got to the field. "Milk, bread, SOS pads. Milk, bread, SOS pads." I got to the woods. "Milk...bread. Milk... Wow, look at the woods! I'm going to the store, I think."

I got to the street and went around the corner. "Oh! What was I supposed to get?" I would just wander around the store, I thought, until I remembered. I got to the dairy case. "Oh, that's right, I was supposed to get milk." Around the corner I saw some bread. "Oh, I think I was supposed to get bread too. Now what was that other thing?" So I wandered up and down the rows. I stopped in the candy department thinking, "Was this what she wanted me to get? No, I don't think so."

And then I remembered. "SOS pads!" So I walked around until I found the SOS pads. I had the milk. I had the bread. I had the SOS pads. And I walked up to the counter.

Now, I grew up a long time ago when they didn't have the nice, computerized cash registers they have today. They had those old-time cash registers. Remember those? The cashier would enter the amount, *click, click, click*, and the register would go brrring! I put my three things on the counter and the cashier went *click, click, click...click, click, click...click, click, click*. Then there was another —*click, click, click*. I put the three dollars on the counter with a smile on my face because I'd accomplished the task for which my mother had sent me.

All of a sudden the cashier looked at me and said, "Three dollars and eleven cents."

"Excuse me, sir?"

"Three dollars and eleven cents."

I didn't have eleven cents. I just looked at him, and he said again, "Three dollars and eleven cents."

I didn't know what to do. So I kind of pushed the three dollars further over the counter. I didn't have eleven cents! I was eleven cents short. I'd gotten the three things my mother wanted, I'd given the cashier the three dollars, and I'd come up short. I could feel the tears welling up in my eyes. What should I do? I was short, and there was nothing I could do....

Sometime later our family moved to Minnesota. There we joined Hope Presbyterian Church which had a church camp called Camp Ojibway. I started going to Camp Ojibway in fifth grade. When seventh grade came, I was ready for the world. Junior high camp is a lot different from elementary camp. You get to stay up a little bit later, there are more responsibilities, and you get to hang around in front of the dining hall before lunch without anyone watching you. It was great!

But then I found out that there was a ninth-grade boys' "rite of passage" that happened every year at Camp Ojibway. The camp wasn't very modern. The land had belonged to a family and the dining hall was the old home which had a garage underneath it on the basement level. It wasn't used as a garage anymore, but was just used for storage. The driveway sloped considerably downhill to tuck underneath the dining hall. On either side of the driveway were concrete walls with the width of probably a car and a half between them. As you looked over the edge of one wall to the other wall, there was about a twelve-foot drop (at least that's the way I remember it). Maybe it was twenty!

I watched the ninth-grade boys in their "rite of passage." They would back up and run hard to leap from one wall to the other wall, impressing the ninth-grade girls!

As I watched this in seventh grade, I prayed I would flunk seventh and eighth grade. I did not want to get to ninth grade! But I was only in seventh grade, so I didn't have to worry about it.

Then eighth grade came. Again I watched the ninth-grade boys backing up and taking a run up to one wall and leaping over. I remember that in the middle of the week one of the boys didn't make it. He hit the wall! As he slid down we could hear him moaning. There were little pieces of him on that wall.

"OK, Lord," I said, "you can always help me flunk eighth grade!" But the summer of my ninth-grade year did come. That summer was just before I got my growth spurt. Some of you may remember from other stories that I was about the same height as I was wide then—kind of a little beach ball, and not designed to do much running and jumping and leaping.

The first day I let the older, more mature, jock-type guys do the jump, and I cheered them on. On Tuesday I did the same. On Wednesday I said, "Ooh, I'm not feeling very well today. There's always Thursday and Friday." On Thursday I said I had diarrhea. But Friday came, and there was no other way to get out of jumping because we were going home the next day. All that morning I was thinking, "Oh my goodness, the day has come. I'm going to have to try to leap over that driveway, and there's no way I'm going to make it." The other kids started teasing me, until finally I'd had enough and I said, "Fine. I'll do it."

I remember backing up to try to get enough of a running start at that jump. I backed up and backed up and backed up. I thought maybe I could back up all the way to Grantsburg, Wisconsin. But I ran into a barbed wire fence. I was at the end of the camp property and couldn't go any further. So I started running.

"Lord, be there for me," I said. I ran and I ran and I ran as fast as my little legs would carry me. I got to the edge of the wall and my foot slipped—but my momentum carried me out over the wall. I closed my eyes and waited for the inevitable—because there was no way I was going to make it to the other side. I was a few feet short for sure. I'd given it my best effort. I'd given it everything, but I was going to come up short. I knew I was going to hit the wall. So I closed my eyes and I waited....

Just a few moments ago we read the story of Zacchaeus. Zacchaeus, as the story tells us, was a little man. In one of the other translations (NIV) it talks about his being a short man. Zacchaeus was a chief tax collector, and to be a chief tax collector meant that you had turned on your own people. You had betrayed them. You were a traitor. You were collecting taxes now for the Gentile Roman rulers and the army that occupied your land.

The Romans offered tax collectors a deal that said basically, "This is how much tax you need to collect from each of the people in your town to send to us. Whatever else you collect, that will be your profit." So the chief tax collector often spent a lot of time cheating his neighbors, his friends (whatever that would mean for him), and probably even his own family, because everyone was subject to the tax. So when Zacchaeus came along, the people passing in the street probably looked the other way. They hated him. They despised him.

Zacchaeus was not only a short man who was probably ridiculed for his height and teased as a child, but he was also caught short in terms of his character. He came up short in his morality, in acceptance by other people, and in terms of feeling loved. He was probably not a likable character. He was probably very lonely and isolated from others, with little future hope in the town and beyond. Until one day....

One day Jesus came to town. Zacchaeus had heard about Jesus. Jesus could do some miraculous, amazing things and turn people's lives around. Zacchaeus wanted to see him.

But when Zacchaeus got to the edge of Jericho on the street that Jesus was traveling, the crowd was already there. And no one was going to say, "Zacchaeus, you're kind of short. Why don't you come up to the front," because they hated him. He was short on love. He was short on character. But then he remembered—"There's a sycamore tree just down the way. I'll bet I could climb up in that tree without anyone knowing, and I could get a glimpse of Jesus."

Do you ever come up short? The apostle Paul declared, "All have sinned and fall short of the glory of God" (Rom. 3:23, NIV). Maybe you're sitting here today saying, "There are a lot of areas where I fall short. I fall short on hope. I fall short on peace. I fall short on being able to make the relationships around me work. I fall short as a parent. I fall short as a spouse. I fall short as a person who has a job. I fall short in terms of my faith, in terms of what God asks me to do, in terms of my future hope." What do you do? What did Zacchaeus do when he fell short? He ran ahead of the crowd, he climbed up in a tree, and he waited.

Now Zacchaeus was a chief tax collector, so it wasn't very dignified for him to shinny up a tree. I can see him in my imagination. As he shinnies up that tree, he has to pull himself out on the branch. And maybe he tries to pull the branches in around him a little bit so no one will know he is there. In his mind he's hidden from the rest of the crowd. He sees in the distance Jesus and his disciples and the crowd following. So he's very, very quiet, hiding in the tree.

Then the very last thing he wants to have happen, happens! Jesus stops underneath the tree. I can see Zacchaeus pulling the branches of the tree in around him even closer. But Jesus says something amazing. "Zacchaeus!" he calls.

"*Cheep, cheep. Cheep, cheep,*" Zacchaeus chirps, hoping it was a mistake.

Jesus says, "Zacchaeus, come down. I'm going to have lunch at your house today."

This man who was despised, who had come up short in every area of his life—this is the man Jesus addresses and invites himself to his house for lunch.

As they're walking along the street, the people around them say: "This sinner! Why would Jesus go to his house? How could Jesus want to spend time with him?" Can you imagine how Zacchaeus must have felt if he heard people saying those things?

At his house Zacchaeus sits down at the table with Jesus. He is so moved by Jesus' love and acceptance that he leaps up from the table and says, "Sir, my life is changed because of you. If I've cheated anyone, I will repay them four times...."

I'm standing at the cash register with tears welling up in my eyes. I'm eleven cents short and there's nothing I can do about it. I'm thinking, "Do I leave the bread? Do I leave the SOS pads? Do I just run away and take nothing home?" Just then, a hand comes up over my shoulder and gently places a dime and a penny on the counter. Quickly, I look back. There stands a man I don't even know. He's just paid the eleven cents. "Maybe you'll pay me back someday," he says. I didn't want to talk about it. I didn't want to think about it. I grabbed that stuff and I ran!

When I came up short, a man I didn't even know paid the price for me....

So I backed up as far as I possibly could at the edge of the property at Camp Ojibway. I gave it my best shot. I ran and I ran. And as I got to the edge of the wall, my foot slipped. As I'm flying through the air, I'm waiting for the impact. My eyes are closed tight—when all of a sudden, I feel a hand on my elbow pulling me over. It's Ron Hoffover. Ron already had a full beard in ninth grade—he was about six foot two, a strong, burly guy. As he stood up at the wall he could see I was in trouble. And as I was about to hit the wall, he grabbed me and pulled me over so that I rolled onto the ground on the other side. "Are you OK?" he asked, as I looked up. When I came up short, he reached out a hand, grabbed me, and pulled me over....

When Zacchaeus came up short, he met Jesus. Jesus loved him and cared about him. If we were on our own and just stopped at Romans 3:23, we would all just come up short: "All have sinned and fall short of the glory of God." Even with God, I come up short. But that's not where the gospel ends. The Romans passage itself goes on to say that all who have sinned "are justified freely by his grace through the redemption that came by Christ Jesus" (v. 24, NIV). When I come up short, I need to remember that Jesus has paid the price for me. When I come up short, I need to know that Jesus reaches out a hand and pulls me over.

I don't know where you feel you come up short today. I just know that we all do, for we are a broken and sinful people. And that's exactly where God's grace becomes real for us. We sang just a few moments ago "Amazing Grace." God's grace is amazing. Because I can't do it on my own. I can't save or forgive myself. I can't heal my soul or reconcile my relationships with others. But Jesus can!

Will you run ahead of the crowd? Will you climb up in the tree? Will you take the risk to see Jesus? Will you be open to God's incredible grace? Grace that has already paid the price. Grace that reaches across the chasms of our lives to save us.

Amazing grace. When we come up short, God is there: "Today

salvation has come to this house.... For the Son of Man came to seek and to save what was lost" (Luke 19:9–10). Praise be to God.

Comment

Cliffhangers. No matter what the medium—from mystery novels to movies to television series—a cliffhanger gets our attention and keeps us wondering. Jeff Lindsay takes us to the edge of the cliff and leaves us there. From the panic of a little boy standing at the grocery store counter, wondering what to do next, to a ninth-grade boy flying through midair, sure to hit a concrete wall, Lindsay adds a distinctive twist to narrative preaching—the cliffhanger. But in doing so, he devotes two-thirds of the sermon to the "introductory" stories. That raises some interesting questions.

In the first volume of *The Library of Distinctive Sermons,* a sermon by Gary Klingsporn titled "$3 Worth of God, Please" does the same. The opening story is lengthy; nearly half the sermon is given to it. The comment writer therefore asks about the nature and function of a sermon "introduction":

> How short or how long should an introduction be? What should its purpose be? How should the introduction relate to the rest of the sermon? Should it be a nice little joke to break the ice, a cute story or quote, often unrelated to the remainder of the sermon? Should an introduction get right to the point of the sermon and present the thesis? Or, can introductions engage listeners, lead them along, and play with them?...[1]

Although the commentator acknowledges that there is no one "correct" formula, he does assert what we all know—the opening is crucial. Within the first few minutes of a sermon, listeners decide whether to stay tuned or to check out. As a preacher looks out over the congregation each Sunday, he or she is looking through a very small window of opportunity to capture the attention of listeners.

Without a doubt, Lindsay accomplishes the first requirement of effective preaching. He captures the listener's attention. For a listener to tune out during this sermon, he or she would have to be semicomatose or seriously preoccupied otherwise. Lindsay's style is personal, warm, winsome, and charming. He doesn't present himself as the all-wise, all-knowing spiritual leader we look to for answers. Quite the contrary. Lindsay lets us into his life. He allows us to see the little boy that has shaped the man before us. As another comment writer has said, "Done appropriately, there is a power in the personal in preaching."[2]

Lindsay goes beyond the personal in this sermon, which brings us back to the cliffhanger. What purpose does this technique serve? In what way do the two personal stories in this sermon enhance the proclamation? To answer those questions, I think we have to look to the text, the story of Zacchaeus. We've all heard it hundreds of times. We've sung it in Sunday school and vacation Bible school. All someone has to do is quote the first line of the lyrics and the tune is immediately going around in our heads: "Zacchaeus was a wee little man, a wee little man was he...."

Although an engaging story for children when told in Sunday school, I think this is a difficult passage to preach effectively for adults. Few adults can relate to a corrupt, arrogant, little tax collector who shinnies up a tree. Most of us aren't curmudgeonly tax collectors cheating our friends and family. And few of us still climb trees. What's the good news in a familiar passage of Scripture heard so often since childhood? The good news is found in the obvious wordplay carried through all three stories: *coming up short.*

From a little boy caught short of money to a teenager falling short of a wall, Lindsay's narrative anticipates the text, leading us to the undeniable reality that we all "come up short." The text is at the center of this sermon, both structurally and theologically. One does not have to do an extensive outline of the sermon to realize that Lindsay tells the stories to set up the text, retells the story of Zacchaeus, then comes back full circle to the two opening stories. Using the ancient Greek literary device known as *inclusio,* Lindsay "bookends" the biblical text by beginning and ending with stories conveying a similar theme or subject. This technique creates a sense of literary symmetry, wholeness and completion. The simple progression is: *Short on money / Short on the jump / Short Zacchaeus / Zacchaeus restored / Money paid / Jump made!*

The simplicity of the sermon combined with effective storytelling—and knowing when to leave the story hanging—is the distinctive quality that makes the sermon memorable. "Coming Up Short" works, in short (no pun intended), by allowing the stories to become the vehicle for the gospel.

Some readers may wonder whether Lindsay's personal stories get in the way of the biblical story of Zacchaeus. Do they dominate too much or overshadow Zacchaeus? I don't think so. I think they help Zacchaeus come alive for modern listeners. But you make the call! The approach Lindsay has used here is *not* for every sermon. But I think it is effective in *this* sermon.

Lindsay's sermon is not a teaching sermon. His purpose here is not to display intricate exegesis of the Luke 19 text. He's not trying to bring theological depth to the pulpit in this particular sermon. But in taking advantage of the childhood association many of his listeners have with this text by telling stories from his own childhood, Lindsay proclaims a profound truth—one that is so simple, many of us have difficulty accepting it.

"When I came up short, a man I didn't even know paid the price for me....I don't know where you feel you come up short today. I just know that we all do, for we are a broken and sinful people....God's grace is amazing. Because I can't do it on my own. I can't save or forgive myself. I can't heal my soul or reconcile my relationships with others. But Jesus can!"

This sermon is a proclamation of grace—what to do when we have searched everywhere and exhausted all of our own resources. It's a simple word for those who would follow Christ. Lindsay preaches the simplicity of amazing grace, "grace that reaches across the chasms of our lives to save us." In the simplicity is the life-changing truth.

SUGGESTIONS

- We must ask the obvious: What childhood stories of your own come to mind when reading Lindsay's sermon? Reflect on those memories. Write them down. Keep them before you as you prepare sermon texts. Is there a sermon in those childhood experiences?
- When working with a familiar text, consider how you can take a narrative and use it to form a vehicle for the sermon, perhaps by telling part of the story at the beginning and concluding the story at the end. As you develop future sermon texts, you might consider using the *inclusio* technique.
- Sometimes a sermon is born from a simple phrase, such as "coming up short." Often the phrase that triggers the creative idea comes from unlikely sources: a child's unexpected comment, a friend's casual words, a conversation you overhear. During the week, listen with attentive ears and write down phrases that strike you as odd or interesting. Those phrases may hold the key to where the Spirit leads as you prepare to proclaim the good news.

Debra K. Klingsporn

Notes

1. Quoted from the Comment section following "$3 Worth of God, Please," a sermon by Gary W. Klingsporn, from *The Library of Distinctive Sermons,* Vol. 1 (Sisters, OR: Questar Publishers, 1996), p. 69.
2. Ibid, p. 71.

All That Lives Must Die

GENESIS 50:15–21; MATTHEW 16:13–28

Rev. Dr. John Mark Jones
Bethlehem United Methodist Church
Bishopville, South Carolina

REV. DR. JOHN MARK JONES

ALL THAT LIVES MUST DIE[1]

GENESIS 50:15–21; MATTHEW 16:13–28, RSV

"All that lives must die." This is the line that Hamlet's mother speaks in an attempt to console her son who grieves the death of his father. Hamlet is looking dejectedly at the ground as if in search of his father's corpse. And Gertrude says to her son,

> Do not for ever with thy vailed lids
> Seek for thy noble father in the dust:
> Thou know'st 'tis common; all that lives must die,
> Passing through nature to eternity.
>   Hamlet: Aye, Madam, it is common.
>   Gertrude: If it be,
> Why seems it so particular with thee?
>   (*Hamlet* Act I, scene 2)

Oh, but death is *particular,* special, unique. Death is particular with us all. The fact that death is common offers no great consolation.[2] For each of us it is troubling, vexing. It is true that "all that lives must die," but with the dying comes our own individual, inconsolable grief.

Our faith forces us to take seriously the reality of death. Never does the gospel belie that reality or try to conceal it from our view. At no place does the gospel attempt to make death palatable. If Jesus agonized in Gethsemane over the death that was coming, then you had better believe that all human flesh is heir to the fear that is summoned by the dark specter.

And yet, though the gospel does not mitigate death's reality, the gospel also does not stop with that reality. The gospel looks death squarely in the eye, and then leaves us all with a daunting question: How shall we respond to the hard reality of death? That is the question we are asking this morning. Given that all that lives must die, how shall we respond to the inevitable fate that awaits us all?

We have been with Joseph's family these past two weeks. We have seen the brothers at war with each other. We have seen their deceit and hypocrisy and violence. We've seen them initiate reconciliation, knowing this is what their aged father desires. And now we see the brothers at their father's tomb. Once again, death has caused disruption. So much chaos that after their father's death, the brothers say, "It may be that Joseph will hate us and pay us back for all the evil which we did to him" (Gen. 50:15).

The brothers are afraid of what Joseph might do to them. And not just afraid; they are feeling guilty. They are doubtful, distrustful, confused. That's a bad position to be in. Walter Brueggemann says, "The space between Joseph and the others is ominous and ill-defined, filled with terror for the brothers." Now that their father is gone, the family balance is upset. The brothers are unsure of themselves, uncertain how to relate to each other. They are terrified. "And no doubt the terror consists largely of unresolved guilt," says Brueggemann. They did Joseph a bad turn years ago. What is Joseph going to do to them now that their father is gone? For the moment, Joseph doesn't do anything. He is "noncommittal. When he is passionate with weeping and not at all cool, we are not sure what it means. [So the brothers] are now set in a dangerous situation of rawness. Old guarantees, protections, and conventions are removed. Now [they all] must face the danger, and none knows beforehand how it will turn out. The risk in the family without the controlling presence of [the father] is [like] every exile in which old systems of support have been lost."[3]

Maybe this is why death is so disruptive. Old systems of support—whether strong or weak—are lost when a family member dies. Somehow the whole family structure changes. We change. Everything around us changes. Go into the house where a parent died, even months later, and see if you don't move differently than you used to move around that house. See if the space in that house doesn't feel different. Death disrupts the whole order of things.

The father of a dear friend of mine is dying in his home. The four children (including my friend) are caring for their father in the final stages of pancreatic and liver cancer. They and their spouses are taking shifts so that someone is with their father twenty-four hours a day. His dying is causing all kinds of turmoil in the family. The other night a sister and a brother got into a fight—a heated argument—over what amounted to nothing. The issue they were fighting over was no issue at all. But, of course, we know that beneath all the little matters that create ruckus in the family is the one issue, the only real issue that stares them all in the face. The only real issue is death.

Death often creates disruption in the family. Crazy disruption. Or rather, the kind of disruption that makes us crazy. So crazy that when a parent is dying, we give vent to hostilities we never knew were in us, give expression to rage we never knew we had. We hurt our brothers and sisters for no real reason other than we want them to hurt. We hurt, so we want others around us to hurt. We take a kind of pleasure in hurting those to whom we are so close that we both love and hate them. We know their strengths. We know their weaknesses. We know how they gratify us. We know how they irritate us.

In the face of death every emotion is intensified. What once was controlled anger becomes outrageous fury. What once was a little anxiety becomes demonic fear. Yes, death does strange things to us all. And, though it is common—"all that lives must die"—death makes us uncommonly strange.

There is a strange irony at play in the church whenever we speak of death. Though our faith forces us to face the issue of death, it is nevertheless very difficult to speak of death in the church. Oh, we do it at funerals. But I know church people who don't even go to funerals because they do not like to be in the presence of death and the grief that death leaves in its wake. And surely, other than funerals, we don't come to church to talk about death. We come to church to talk about life, resurrection, hope, faith, victory. In fact, the gospel preached in some churches is a gospel of success, prosperity, achievement. No mention of failure, defeat, or death. The gospel is *good* news. Let's keep it light, easygoing, pleasant.

Understand this is not merely a modern view of life. Televangelists did not invent the gospel of success and happiness. No, people have wanted to keep it light and easygoing and pleasant for a long, long time. Look at the Gospel lesson for today. Peter doesn't want to hear anything about failure, defeat, death.

What does Peter say when Jesus asks him, "Who do you say that I am?"

"You are the Christ, the Son of the *living God*," says Peter (vv. 15–16, italics added).

"Good response, Peter," Jesus tells him in effect. "You got it right. Or better yet, God in heaven gave you that understanding." But then he goes on, "And I tell you, you are Peter [which means 'rock'], and on this rock I will build my church, and the *powers of death* shall not prevail against it" (v. 18, italics added).

Death? Why this mention of the powers of death? Peter is speaking of the *living* God. No need to speak of death.

But Jesus does. And he says more. He speaks of his own suffering and death. Then Peter gets angry. "God forbid, Lord! This shall never happen to you" (v. 22). Which is to say, "It will also never happen to me, since I'm your follower. I'm your man, Jesus. And since you're not going to suffer, I'm not going to suffer. I'm following you because you will keep me safe."

To which Jesus says, "Get behind me, Satan!...You are not on the side of God, but of men" (v. 23). That is to say, "Peter, if you can't face the reality of death, you have no part of me, you have no part of God. And besides, the only part of God that really matters is the part that lies behind the veil of life and death."

Peter is afraid of death, as we all are. And what does the fear of death do to Peter as he relates to Jesus? It makes him want to control Jesus, to put Jesus in a box where everything is safe and predictable. Peter might as well be saying to Jesus, "If you're the Messiah, then you've got to respond to my every need. You've got to shelter me from pain and suffering, defeat and death. You've got to make it easy for me, Lord. Lift all my burdens."

"I can't do it, Peter," Jesus tells him. "I can't make it easy for you. I can't shelter you from pain and suffering, defeat and death. Peter, I can't even shelter myself."

Friends, if the gospel is about bringing us face to face with Jesus, it's also about bringing us face to face with life's hardest realities—the same realities that Jesus himself faced. And certainly the hardest of them all is death. So the gospel is about bringing us face to face with the reality of death. But the gospel doesn't stop there. The gospel poses the question for each of us to answer: How shall we respond to the reality of death?

I tell you death does strange things to us. It disrupts the family. Makes brothers and sisters fight. Summons our deepest fears. Makes cowards of us all. Is there a way to face the fear of death, and possibly move beyond it into something greater than fear?

Consider how Joseph responds to his brothers' fear. He does have the right and the power to punish them. They did betray him...and he them. There have been a lot of bad turns on both sides. Joseph is in a position to gain revenge. And many in his position would.

But what does Joseph say to his brothers? "As for you, you meant evil against me; but God meant it for good, to bring it about that many people should be kept alive, as they are today" (v. 20).

I don't know what you think of that statement. You may think that Joseph can actually read the mind of God, really know what God intends. But I don't think Joseph can do that. I don't think the smartest person in the world can read the mind of God. But I do think that Joseph is a man of faith. A man of faith who dares to see the hand of God in the most difficult of circumstances. A man of faith who dares to seek the presence of God and even wrestle with God in the midst of life's enormous difficulties. A man of faith willing to use all the strength and cunning God gave him to make good on a raw deal.

"You meant evil against me," he says. They not only meant evil; they did evil. But so did he. Evil swings both ways in almost every human encounter. "You meant evil against me; but [I believe] God meant it for good."

What Joseph is saying here is that, in his mind at least, the plan of God defeats the plan of evil.[4] And that, dear friends, is faith: to believe that in the face of evil, God can use us to prevail. And use us in such a way that even brothers who stand over the grave of their father can see beyond the madness of their fear to the power of reconciliation. But notice, it is not the kind of reconciliation that shields them from suffering and death. It is the kind of reconciliation that enables them to face death. They are reconciled over the grave of their father.

Likewise, Jesus in the Gospel lesson looks death squarely in the eye—and tells Peter to do the same. The "living God" does not shield us from the reality of suffering and death (v. 21)—either death in literal terms or death in figurative terms. Not just the death of the body, but the death of the ego, the giving up of those things we have always used to shield us from the hardest realities of life—the hardest realities of our own lives. How does Jesus put it? "Whoever would save his life will lose it, and whoever loses his life for my sake will find it" (v. 25).

"All that lives must die...Why seems it so particular with thee?"

Because death is particular with us all. But reconciliation over the grave and the redemption of life are also particular. Particularly aimed at you and me and all God's children.

Notes
1. The title is taken not only from William Shakespeare's *Hamlet*, but from an article by J. Bottum, "All That Lives Must Die," *First Things* (May 1996), pp. 28–32. I am indebted to Bottum for some of the ideas articulated in this sermon.
2. See Bottum, p. 29.
3. Walter Brueggemann, *Old Testament Theology: Essays on Structure, Theme, and Text*, ed. Patrick D. Miller (Minneapolis: Fortress Press, 1992), p. 207.
4. Ibid., p. 213, though I am veering from his view a bit.

COMMENT

John Mark Jones knows with Shakespeare that however "common" death may be to the human experience, it confronts every individual in a "particular" fashion. He also knows that "our faith forces us to take seriously the reality of death" in a culture which often attempts to blunt the effects of death. In the opening paragraphs Jones clearly poses the central question of the sermon: How does a Christian face death?

Among the obvious merits of this sermon is the willingness to tackle a difficult subject. In a culture which craves user-friendly products, there is considerable pressure on preachers to provide biblical inspiration for self-esteem and feeling good about oneself. The congregation at Trinity United Methodist Church in Columbia, South Carolina, was not pampered with soothing counsels for prosperity or reassuring remedies for inner peace.

The preacher of this sermon is to be commended for his courage in taking up this difficult subject from which the more fainthearted might back away. He doubtless addresses the concerns of many in his congregation. He avoids frivolous illustrations and cutesy prose. He offers no facile answers to the concerns people have about death. He should be applauded for his serious and thoughtful labor.

Jones's resolute grappling with the theme of death by his reading of Genesis 50:15–21 and Matthew 16:13–28 presents an opportunity to think about a perennial and unresolved issue in preaching: the relationship between exegesis and the sermon. How does one move from text(s) to sermon? Jones instructs us by the way he carries out the task. But because multifaceted texts may address many concerns, we shall explore other (not necessarily better!) ways to use these texts in preaching.

Faith Confronting the Reality of Death

In his introductory comments, Jones gains our attention with the citation from Shakespeare that says however "common" death is, it always confronts us in a "particular way." The first major section of the sermon emphasizes that faith takes seriously the reality of death, as seen in the Joseph story (Gen. 50:15–21). Jones develops this theme by suggesting that (a) death shatters old systems of support; (b) death disrupts family relationships; and (c) death intensifies every emotion. These reminders surely touched on concerns of many in the congregation.

The second major section of the sermon notes that although faith forces one to face the reality of death, "it is nevertheless very difficult to speak of death in the church." For Jones the story of Peter's confession of Jesus as the Messiah in Matthew 16:13–28 indicates that "Peter doesn't want to hear anything about failure, defeat, death." The one who recognizes Jesus as the "Messiah, the son of the *living God*" (v. 16, Jones's emphasis) will not countenance any discussion of death and suffering (see especially v. 22). By following the RSV translation of Matthew 16:18 and placing emphasis on the last phrase ("and the *powers of death* shall not prevail against it [the church]"), Jones concludes that Jesus is speaking primarily about death in the passage. He notes that Peter's refusal to recognize Jesus' suffering reveals that Peter "can't face the reality of death." He concludes this second section of the sermon by advancing the thesis that "the gospel is about bringing us face to face with the reality of death."

Jones then considers a related question which he holds that the gospel poses: "How shall we respond to the reality of death?" The conclusion of the sermon focuses on pivotal ideas which Jones finds in the texts from Genesis and Matthew. Returning again to his reading of the Joseph story, Jones looks at fear in the presence of death. Faith, he suggests, enables the brothers of Joseph to "see beyond the madness of their fear to the power of reconciliation." He adds that this reconciliation, which takes place "over the grave of their father," also "enables them to face death." The passage from Matthew 16 indicates that Jesus "looks death squarely in the eye." Consequently, Peter and present-day Christians are invited to do the same.

The Theme of Death and the Scripture

In this section of the "sermon comment" I want to help us not only to learn from the sermon itself, but also to think about how one deals with the reality of death in preaching. More generally, how does one move from text to sermon, or move from a general theme such as "death" to an appropriate passage of Scripture?

It goes without saying that there is no single biblical view of death. Rather there are a variety of perspectives on death in Scripture. Rarely does one find a biblical passage directly addressing the subject of death. Most often, a perspective on death surfaces in the context of a wider discussion. While death is not absent from many of the teachings of Jesus, death is never viewed as the central problem to be resolved. Thus our questions today about death may differ from questions raised in Scripture.

Jones deserves thanks for exploring in this sermon how the reality of death connects with human emotions. For instance, he gives vivid examples of the anger that may be evident when a parent is dying. He doubtless would recognize, of course, that not every situation in the presence of death is marked by anger and a desire to hurt others. But he surely is on target in reminding us that "in the face of death every emotion is intensified."

Jones gives us a responsible treatment of the theme of death. With appreciation for his efforts, we might also ask whether there are other passages which might more compellingly deal with the topic, among them 1 Corinthians 15, 1 Thessalonians 4:13–18, and 1 Peter 1:3–12 which emphasize that because Jesus was raised from the realm of the dead, the domain of death is no longer a tyrant. Yet 1 Thessalonians 4:13–18 shows that the affirmation of resurrection victory did not spare some of the Thessalonians from agonizing over the deaths of Christians. Moreover, the Pauline connection between death and sin, albeit cast in mythological language, may today raise questions which invite careful theological reflection (see especially 1 Cor. 15:53–57). Further, in Pauline thought, it is not only the single individual who is subject to death, but the whole creation (see 1 Cor. 15:20–28; Rom. 8:18–25, 35–39).

ANOTHER PERSPECTIVE ON MATTHEW 16:13-28

Jones's use of the passage from Matthew suggests a particular reading which concentrates on the theme of death. A more traditional exegetical approach suggests that the passage is not so much chiefly about death as it is about the significance of the suffering death of Jesus. A strict reading of the text—not always required in sermons—might not lead to the same conclusion as does Jones's sermon in its paraphrase of Jesus' response to Peter: "That is to say, 'Peter, if you can't face the reality of death, you have no part of me, you have no part of God. And besides, the only part of God that really matters is the part that lies behind the veil of life and death.'" Jones's sermon pushes us to think about how strictly one must adhere to the meaning of the text disclosed by exegesis.

Perhaps we can make the point more sharply by another look at the Matthean text. Jones surely has seen aspects of the text touching on death. Yet the part of the passage in which he finds the theme of death actually places the spotlight on the Rock (Peter) on which Jesus will build the church. Verse 18 is not primarily about death; it asserts that Jesus will build the church on Simon Rock. Of course, Simon is Rock because he confesses Jesus as Messiah. The passage emphasizes the unique role of Peter in the founding of the church. Each generation does not begin anew. There are founding figures who provide guidance and nurture for subsequent followers of Jesus. One might want to move from text to sermon along these lines.

Jones finds the theme of death especially in the RSV translation of verse 18. He places the pivotal phrase in italics: "And I tell you, you are Peter [which means 'rock'], and on this rock I will build my church, and the *powers of death* shall not prevail against it." The NRSV, however, reflects literally the Greek. In place of "powers of death" the NRSV has "the gates of Hades."

"The gates of Hades will not be stronger than the church" (my translation). Hades was viewed as a place of many gates where the dead would remain until the final resurrection (cf. "gates of Sheol" in Isa. 38:10, NRSV). The "gates of Hades" represents the power of the realm of the dead. The church will be stronger than all the mighty power of death because the Risen Lord promises to be with his followers "always, to the end of the age" (Matt. 28:20; cf. Isa. 28:14–18). Even in this present age, the church will share in the resurrection power of Christ. While the RSV translation, "powers of death," does seem to warrant a reference to death, the Greek phrase itself suggests that a general view of death is not the primary meaning. The passage really speaks of the church.

In fact, the subsequent verses suggest that the theme is about the church, not death. The "keys of the kingdom" in verse 19 is reflected in 23:13 in the charge that the Pharisees "lock people out of the kingdom of heaven." Peter is given the "keys to the kingdom of heaven" to emphasize his role as doorkeeper in the kingdom for the well-being of the community. The duties surely include missionary activity, teaching, and discipline.

The work of binding and loosing (16:19b) refers to judicial decisions related to disputes in the community. This duty is not only granted to Peter here but is also granted to the church in 18:18. These verses remind readers today that the church of Matthew's time and subsequent ages must deal with disputes, with the discipline of members, and with false teachers. Church decisions must be made by humans.

However prominent Peter is among the disciples, he is not idealized in the New Testament writings. For example, Matthew alters in a notable way Mark's rendering of Jesus' rebuke to Peter. Jesus tells Peter in Mark 8:33, "You are setting your mind not on divine things but on human things" (NRSV). Matthew, however, presents Jesus as saying in 16:23: "You are a stumbling block [literally, scandal] to me." The citation of Isaiah 8:14 in Romans 9:33 and 1 Peter 2:8 speaks of a rock (Greek: *petra*) of stumbling or scandal (i.e., "a rock that makes them fall", NRSV). The disciple who is the "stumbling block" in Matthew 16:23 is also the foundational rock on which the church is built! Peter is both the rock of stability for the church and the rock for stumbling. It is an act of God's grace that the church can be built on Simon Rock.

These exegetical observations point to other directions to move from text to sermon. Jones's helpful sermon gives us one approach. His sermon also encourages us to reflect on ways Scripture should be used in preaching. This sermon can encourage those who preach to ask the hermeneutical question. Jones has served us well through the sermon itself and the important discussions it generates.

James J. H. Price

A CRAZY, HOLY GRACE

MARK 1:9–11

DR. GARY W. KLINGSPORN
COLONIAL CHURCH
EDINA, MINNESOTA

DR. GARY W. KLINGSPORN

A CRAZY, HOLY GRACE

MARK 1:9-11, NRSV

Bedtime for our two little girls, Katy and Kari, as in any family with small children, can be a very elaborate process. Bedtime usually begins about 8:15 or 8:30 with a search for all the paraphernalia Debra and I are going to need for this major nightly undertaking in our lives.

First, it's which "jammies" and where are they? Will it be Beauty and the Beast, Mickey & Minnie Mouse, Petal Power, or the Goofy nightgowns tonight? After a protest or two ("But I'm *not* tired yet!"), they give it up and the jammies finally go on. Then the search for "blankies" begins—the torn, ragged pink one for Kari, the quilted blue one from Grandma K for Katy. Then what doll or stuffed animal goes beddy-bye tonight? The critter search begins throughout the house.

Oh, and don't forget the water—in two "Tippy" cups. Katy always gets the blue one. Kari gets the other one. Then two little cups of snacks: a few Cheerios, graham crackers, Alphabits, or Lucky Charms. Most of you know how it goes. If any of this is missing, you hunt until you find it! Everything has to be there. It's the same ritual every night.

Finally we move our little bedtime party upstairs to sit on the floor between two twin beds, with pillows propped behind our backs, for story time. Who chooses the story tonight? Who chose last night? Who remembers? Who cares? After some weary negotiating, the story finally gets underway to the crunching of cereal in one ear and the hum of Kari's little bedtime tune in the other ear.

The story over, my favorite time is here. We dim the lamp on the chest between the two beds until there's just a hint of light in the room. There in the darkness it's time for a final snuggle and a little conversation with each girl. We lie on the bed looking up at the ceiling or at a little face framed with blond curls, still reflecting the glow of the day. "How was your day?" we sometimes ask, or "Tell me something you did today that was fun!"

One night not long ago during this snuggle time, my wife Debra asked Katy, "What could you do that would make me *not* love you?" It came as a surprise and a hard question. All Katy could do was suck her thumb, pull her blanket to her face, and give a big shrug. "Well," said Debra, "if you made a real mess in your room, do you think that would make me not love you?"

"No," said Katy.

"That's right," Debra said. "How about if you got into Mother's make-up in the bathroom and smeared it all over yourself and all over the bathroom, do you think *that* would make me not love you?"

There was a long pause, then finally, "No."

"You're right," said Debra. "What if you got really, really angry with me and ran away from home, do you think that would make me stop loving you?"

Another shrug.

"Well, what if I got really, really angry with you, Katy? Would that mean that I no longer love you?"

Katy catches on quickly. This time the response was an emphatic "*No!*"

That's right!" said Debra. "I might not like what you did, but I would still love you."

That little conversation took place in much the same way the next couple of nights, with Katy a little hesitant, uncertain. But the fourth night Debra asked the question again. "Katy, what could you ever do that would make me not love you?" Without a moment's hesitation, with a big smile from behind her blanket, Katy said, *"Nothing!"*

"You're exactly right," said Debra, "and don't you ever forget it!" So it has been ever since, and so it will be.

Among the deepest of our human needs is the simple need to be loved and accepted. To know that someone loves us as we are, not because of something we have accomplished or achieved, but just because we are who we are!

The whole world is crying out for this kind of love and affirmation. It is the outer side of a deeper need—the need for self-acceptance—to feel good about ourselves, to accept ourselves as we are. Criticism and rejection are found everywhere around us—from others and from within ourselves. Underneath much of our loneliness, much of our pain and woundedness, much of our need to perform, is the basic fear that our lives will have no meaning, that we will not be loved, that we will always be searching, never finding the ultimate acceptance we seek.

"Please love me" is a need that never goes away. The fear that we will not be loved or that we will lose the love and acceptance of others fuels many of our compulsions and contributes to much of our pain and brokenness. We long for someone to ask, "What could you do that would make me not love you?"—and to be able to answer, "Nothing!"

Here we are in worship this morning, longing for a word to address our deepest needs. Christmas is over. It's back to the hard, bare realities of our lives in the frozen cold of this new year with a lot of winter yet ahead. The sanctuary is so bare. Only a week ago the warmth and joy of Christmas were still present. The Advent wreath was still at full blaze and the tall elegant trees were still flanking the pulpit with the bright red poinsettias at their base. The large wreaths with their red bows were still on the walls and in the windows. The garlands were still on the staircases. But this week it all came down amid the muffled voices of custodians with their ladders and their vacuums. They tore it all down, cleaned it up, put it away.

Perhaps some of us are glad that Christmas is over. Perhaps others are sad and finding the transition back to real life a difficult one. But for all of us there is the lingering question, What was it finally all about? What did it all mean for me, for you? What difference did it make?

On this first Sunday after Epiphany, the manger is gone. The angels and shepherds have vanished. The Magi have long since left their gifts and gone home. The star of Bethlehem has faded from view. The Child has become a man and, like all of us, is caught up in time, in change, and mortality. He comes to the Jordan River, stands among sinners, to be baptized by John. Then, as Mark tells it, "Just as he was coming up out of the water, he saw the heavens torn apart and the Spirit descending like a dove on him. And a voice came from heaven, 'You are my Son, the Beloved; with you I am well pleased'" (Mark 1:10–11).

In Mark's Gospel this story establishes the identity of Jesus before he begins his public ministry. For the reader the story is an "epiphany," a revealing or "manifestation" of who Jesus is. In the coming of Jesus, Mark proclaims, something radically new has occurred. The heavens are "torn apart" by God, a sign of the breaking-in of a new age in human history and in the purpose of God. The Spirit descending upon Jesus reveals that he is the One greater than John, anointed and empowered by God. The voice from heaven affirms Jesus as the beloved Son of God whose relationship with the Father is very special and pleasing.

That sentence, "You are my Son, the Beloved; with you I am well pleased," is the joining of two well-known phrases from the Old Testament. Half of the sentence is from the coronation hymn in Psalm 2, "You are my son" (Ps. 2:7); the other half is from the first Servant Song of Isaiah, "Behold my servant...my chosen, in whom my soul delights" (Isa. 42:1, RSV). In a word, the voice proclaims that the baby Jesus of Bethlehem, now a young man on the verge of his ministry, is indeed the royal Son of God, the Sovereign Lord of all, and the Servant of all—One who will ultimately suffer for all, One in whom God takes great delight and pleasure. The voice in Mark's Gospel is an affirmation of Jesus that tells us who he is and points to his mission as the Servant-King.

Mark proclaims in this scene that in Jesus the new age of salvation has dawned. God has opened the heavens and spoken in a decisive way. God's Spirit is now active in the world. God has acted in his Servant-King Son to bring God's salvation to all people.

"What could you ever do that would make me *not* love you?"

For us on this January Sunday in the season of Epiphany, this heavenly voice is not only about who Jesus is—it is also about who we are—we who have such great need to love and to be loved, to know that we are accepted, affirmed, loved by someone who will never stop loving us.

We come this morning from complex lives of single parenting and blended families, of economic uncertainty and corporate takeover, of cancer and Alzheimer's, of busy young families, of the passages of midlife, and the loneliness of aging. We come from a world of oughts, musts, and shoulds, where criticism and rejection are easily found, where unconditional acceptance and affirmation are rare.

In a world filled with other voices telling us we are somehow less than adequate, that we have to "prove ourselves" or earn acceptance, we come this morning longing for a word to address our deepest needs. There is a voice—the same voice that spoke to Jesus at his baptism, saying now to us: "You are my beloved!"

They are words spoken to Jesus before he had done anything in his ministry to "prove" himself. They are words telling us we don't have to "prove" ourselves worthy of the love of God. We cannot make this love happen. It is a gift that God offers us, already freely given, the promise that, as Paul says, in Christ Jesus we are all children of God through faith. "For as many of you as were baptized into Christ have put on Christ. There is neither Jew nor Greek, there is neither slave nor free, there is neither male nor female; for you are all one in Christ Jesus" (Gal. 3:26–28, RSV).

Jesus' baptism at the Jordan is not only an "epiphany" of who Jesus is—it is an "epiphany" of who we are as we receive Jesus Christ by faith. In the words of our own baptism we hear the same heavenly voice, "You are my beloved son, daughter, with whom I am well pleased." These are words that answer our deepest need to be loved, accepted, affirmed.

"What could you ever do to make me not love you?" The good news of the gospel this morning is this word of God's grace: *"Nothing!* You are my beloved!" The word of law condemns, demands, threatens, drives. The law triggers the rebel in us all. The word of law cannot change us or transform us into God's people. But as John Claypool says, "If I am effectively told that there is nothing I can ever do that will make God love me any more than God loves me this moment, that there is nothing I can ever do that will make God stop loving me, then enormous powers of motivation are released in me, and 'the perfect love that casts out fear' begins to blow like wind in a sail to move me forward."[1]

The season of Epiphany is about who Jesus Christ is for us: Son of God incarnate and Servant-King baptized at the Jordan; Savior who came to teach, heal, forgive, die for us, and reconcile us to God—because God loved the world and loves us. You and I are loved, not because of what we have done, but because of who God is in his deepest nature. The season of Epiphany is also about who *we* are: beloved sons and daughters of God in Jesus Christ.

The challenge for us is to listen to that heavenly voice telling us who we truly are—"the beloved"—to listen together as the church, the community of faith, and to proclaim in word and deed this same love of God for the world.

In Jesus Christ, God's own Son, the heavens have been torn apart. The Spirit has descended upon us and is on the loose. The voice of God has spoken and continues to speak: "You're mine. You're unique and special. I'm pleased with you! I love you."

So in the bedtime lamplight comes the question, "Katy, what could you do that would make me not love you?" And now, without a moment's hesitation, Katy responds emphatically, *"Nothing!"*

In the bright clear light of this Epiphany morning, God asks us, "What could you do that would ever make me stop loving you?" Can we answer without a moment's hesitation, *"Nothing!"*?

Frederick Buechner is right. This is a crazy, holy grace. "Crazy because whoever could have predicted it? Who can ever foresee the crazy how and when and where of a grace that wells up out of the lostness and pain of the world and of our own inner worlds? And holy because these moments of grace come ultimately from farther away than Oz and deeper down than doom, holy because they heal and hallow."[2] This grace transforms our lives into sacred journeys in which we in turn reach out to others in love, justice, and mercy and say, "I love you. I want to love you, because I have been loved and I am loved of God."

Whatever the sin, the pain, the brokenness in our lives and in our world, we cannot make God stop loving us.

May you and I enter and live more deeply in the relationship God offers us in Jesus Christ. May each of us know and respond to the love that is offered. And in it, may we find healing and hope for our lives and for our world.

May this crazy, holy grace heal, restore, uplift, and bless you on your way today, tomorrow, and in all the seasons of your life, until at last we stand together in the presence of the One who loves us always. So be it! Amen.

Notes
1. John R. Claypool, *The Preaching Event: Lyman Beecher Lectures* (Waco, TX: Word Books, 1980), p. 134.
2. Frederick Buechner, *The Sacred Journey* (San Francisco: Harper & Row, 1982), p. 57!

COMMENT

Everybody wants somebody to bless them. Little children and even grown-up children long to hear their parents say, "I love you!" or "I'm so proud of you!" The graduate student labors long in hopes of obtaining the blessing of her supervisory professor: "You have done well. This is an excellent paper." Any minister in any congregation counts it a good day when a parishioner expresses appreciation for some particular work of ministry. Blessing renews our self-confidence and our hopes for the future. Blessing restores our sense of purpose and self-esteem. We all want to be blessed.

In his sermon, "A Crazy, Holy Grace," Gary Klingsporn appeals to this universal need and desire for blessing to present the story of Jesus' baptism in an altogether different light. He contends that the heavenly voice that bestowed blessing is "not only about who Jesus is—it is also about who we are."

PROBLEM

Klingsporn devotes the first portion of this sermon to an episode within his own family. One evening, as he and his wife were putting their children to bed, he heard his wife ask of one of their daughters this provocative question: "What could you do that would make me not love you?" Repeatedly, his wife presented hypothetical situations and asked, "Would that make me not love you?" Each time, Katy answered no. Through this give-and-take the little girl learned something very valuable from her mother: nothing she could do would ever make her parents not love her. They love their daughters no matter what. They accept their children no matter what.

According to Klingsporn, this unconditional love and acceptance is what all of us want more than anything. We want to know that nothing we do can make someone not love us. We want to know that "someone loves us as we are, not because of something we have accomplished or achieved, but just because we are who we are!" This universal desire provides the foundation for the sermon. Klingsporn has crafted the message to address our "simple need to be loved and accepted."

TEXT

The sermon focuses on Mark's account of Jesus' baptism. Klingsporn faithfully retells the story. In doing so, he unpacks the significance of Mark's imagery ("the heavens are torn apart") and relates some helpful background information on the word from heaven, "You are my Son, the Beloved; with you I am well pleased." This portion of the text serves as the focal point for the sermon, as Klingsporn seeks to relate that heavenly affirmation to earthbound folks.

PROCLAMATION

The question, "What could you ever do that would make me not love you?" structures Klingsporn's entire presentation. This question is repeated at least eleven times within the sermon. Repetition of the question keeps the sermon focused and leaves no doubt as to its subject. The preacher uses the question in connection with Jesus' address as "the Beloved Son" to proclaim the good news for all of us: "There is a voice—the same voice that spoke to Jesus at his baptism, saying now to us: 'You are my beloved!'"

In this way, Klingsporn models what all preachers should do. He bridges the distance between the text and the contemporary audience. Although he effectively tells us what happened when Jesus was baptized, he connects it to us, illustrating its significance in the here and now. He makes this connection most clearly when he says, "For us on this January Sunday in the season of Epiphany, this heavenly voice is not only about who Jesus is—it is also about who we are." Too many preachers excel in unpacking the historical material of the text. They can dazzle their congregation with their knowledge of antiquity. But most listeners leave such presentations asking, "What's that got to do with me?" On the other hand, many preachers fall short in the opposite way. They care little for the history and context and immediately jump to the significance of a text for someone in today's world. Divorced from its roots, the biblical text may yield a message, but quite often it is a message far removed from that intended by the biblical writer.

Perhaps the best illustration of Klingsporn's reading of the text in terms of what happened then and its significance now lies in his observation that God affirmed Jesus as his Beloved Son "before he had done anything in his ministry to 'prove' himself." That's gospel!

Response

This sermon was preached during Epiphany, in the aftermath of Christmas. After the Christmas rush, most of us feel a little down. Perhaps we didn't get what we wanted for Christmas—not so much in gifts but in expressions of love and appreciation. Through this sermon, Klingsporn seeks to encourage those who have been laid low by the holidays. In keeping with the theme of the sermon, he doesn't ask his audience to do anything. He doesn't call for the performance of extravagant service. Instead, the invitation Klingsporn gives is to listen. He calls on all of us in the church to listen to God's voice, the one that speaks to us before we've done anything at all. The voice that tells us that we are his beloved people. The message bears an implicit invitation to accept the fact that we are accepted.

Suggestions

- This sermon uses the repetition of a question as a rhetorical strategy. This repetition keeps the subject clearly in front of the listener and provides a means of linking the different segments of the sermon. This move leaves no doubt as to the subject of the sermon. Sometimes repetition comes off as hokey and contrived: Here it works. Read through the sermon of past masters of preaching and good preachers today with an eye to the ways in which they effectively employ repetition. Experiment with your preaching. Utilize repetition of a key idea to present your message. Elicit feedback

from members of your congregation to see if they heard what you wanted to say.
- The best preaching always bridges the distance between what happened then and what it means now. Review your sermons from the last three months. Did you give necessary attention to both dimensions? Are your sermons balanced between background material and the points or lessons you wished to draw? Is your message faithful to the text?
- Good sermons are appropriate to the seasons of listeners' lives. We are not always up; neither are we always down. Faith is not lived on a perpetual mountaintop; nor does it reside exclusively in the valley. Effective ministry demands that we listen to our people, knowing when to encourage and when to challenge. One-note preaching always delivered at the same volume soon wears thin.

William J. Ireland, Jr.

A COMFORT, DEEP AND LASTING

ISAIAH 40:1-2

REV. DR. F. DEAN LUEKING
GRACE LUTHERAN CHURCH
RIVER FOREST, ILLINOIS

REV. DR. F. DEAN LUEKING

A COMFORT, DEEP AND LASTING

ISAIAH 40:1-2, NRSV

How universal is the yearning for comfort! From the first day of life onward it's there. Think of that marvelous arc of a mother's (or father's) neck and shoulder on which a toddler nestles for comfort when afraid or sleepy. That's a place of comfort, and blessed is the child who receives that reassuring hug.

Sometimes comfort comes in an unforgettable dramatic moment. A month ago a father and son were out sailing on Lake Michigan when a sudden gale overturned their sailboat. For nine hours they somehow held on to the hull and each other in icy waters which grew stormier as night fell. They had prepared each other for death after struggling again and again to pull each other back onto the upended hull as the waves washed over them. Suddenly, out of pitch-black darkness, a strong beam of light from a rescue boat spotted them. Imagine the comfort that ray of light brought. Imagine their delirium of joyful comfort when that heroic fisherman hauled them on board, totally exhausted by the ordeal. The letter of thanks they wrote in the Washington Island, Wisconsin, newspaper included this: "We give thanks to God through Jesus Christ our Savior for his mercy in sending Ken Koyen out into that wild storm, risking his life to save ours."

Somewhere along the spectrum between the comforting hug of a caring parent and the incredible drama of rescue of that father and son, we have our place as people both in need of comfort and with comfort to offer in matters large and small that make up the daily round.

A Voice of Comfort

Comfort means many things to many people. Southern Comfort (beware)! The comfort women of Korea forced into prostitution for Japanese troops in World War II (a travesty of the word). The incessant promises of comfort if we will buy this or subscribe to that (short term, at best).

Now comes the best word on comfort, a comfort deep and lasting, a comfort that has Advent promise and power. Hear the word of the Lord:

> Comfort, O comfort my people,
>   says your God.
> Speak tenderly to Jerusalem,
>   and cry to her
> that she has served her term,
>   that her penalty is paid,
> that she has received from the Lord's hand
>   double for all her sins (Isaiah 40:1–2).

Thus did the prophet speak to an exiled people, dragged off by their Babylonian captors in 586 B.C., an all-important date to remember, when Jerusalem was sacked, the great temple of Solomon burned, and the long years of exile began. It was a bitter time of chastisement for God's people who never believed that the warnings against idolatry, injustice, and immorality were meant for them, as well as for the pagan nations around them.

As exiles far from home, they despaired of comfort. Their lament comes through in these words from Psalm 137:

By the waters of Babylon—
    there we sat down and there
we wept
    when we remembered Zion.
On the willows there
    we hung up our harps.
For there our captors
    asked us for songs,
and our tormentors asked for mirth, saying,
    "Sing us one of the songs of Zion!"
How could we sing the Lord's song
    in a foreign land? (vv. 1–4, NRSV)

The Babylonian exile was long ago and far away from us. The despair over ever finding comfort is not. An abused child knows it. A man or woman caught up in a long-dying marriage can feel its creeping numbness. Think of the refugees of the world, twenty-three million of them, who are pawns of insatiable tyrannies that never intend to offer comfort to their victims.

Such long-term woes can strangle hope and nullify comfort. When that happens something even worse follows. The very word *comfort* is resented. Life is defined by being a victim. Comfort is refused. To hope for it seems a mockery. To accept it would mean coming out of a black hole of helplessness. A paralysis grips the inner spirit, a dead-end paralysis that shuts the door against even imagining what comfort could mean, let alone hoping for it.

We catch glimpses of this in the Scriptures. Job's wife, battered by disastrous loss, can only tell her disconsolate husband to curse God and die. An embittered Naomi, bereft of both husband and sons, tells her widowed daughter-in-law to go on without her since the hand of the Lord has gone against her. Rachel's barrenness drives her to chicanery. The mothers of Bethlehem, their little sons slaughtered by Herod's madmen, are inconsolable—like Rachel of old. Judas despairs of any comfort equal to the monstrous betrayal he had carried out, and chooses instead the end of a rope.

Be on guard against this terrible blight of soul that keeps comfort out of reach. It can become a way of life, a license to give up because all is lost. It is the sure mark of unbelief, a defiance of God who can and does work together for good in all things. Dietrich Bonhoeffer has a haunting phrase for living in despair, "Like a beaten army, fleeing in disorder from victory already achieved."[1] That bleak condition of soul may take the form of defiance. Or it may come in the form of a numb passiveness that accepts meaninglessness in life as the norm, seeing no exit.

A God of Comfort

God's will is to bring comfort, deep and lasting, as only God can.

> Comfort, comfort my people, says your God.
> Speak tenderly to Jerusalem,
>   and cry [not just tell] to her
> that her warfare is ended (Isa. 40:1–2, RSV).

The war is over. Such passion in that call!

It took courage for the prophet to declare that comfort was at hand when no sign of it was obvious. It always takes courage to declare a promise of the Lord before it comes about. But that's the nature of a promise, and the power of faith is to believe the promise.

The release did come. The exiles did return home. The old pagan Cyrus was God's anointed servant of deliverance, in one of the marvelous ironies of divine providence. The Jewish people went back to rebuild the temple and the nation and to remember the covenant that gave them a future.

Learn what comfort is from this great text. Comfort is not sin denied; it is sin forgiven. Comfort is not exile avoided; it is exile endured. Comfort is not getting our own act together; it is entering into the saving acts of God. Comfort is not a skin-deep course correction; it reaches through to the very core of the humbled heart. Comfort is not everything in place and under our control; it is a still calm with plenty of storm still around. Comfort means that there is a pathway through the dilemma, a call to go forward with God's hand leading.

Above all, comfort comes in the trust that God is at work, that God keeps his word, that his judgments are well deserved, that his overflowing mercy is not deserved. From this trust comes the peace that passes all understanding.

Comfort is Jesus Christ crucified and risen. For you and me and for the world, he left eternity and entered time in humility. He suffered. He died. He rose again in glory. "Comfort, comfort my people" is God's resurrection word for us today. Here. Now. It is ours for the asking.

A Deep Comfort

The Gospel reading today from Mark 1 features John the Baptist "proclaiming a baptism of repentance for the forgiveness of sins" (v. 4, NRSV). Why did this stark proclamation draw the people of the whole Judean countryside and Jerusalem out to the desert? I don't have the full answer by any means, but one sure part of the answer is that John told the truth at the right time, in the right place, for the right reasons, to those who were ready to hear it. In the mystery of God's ways, the time was right for a deep comfort to set in because a deep repentance opened the way for it.

I knew a man, no longer with us, who was the head of a prominent hospital in Chicago. He was gifted, successful, admired by many. While climbing the ladder of success, he had neglected some basics, including his family and his spiritual life. For reasons unclear to me, however, he found his way one Sunday to a small country church in Wisconsin and sat in the back row. Half-listening to the sermon, he did hear one sentence from the preacher that went something like this: "Jesus never turned his back on anybody." Just that. Upon hearing it, really hearing it, he could not hold back the tears. When asked by his friend what was happening, he said, "I turned my back on my son...and lost him." Never before had he opened up that deep place in his soul where the truth could finally reach. It began a journey for him that led to a comfort before he died, a comfort with depth because the truth of a merciful God reached the heart of a humbled father.

Comfort That Lasts

The apostle Paul taught the truth that comfort lasts as it is shared. We hear it in the liturgy of burial which begins with thanksgiving to the God "who comforts us in all our affliction, so that we may be able to comfort those who are in any affliction…" (2 Cor. 1:4, RSV).

Here is the story of one who knows. She is an attractive and capable young woman in her early thirties who recently joined friends for a few days of rest on the West Coast. At an evening gathering, another woman twice her age looked her over and blurted out, "Well, honey, I see you've transferred that gorgeous ring from your left to your right hand. Tell me, when did you dump your husband?" The young woman swallowed hard, struggling to hold on to her emotions, but then said with an even voice, "I buried my husband four weeks ago; he was drowned while on a medical mission off the northern coast of Alaska."

The older woman was stunned with embarrassment, and rightly so, unable to say anything. The young widow gathered up the enormous strength and durability of a God-given comfort (*cum forte,* meaning "with strength") and quietly began a conversation that reached out to the other. In time she learned that the older woman had lost her daughter to leukemia at age thirteen. Into that long-kept, unhealed wound, was poured the oil of solace, the balm of the gospel. Comfort lasts as comfort is shared.

Give that comfort in these days. Comfort those who have everything else but comfort. Speak tenderly to those who have not heard tender speech for too long a time. Speak truth with love. Show how deep and lasting is the comfort given by the Holy Spirit, whom we name the Comforter.

It may be that comfort is not currently on your wish list. You may feel that this testimony to the comfort with which God comforts is for others. I must say to you, speaking the truth in love, that the time will come in your life when you will need this comfort, deep and lasting, in ways you cannot now know or believe. Then you will know the truth of the psalmist's word about what we can lean on in the valleys and shadows yet to come: "Thy rod and thy staff, they comfort me."

Note
1. Dietrich Bonhoeffer, *Letters and Papers from Prison*, ed. Eberhard Bethge (New York: Macmillan Publishing Company, 1971), p. 348.

Comment

Where do I go when I need some comfort? Modern writers tell us that our reality is defined by "anxiety." In the event of a failure of nerve, we become like little children seeking solace from our moms or dads. This quest is universal in our culture—regardless of status, class, race, or gender. While we express the need for comfort in millions of different ways, we will all seek, at some point in our lives, a shelter from the storm.

In this sermon, Dean Lueking addresses this need we have to find a way out of lives of "No Exit" (to use Jean-Paul Sartre's despairing term). While Lueking's focus is on biblical comfort, he helps us deal with an underlying anxiety that can steal our hope, paralyze our inner spirits, and blind us to deeper truth. As we reflect on this sermon, we will ponder how we can lead our congregations in healthy, positive, Christlike ways to the "Great Comforter."

Problem

Lueking likens our lifelong quest for comfort to a baby receiving a hug or a victim being dramatically rescued from certain death. Later he further defines the problems which stem from a lack of comfort. The "blight of the soul" leads us away from God into a life of unbelief and defiance that makes meaninglessness the norm of life. We live "lives of quiet desperation," as Thoreau suggested, because we have not experienced the courage and compassion that divine comfort can bring.

Text

Lueking develops this sermon from the Isaiah 40 text made famous by Frederick Handel's *Messiah*. Handel's music beautifully captures our yearning to be comforted. "Comfort ye, comfort ye my people, saith your God. Speak ye tenderly to Jerusalem" (KJV). In contrast to the circumstantial discomfort of the Jerusalem exiles six centuries before the Incarnation of Christ, Isaiah passionately calls them, and us, to believe in a personal God who deeply cares for us in our suffering. We are not abandoned like orphans in the storm, nor are we left to our own resources.

The seeds of despair are planted deep within our souls. Lueking repeats the Isaiah text early in the sermon to remind the congregation of the desperate need the exiles had to find hope in a strange and faraway land. He also quotes Psalm 137 which reflects their despair. How many of our hearers share that sense of exile, that numbness of spirit that comes when we have experienced too much evil?

PROCLAMATION

Lueking hints at some good news in a negative way when he quotes Dietrich Bonhoeffer's phrase, "Like an army fleeing from a victory already won." God's comfort is not something to be experienced only in an eternal future. It is already available because of God's victory in Christ's death and resurrection. Comfort can be claimed immediately! Despite circumstances, we can be carried through deep waters as a little lamb might be carried by a shepherd across the raging waters of a spring torrent in Israel.

The message given to exiles in Babylon rings true for us today. God gives us comfort for the asking. This is the good news of the gospel. We can live life "with strength" because of the power of the Holy Spirit—if we choose.

RESPONSE

Throughout this sermon, Lueking invites his hearers to four action steps. First, we need to believe the promise of comfort. We must step away from our natural inclination to deny our need for comfort or to seek it in "all the wrong places." Second, we need to ask for comfort instead of closing the door to it because of fear. Our despair can lead us away from the very source of our healing. Third, we need to repent. Comfort comes when we turn from the lies and untruths that imprison us and lead to self-defeating behavior. Repentance paves the way for deeper truth to be revealed. The truth will set us free. We can live empowered lives if we choose to accept

God's comfort. And fourth, we need to share comfort with others. A life of compassion leads to a lifestyle of comfort for others and ourselves.

I read this sermon at the same time I was reading articles on courage in the journal of Christian spirituality, *Weavings*.[1] It struck me that comfort and courage are two ways of addressing the same theme. Faith in the face of hopelessness or despair is always a choice to "put our hand in the hand of the Man who stilled the water." It takes courage to persevere against the odds and, despite the facts, to live by faith.

But living with the expectation of winning in the end is contrary to our culture. This is especially true of our younger people. Conditioned either by the tragic suicidal deaths of their contemporaries who have given up hope, or even by the silly video games where the player always "dies" or can never really win, people often believe that life is essentially meaningless. There is no reason to risk because there is no hope of winning. There is no place for heroism because life is only a futile attempt to grasp brief moments of pleasure before the pain begins again. Courage is reserved for other folk who will risk it all and perhaps make the news or a *Reader's Digest* article for their brief moment of recognition.

Without comfort, we can hardly have courage. There is too much evidence that life is a meaningless song sung by fools. And without courage it is difficult to have compassion. While there may be fraternities of pain to help us make it through the night, there is little hope we can really make a difference in the world.

Jesus said in a passage I often find myself turning to, "In this world you will have trouble. But take heart! I have overcome the world" (John 16:33, NIV). Jesus was keenly aware of the difficulty of maintaining faith in the face of circumstances, but he was also here to provide a means of experiencing the truly abundant life—a life of comfort, courage, and compassion.

As we preach the word of God, we may sometimes feel we are spitting into the furious winds of evil that threaten to overwhelm us and undo our faith. We can tread the same pathway Lueking recommends and that Isaiah calls us to follow. We can claim the victory Jesus offers.

We can proclaim the good news that God's comfort gives us the courage to face each day. We can believe that we will receive the grace to make it through. By God's grace, we can face troubles, not as losers despairing of life itself, but as winners who can help others find God's comfort also.

SUGGESTIONS

- Consider the relationship between comfort, courage, and compassion. Why not preach a sermon or series of sermons dealing with the relationships between these in the life of faith?
- How have you experienced the universality of the need for comfort in your life? How can this illustrate your preaching?
- Lueking says in this sermon: "Comfort is not sin denied; it is sin forgiven. Comfort is not exile avoided; it is exile endured. Comfort is not getting our own act together; it is entering into the saving acts of God." Do you agree? Explore these ideas in a sermon of your own. In addition to Isaiah 40, what other texts might you explore on the theme of comfort?
- Are you familiar with the publication *Weavings*? I recommend it for your personal reading.

Gary W. Downing

Note
1. *Weavings: A Journal of the Christian Spiritual Life,* John S. Mogabgab, ed. (Nashville, TN: The Upper Room), vol. 12, May/June 1997.

Freedom!

MARK 12:13–17

MARY RUTH HOWES
LAY LEADER
TRINITY UNITED METHODIST CHURCH
JERSEY CITY, NEW JERSEY

FREEDOM

MARY RUTH HOWES

FREEDOM!

MARK 12:13-17

Have you ever wanted to be totally free? Free of every obligation? Free of every restraint? Free from everyone's demands on your time, your money, your talents? Especially free from the demands the government makes on your time and money?

A man by the name of McLaren has made the news these last weeks, because of his desire to be free. He set up his own separatist Republic of Texas out in the Davis Mountains in West Texas, so he wouldn't have to pay taxes to the state. As we watched the siege of his little Republic on television, and heard his statements quoted, some of us may have been tempted to call him silly, a megalomaniac, or just plain stupid. But he was acting on the desire every one of us has in some measure—to get out from under a burden.

Something of McLaren's attitude was behind the question the Pharisees put to Jesus in the temple that last week before the crucifixion.

"Why should we have to send money to a government which cruelly conquered and unjustly occupies a land which was not originally theirs?" is the thought behind their question. "Should we pay taxes or not?—paticularly since we owe our basic allegiance to God," they added under their breath!

Today we might ask, as some American citizens do, why should we pay taxes to a government that is wasteful, spendthrift, riddled with corruption, and just gets bigger and bigger so it can pay itself more and more without doing anything more for the common person—for us, for me? Why should everything I earn through May, in effect, go to the federal government?

The Pharisees' question, though, was a trick question. Whichever way Jesus answered he'd be in the doghouse with someone, with some group. The Romans took very seriously anyone who refused to pay taxes or who was thought to be advocating independence—just as the U.S. government took McLaren's group very seriously, particularly when they threatened other citizens and law officers. On the other hand, Jews in general hated anyone who publicly advocated supporting the evil Roman conquerors and would refuse to follow anyone who took such a position.

Jesus was caught in a bind, so the Pharisees thought. Unfortunately for them, they didn't realize how accurate their flattery of Jesus really was. You are *sincere,* they said when they came with their question; you teach in accordance with the *truth,* and are *not biased.*

This is exactly what Jesus is, whether the Pharisees believe it or not. He sees all sides of an argument. He isn't biased. He sees the truth—that he is being flattered and also asked a trick question. "You hypocrites," he calls his questioners. Perhaps he does so with a bit of a twinkle in his eye—letting them know he understands the trick and is willing to treat it as a joke. Today perhaps we might say, "Come on, you guys. You already know the answer to the question. You don't really believe all that about me. Get real!"

Then, in one fell swoop, he demolishes the Pharisees' position and every argument any one of us might have for reneging on our tax debt. If you use the government's services in any form, you owe the government taxes! Money, roads, utilities, programs—you got 'em, you use 'em, you pay for 'em. "Give Caesar what is Caesar's."

"Oh boy!" we say, settling the national debt and real estate taxes back firmly on our shoulders, all set to go on with our ordinary, tax-burdened lives.

But Jesus isn't done. "That's not all," he tells the Pharisees—and us. "You owe a bigger debt."

We do? To whom? To First National Bank? To Colonial Mortgage Company? To Sterns? To the local pawn shop?

"To God! Give God the things that are God's."

Jesus doesn't tell us what belongs to God. The Greek text says rather cryptically that he told the Pharisees, "Give Caesar Caesar's and give God God's."

Caesar's stuff we can tell, because it has his name and/or his face on it. We're seeing all sorts of "Caesars'" faces all over our town these days, as we face our elections. "Courtesy of the mayor, the county commissioner, the governor, our state senator."

But God? Where does God write his name to let us know what belongs to him?

Where? Everywhere? You and I, like Adam and Eve, are made in the image of God. God's image may not always be clear, but it's there. What that means is my life comes from God. My time comes from God. My abilities come from God. Even my nonabilities come from God (that is, when I'm asked to do something I think I can't do).

"You mean I can never get free of my obligations, the demands on me and my time and talents?" you ask.

Only by giving them to God and letting him give them back to you and me with his strength and power, so that we may freely serve him. Then we can take up our responsibilities with joy, knowing that God himself is with us.

God has given me everything. So I will live from now on as Jesus asked me to—deliberately, accepting my whole life as God's gift, and giving every moment back to him. It's the only way to true freedom. Will you join me?

COMMENT

Behold, the short sermon! Hallelujah! Call it a meditation...a thought for the day...a sound byte of gospel. Regardless of how one looks at this short message, it is another reminder to all who preach that depth does not necessitate length. Worthiness is not measured in wordiness. Mary Ruth Howes has given us a sterling example of a concise, effective presentation of the gospel in this brief exposition of Mark 12:13–17. While Howes is a "lay leader," let's hope it doesn't take someone outside "the cloth" to teach us "professional preachers" how to ply our craft more efficiently. In truth, this is precisely what she does, and she does it precisely.

PROBLEM

From Howes's first word, there can be no doubt where this sermon is going. No jovial warmup or beating around the bush. Howes goes straight to the subject at hand. In fact, the title of the message says it all, "Freedom!" What is the sermon about? You guessed it—freedom. The opening line lays it out directly to the audience: "Have you ever wanted to be totally free?" Who of us hasn't? Isn't freedom what America is all about? The pursuit of individual freedom is, arguably, the single greatest impediment to faith-filled living in this country. Individualism is a virtual religion in America. Howes obviously knows this and capitalizes on it for the sake of her message. We Americans will go to any extreme to liberate ourselves from strictures on how we spend our time, money, and talents. This is why Howes hits the nail right on the head with her three introductory questions. She effectively sets the stage for a biblical answer and a personal response.

To bring the issue closer to home, Howes refers to some Texas separatists who, at the time this sermon was preached, were in the midst of a confrontation with government authorities. If you want to make a concept real, give it a name. Better yet, give it a name that is immediately recognizable to your audience. Howes does precisely that; she gives the problem an identity. His name is McLaren, and because the media have already told us his story, Howes can use it as a modern parallel to the confrontation between Jesus and the religionists of his day. More than that, she enlists McLaren's separatists to illustrate the greater problem humanity has faced since the earliest of days, namely, our desire for spiritual autonomy. McLaren, the obstinate Texan, personifies that sinful self within all of us which balks at submitting to another, whether the "other" is a person, a government, or even God.

TEXT TO PROCLAMATION TO RESPONSE

Reread the sermon and notice how quickly and efficiently Howes moves through her presentation. First she briefly describes the McLaren incident. Then she quickly segues into the gospel narrative, making it the heart of her message. Finally, she wraps it all up with the question she wants us to ask ourselves: "Am I willing to give God full ownership of my being?"

There is nothing wasted here. Nothing to distract. Howes follows a straight line through her presentation, remaining absolutely faithful both to the evangelist's intent and to Christ's challenge. Mark's narrative is not about civil disobedience; it's about the disposition of every human heart. What begins with a Texas dissident ends with us having to face ourselves in the mirror. This is the ultimate goal of all good preaching: to transport the listener from objective truth to personal evaluation and, finally, to action.

Does Howes handle the text responsibly? Absolutely. The point of the narrative is not whether we should pay our taxes; it is to acknowledge to whom our souls belong. When the Pharisees hand Jesus the coin in hopes of entrapping him, he adeptly evades the tax question ("Give Caesar what is Caesar's") in order to get to the crux of the matter ("Give God what is God's"). The question about the coin is a throwaway. But the question of spiritual obligation is a keeper, and the sermon's final two paragraphs leave this question ringing in our ears. The preacher expects a response. "You mean I can never get free of my obligations, the demands on me and my time and talents?" According to Howes, no, we can't. We will only find "true freedom" in seeing the totality of our life as God's gift and then "giving every moment back to him." The closing words, "Will you join me?", invite us to respond by committing our lives to God as the way to that freedom.

SUGGESTIONS

- Using Howes' succinct message as a model, drop a plumb line through one of your own sermons and see if the string passes through every point along the way. If a message is padded with tangential material, it's likely wasted material which diverts listeners away from your central focus. Nowhere is it written that a sermon must fill twenty minutes to a half hour, so why do we consistently do so Sunday after Sunday? Do we rule the clock, or does the clock rule us?
- There is a simple "oneness" about this message. Howes asks one question: "Are we free to live apart from obligation to God?" She sticks to one biblical text: Mark 12:13–17. She uses one contemporary illustration: McLaren. And she reaches one conclusion: We owe it all to God. Simple but not simplistic. If preaching is about clarity—which most of us would agree it is—then why muddle it up with complexity? Someone once said a good speaker follows three simple rules: 1) Tell them what you're going to say; 2) Say it; and 3) Remind them what you've just said. Howes obviously plays by these rules. Do you?
- Choose another of the controversy stories in Mark 11:27–33 or 12:18–37 (or from parallel passages in Matthew 21–22 and Luke 20) and develop a sermon using Howes' simple model: one question, one text, one illustration, one conclusion.

Richard A. Davis

THE CHRISTIC JOURNEY

HEBREWS 11:29–12:2

REV. DR. GILBERT R. FRIEND-JONES
CENTRAL CONGREGATIONAL CHURCH
ATLANTA, GEORGIA

REV. DR. GILBERT R. FRIEND-JONES

THE CHRISTIC JOURNEY

HEBREWS 11:29–12:2, NRSV

Looking to Jesus the pioneer and perfecter of our faith, who for the sake of the joy that was set before him endured the cross, disregarding its shame, and has taken his seat at the right hand of the throne of God. Hebrews 12:2

The bright florescent lights filled the room, while the dark wood veneer tables formed its solid center. A few metal folding chairs testified beyond any doubt to its institutional character.

The nurses and staff wheeled them in: Margaret, Jeff, Connie, Bill. One by one they came through the doors into this room, this room where now they passed their days. Here they ate their meals; here they read the paper; here they sang together and conversed. Or tried to.

One was the mother of twelve; another had been a physicist before he arrived. One had been a brother at Saint John's Abbey; another had driven big truck rigs in her "former" life. Most were young adults or middle aged, very intelligent, very eager to make contact with each other, the staff and their visitor from Mayflower.[1]

It was my first visit to the Huntington's chorea unit of the Good Samaritan Society's University Center. This is one of the few units in the country that specializes in giving the extraordinary quantity and quality of care which persons who have this disability require.

I wanted to be respectful and not intrusive as they gathered to worship. Would I be seen by them as an able-bodied interloper? A voyeur of their private anguish? The uncontrollable muscular contractions—the sudden and seemingly violent spasms of arm or leg or head—these are embarrassing to many who suffer Huntington's. This unit is their home, their safe place, their refuge. Here they know they are understood. Here they are accepted. Here they are free—free from scorn, free from the well-meaning but often demeaning "help" of nice people, free even from any responsibility to make others feel comfortable with their involuntary grimaces, their uncontrollable exclamations, their incessant movement.

This rare disease passes through families. Each child has a 50 percent chance of inheriting Huntington's chorea if a parent has it. Most of the time the disease lies dormant until the affected person becomes an adult. It is progressive and incurable and follows a predictable course that includes multiplying physical disabilities, the loss of muscular control, the progressive loss of speech, a gradual transformation of the personality, and increasing dementia. Death comes after many years by choking, infections, or suicide.

My dictionary describes Huntington's chorea as a disorder within the cerebrum, but it is a "disorder" in the same way that Bosnia is a "skirmish" or the Titanic's sinking was merely "unfortunate" for those on board. Rather, this degenerative nerve disease is a full-blown assault on the personhood of its victims—on their bodies, to be sure, and their minds, but also on their spirits. Every conceivable value is tested; every hope is stretched to the breaking point.

Many of the people in this unit have seen a parent, an aunt, an uncle, a cousin die of Huntington's; they know what lies ahead. Some have children. Imagine the terror of not knowing whether your child will face what you are facing. Imagine the helplessness beneath this terror, and perhaps the despair beneath this helplessness.

In that room were authors whose books never will be written, lovers whose trysts never will be consummated, travelers who never will leave for distant shores. Around these tables, as surely as around the kiosk at the mall or the tables in Mayflower's dining room, gathered a cross section of our common humanity—saints and sinners, losers and winners whose tastes, abilities, and interests are as varied as yours and mine. Here were my sisters and my brothers, my mothers and my fathers, my flesh and blood.

A home, a garden, a "normal" family life—is that too much for them to ask? To make a contribution in the world—is that too much for them to hope? To dance across the ballroom floor, to skip a "smoothie" across the lake, to share a cup of tea with friends—why are such simple pleasures denied?

The greatest of life's questions hover anxiously around this unit: questions about meaning and purpose, questions about the goodness or fairness of life, questions about faith and hope, the past and the future, God and the nature of the universe.

One must give credit to the staff and volunteers who choose this unit. With their compassion, and their obvious respect for the intrinsic dignity of these individuals, they are creating a safe and affirming shelter. Margaret, Jeff, Connie, Bill, and all the others can relax, share the news, talk about their families, and face the great challenge life has set before them.

I need not have worried about how I would be received. My welcome was warm and immediate. Here were people eager to talk, eager to extend the gift of hospitality to an outsider. I was invited to the table to join them, given a hymnal to share, and encouraged to add my voice to theirs:

> Oh, for a thousand tongues to sing
>   My great Redeemer's praise,
> The glories of my God and King,
>   The triumphs of his grace!

Although I have sung this hymn all the years of my life, Charles Wesley's words were never so poignant nor so real to me as they were that morning. I looked around the table. I looked from face to face and eye to eye. I don't know what, exactly, I was searching for. Perhaps I thought

I would glimpse the hopelessness I was sure was there or the rage or the cynicism of singing God's praise in such circumstances. "Oh, for a thousand tongues," when even the one refuses to articulate what the heart commands. What "glories" should we point to? What gracious triumphs justify our praise?

I looked at Margaret. She was singing lustily away, and practically dancing in her chair. Jeff was singing the words just as loudly. The quiet Benedictine brother from Collegeville, his head bowed, was silently, reverently praying this hymn:

> My gracious Master and my God,
>   Assist me to proclaim,
> To spread through all the earth abroad
>   The honors of thy name.

There was no hint of cynicism, no rage, no despair in these faces. Even the eyes of those who didn't sing brightened; the room was filled with a sense of blessing and peace. In those brief moments, I became a part of their fellowship, and they became a part of mine. We were singing our joyful prayer of thanksgiving with an earnest and heartfelt desire. We were surrounded by an invisible "cloud of witnesses" singing with us—all those dear people in our lives, living and dead, near and far, who with us weave together the timeless, seamless web of sacred life.

> Glory to God, and praise and love
>   Be ever, ever given
> By saints below and saints above,
>   The Church in earth and heaven.

The rest of the liturgy was every bit as meaningful. The Scriptures, the chaplain's prayers, her words of reflection, were in no way condescending or pleading. We concluded our worship with an even greater hymn, sung with even greater gusto—Henry van Dyke's "Joyful, Joyful We Adore Thee"—set to Beethoven's famous "Ode to Joy." Joy. Dignity. Grace. Fellowship. Life. This is what I encountered. This is what I received. This is what I took with me into my day.

Later I reflected on my experience. Naturally I realized how much about my own life I take for granted, how mindlessly ungrateful I often am, and how at any time the course of my life could change unpredictably. But what struck me most forcefully was the utter appropriateness of our worship, of praise in the context of suffering and of prayer in the presence of death. Allow me to digress.

Many centuries ago, the great doctors of the church summed up the whole of Christian teaching in one pithy statement: "God became man, so that man might become God." This is hard to render into gender-inclusive language. It is harder still to affirm in the context of Huntington's chorea. God entered our flesh, so that our flesh might experience its own divinity. God entered our nature, so that our nature might know its divine origin and destiny.

There are two pieces to this traditional teaching that continue to surprise and challenge us. One concerns who we are. The other concerns who God is.

Each of us bears the image and likeness of the Sacred; we are intrinsically lovely. We are cherished by God. We come from, dwell in, are surrounded by, and return to God. Our true nature is divine. The meaning of our lives can never be fully grasped within the confines of time and space as we are accustomed to understand them. Our real life is much larger than we imagine. This is true for all of us, whatever our circumstances may be.

And God? Many of us still cling to the ideas and ideals of God that are essentially Olympian. God stands above our personal dramas and beyond the human fray. Like Zeus of old, or like the warrior gods of many ancient texts, God retains an awesome power to intervene in our circumstances and bend them as God sees fit. The best we can hope for is to placate this God or to influence God to act according to our wishes.

For others among us, God has become more abstract: the "Force," the First Cause, the explanatory principle, the ultimate answer to the ultimate question of "Why?" Not to placate, but to perceive, to know, to understand, is their primary reason for believing.

For still others, God represents the moral agency of the universe, the divine order of righteousness, the ultimate source of judgment about what constitutes good or evil. Either through revelation or natural philosophy, God's will emerges as the single most important factor determining proper relationships in our world. Not to placate nor to contemplate, but to align our will with God's righteous will is the goal of their faith.

Whether Ruler, Principle, or Moral Agent, it would be a cold, cold God who could look down in Olympian serenity on the misery and evil in our world, indifferent and untouched by our common lot. If the suffering of the Huntington's unit does not reach into the very heart of God's eternal being, then what, indeed, is God?

Power? Explanation? Righteousness? These may convey significant aspects of the one in whom "we live and move and have our being" (Acts 17:28). But the God mediated through our Scriptures and traditions is a wholly different God, and not to be found in such obviously "godly" places. It is a God who exists in and for relationships, who is truly hungry for our intimacy and thirsty for our freely given love. It is the God of our hearts as well as our heads, a God who is vulnerable to our wounds, a God who enters fully into our life and our flesh.

Our text points us in this direction. Chapter 11 of the Letter to the Hebrews is a long testimonial to our ancestors in faith. But while there are heroes and heroines among them, this recapitulation has been described as a veritable "rogues' gallery of the redeemed." The best and worst of our common humanity is gathered into this lineage, men and women with all the imperfections, anxieties and heartaches which we know so well. They were kith and kin to Margaret, Jeff, Connie, Bill, and me.

What do we have in common—Rahab and Margaret, Jeff and Jephthah, Samson and me? Each of us knew or knows profound disappointment and the pain of promises unfulfilled. Each of us lived or lives with incomplete knowledge, imperfect motives, and a deep, deep yearning to be made whole. Here, I think, is the key.

The God of our text does not seem to exist for the successful and self-sufficient among us. The God who is capable of giving true dignity, joy, grace, fellowship, and life itself, the God who can restore meaning to our existence, this God comes to us when we are vulnerable, when we have been humbled by forces more powerful than ourselves. Our vulnerability meets with God's deepest love; into our humility flows the divine essence of God's being. When our masks are torn from us, our true identities are revealed. These are more lovely than any personae we have been able to maintain. Even in the midst of our greatest suffering and limitation—perhaps especially then—we may come to know the radiance of life and the utter gratuity of being.

Who is this God? It is the God of the Christic journey—the journey from Godhead to flesh, through death, to flesh, to God. "In life at its highest degree of intensity," said Nicholas Cabasilas, "death and life are not opposed anymore, but they are entwined in the liberating figure of the Cross."[2] The Christic journey was called *kenosis* by the ancients, or the emptying of self. It is a journey from wholeness into nothingness and a return to wholeness. It is descent and ascent, from light to darkness into light, from life into death into authentic life.

Would you know God? Then meditate on Jesus, "the pioneer and perfecter of our faith,"—its beginning and its end. In Christ we finally see into God's fundamental nature. Do we see Power? Explanation? Righteousness? No. We see rather a person filled and overflowing with love. In love God renounces everything "godly," according to Paul, and takes the lowly form of a slave. God embraces our flesh, our humanity, and our nature. If that isn't enough, God becomes ever more empty—to the point of undergoing a painful and shameful death (see Phil. 2:5–11).

Yet it is this "kenotic" or self-emptying love which you and I exalt above every other. This love is what we worship today. Its peculiar power transforms all it touches. Its wisdom transcends mere explanation. Its goodness encompasses more than abstract righteousness.

I don't think I ever understood this text until I worshiped in the Huntington's chorea unit that morning. It was not enough that God became flesh so that flesh could become God. God had to become *this* flesh, this palsied, jerking, spastic flesh, so that *this* flesh could begin to realize its divinity. If God cannot reach into this unit and become incarnate in this situation, then all our theologizing and all our spiritual practice is in vain.

But God was there. As surely as I have felt God's presence anywhere, God was in that room. God was in the singing and the praying and in the eyes that met across the table. God was in the laughter and the tears and in the uncontrollable vocal explosions. God was in the wildly exaggerated signing of the cross made by a Catholic resident. God was in this flesh. In our few moments of intimate worship, I glimpsed a raw and radiant wholeness in the facial expressions of the residents as we sang:

> Oh, for a thousand tongues to sing
>   My great Redeemer's praise,
> The glories of my God and King,
>   The triumphs of his grace!

These brothers and sisters of ours are well into their own Christic journeys. Many of them know what many of us but dimly intuit: that the life we enjoy or suffer is both much less and much more than we imagine. Life is not the food we eat, the clothes we wear, the cars we drive, nor the computers we manipulate. It is the love we receive and give. Though these residents are confined to a few rooms and hallways, some have made a home in a vaster universe than you or I inhabit. If ever I have experienced authentic worship, a genuine celebration of grace, a true adoration of God, a service of praise and thanksgiving, it was there, in the Huntington's unit of the Good Samaritan Society's University Center.

Notes
1. This sermon was originally preached while Dr. Friend-Jones was Senior Minister of Mayflower Church, Minneapolis, Minnesota.
2. Nicholas Cabasilas was a fourteenth-century lay theologian in the Eastern church. Here he is quoted by Francois Varillon in *The Humility and Suffering of God* (New York: Alba House, 1983), p. 101. Though it may be a bit technical, I find Father Varillon's work extremely rewarding for those who are grappling with suffering in all of its manifestations.

Comment

Biblical Text

The lesson for Gilbert Friend-Jones's sermon is the concluding section of a sequence in Hebrews that begins with 11:1. The author of Hebrews first proclaims faith as "the assurance of things hoped for, the conviction of things not seen." What follows is a collage crammed with images of faithful persons within the biblical narrative. The entire passage is shaped by the visual motif of things seen and unseen. We are reminded at length how the characters of the history of salvation lived before God by faith, beginning all the way back with Abel, then moving on to Abraham and Sarah. At this point, the author interjects the comment that "All of these died in faith without having received the promises, but from a distance they saw and greeted them" (11:13). The visual orientation of the passage persists. From a distance, Abraham and Sarah "saw" the promises.

The chronicle then continues by way of recounting the patriarchs, Moses, and an interesting conglomerate of heroes—Rahab, Gideon, Barak, Samson, Jephthah, David, Samuel, and the prophets (11:31-32)—among those who lived by faith and trusted the promises. Then there occurs a shift, albeit subtle, focusing our attention on the heroes of the New Israel in Christ. Their suffering and persecution are portrayed in graphic detail. Yet even enduring all of these hardships, these Christians kept the faith and were commended by God.

Now the writer of Hebrews shifts the focus to the question of the identity and faith of the followers of Christ. Surrounded by a great cloud of witnesses, we are urged to lay aside the weight of sin and run the race *(agona)* with perseverance. Like any good runner, we should keep our eyes fixed on the goal—Jesus "the pioneer and perfecter of our faith" (12:2). Jesus' own *agona* is then portrayed, as he endured the shameful cross before taking his place in glory. All of this, of course, was in order that the promises once held by faith may now be seen fulfilled by the faithful.

Context

The context for the sermon, "The Christic Journey," is a parish setting on the Lord's day. It is preached by a pastor to his congregation. This is not a "visiting firefighter," blowing in to lay the Word on hearers before blowing out again. Friend-Jones is preaching to a people he knows well.

There is another context for the sermon that also claims the attention of the hearers: the Huntington chorea unit of a local hospital. It is into the latter context that the former are invited. The people worshiping at the Mayflower Church are invited to join the worship with their pastor and the patients at the chorea unit. By way of this journey—the Mayflower worshipers' journey to the hospital—another clue to the context for the sermon is disclosed. The sermon is also addressed to everyone who is enduring their cross, either in their own journey or through that of a loved one.

Performance

One of the awesome capabilities of language is that it can shape a "world" within the consciousness of the listeners. The preacher's words can build a world, much as the words of Scripture build a world within which we find our identity and purpose as a people of faith. Most obvious is the way in which biblical narrative can work to locate us within its world. We go with David against the towering Philistine; we listen to Sarah's laughter or Jeremiah's lament; we are there to rejoice when the prodigal returns home, or we can join with the prodigal's elder brother outside and remain there. All the elements of narrative work together to perform this achievement, including the hearers within the story. The voice of the narrator, the distinctive characters, the story's setting and tone, even the sense of a story's time, function both to build a world within the communal consciousness and to invite us to inhabit that world. Homiletically speaking, once we have come to listen to the story and find our location within it, it is difficult for us as hearers to relocate elsewhere.

In its opening lines the sermon begins to establish a world for the hearers and invites them to inhabit it. It is not a pleasant world at all; chorea is not in any way a pleasant disease. The preacher eases us into the world of the chorea unit, inviting us to share his point of view, for he is offering a first-person account to the congregation. Soon, however, we are watching the patients along with the pastor. We see their uncontrolled movements. We hear their distorted speech. We are there—whether we like it or not. We come to the unit with some reservations, both about ourselves (how we will respond to such persons) and about the patients (will our visit be received as "demeaning 'help' of nice people"?). After this initial entrance into the unit, the preacher backs off and allows us to do some "head" work. He gives us further information about the disease—how it is inherited, how it progresses, and how it kills, "by choking, infections—or frequently suicide." Friend-Jones then adds an effective rhetorical system that summarizes what has just been said and also suggests some initial reflection for hearers. Watch how the language is shaped in this summarizing and reflective move:

> My dictionary describes Huntington's chorea as a disorder within the cerebrum, but it is a "disorder" in the same way that Bosnia is a "skirmish" or the Titanic's sinking was merely "unfortunate" for those on board. Rather, this degenerative nerve disease is a full-blown assault on the personhood of its victims—on their bodies, to be sure, and their minds, but also on their spirits. Every conceivable value is tested; every hope is stretched to the breaking point.

The imagery is powerful and effective. The hearers are now focused on the issues of hope and despair.

With such a rhetorical system now in place, the preacher faces an important question in homiletic strategy: Where do I go now; where do I invite my hearers to journey next? The system he has used at this point in the sermon creates closure to what has gone before it. A "seam" has been formed within the homiletic plot. At this point we might pause, too, and consider some of the options the preacher has for his next sequence in the sermon.

The first option is that Friend-Jones could now pick up the first-person narrative and further describe the story of his visit to the unit. He will do that, but not at this point in the sermon. Second, the preacher could now pick up on the issue of suffering and how this kind of tragedy attacks every value and hope. The reflective mode of the closure system certainly invites such a next move. Third, the preacher could have put the entire sermonic plot on hold and given an illustration of the "point" he has just made. Fortunately, he avoided this temptation. A powerful contemporary story has already been formed in the consciousness of the hearers and profound questions have already been raised. What other story could "illustrate" the one that has just been formed in our hearing?

What the preacher does decide as a next course of action is to explore more deeply the complex character of Huntington's disease. In this regard, he is reentering the reflective mode with the hearers and expanding on the information already presented. Since chorea is inherited, the patients in the unit have already seen its dreadful course in the lives and deaths of loved ones. Friend-Jones then expands on this new information with a rhetorical system arranging a "what-might-have-been" kind of lament, and then adding, "Here were my sisters and my brothers, my mothers and my fathers, my flesh and blood." He explores further "what-might-have-been" scenes with another tag line: "Why are such simple pleasures denied?"

Now come two further shifts in congregational consciousness, both offered in rapid succession. A gesture is made toward the issue of the great questions of life's meaning and purpose. But those questions are left unexplored for now, and the sermon shifts our focus over to the context of the chorea unit, including the caring and compassionate staff. This focus, also, is only briefly stated. Within a very brief time, the congregation has been invited to focus in several different directions. Now the issue for the preacher, once more, is where to move next in the homiletic plot. In my view, it is likely that these brief and rapid shifts in point of view do not work well in a congregation's hearing. Congregations have difficulty "tracking" rapid shifts in perspective and content. These two brief passages may simply delete from the congregation's consciousness.

Now the homiletic plot gains a clear direction and the perspective remains constant. The sermon once again picks up the story introduced at the beginning. The preacher recounts his entrance into the unit, the hospitality of the patients, and the joy of their worship. He names some of the patients and expands their identity. The motif that connects through this narrative is Wesley's hymn, "Oh, for a Thousand Tongues to Sing." Sandwiched between verses are the anecdotes about the individual worshipers and their participation in the act of praise. At the end of this narrative section dealing with the worship, Friend-Jones mentions the other parts of the worship where the same realities were present—"Joy. Dignity. Grace. Fellowship. Life." A closure system indicates that a new section of the sermon is now about to begin: "This is what I encountered. This is what I received. This is what I took with me into my day." Clearly, we are at the closing of the previous focus on the worship service in the unit. We are now ready to hear what the preacher has to say next.

What is next is the issue of suffering, and particularly "the utter appropriateness of our worship, of praise in the context of suffering, and of prayer in the presence of death." This "utter appropriateness" is possible only from the perspective of Incarnation, of God becoming human in order that we humans might become divine. Friend-Jones splits the focus in two directions—our own identity as mortals, and the identity of God. The former question—our human identity—is developed within the context of the doctrine of the *imago Dei*. We are created in the image of God. We are therefore loved by God, have our source and destiny with God. Put simply, "our true nature is divine." The focus on the *imago,* however, is quickly put aside. Friend-Jones gives much more attention to the identity of God. Without imagery to support this proclamation of our identity as bearing the image of the Divine, it will be difficult for it to form in congregation consciousness.

A word of caution. Even the best preachers will occasionally leave an important portion of their sermon presented only conceptually. An issue or affirmation will be "talked about," but not "spoken of" (David Buttrick). There is some irony in the fact that a move within a sermon dealing with the image of God is left imageless! Our learning from this omission? For our conceptual discourse to be heard, we will need to image that material out of the lived experience of the congregation.

What is nicely imaged, however, is the section that follows on the identity of God. A series of "not this" negations forms a clear rhetorical system. God is not "like Zeus of old," not "the 'Force,'" not simply "the moral agency of the universe." Those kinds of divinity could never become involved in the human suffering, especially the kind of suffering found in the chorea unit. So Friend-Jones asks, "If the suffering of the Huntington's unit does not reach into the very heart of God's eternal being, then what, indeed, is God?" The answer for us is provided within the Scripture. The God of Israel and the New Israel does not remain far off from the creation, but longs for relationships. Indeed, that longing finds its fullest expression in the Incarnation. Revealed in Scripture is "a God who is vulnerable to our wounds, a God who enters fully into our life and our flesh." Now the text from Hebrews is introduced for consideration. A sermon does not have to begin with the biblical text in order to be a biblical sermon. Here, an extended focus on a contemporary situation has raised the questions and concerns which the text can address.

The preacher has just presented a "not this" listing of ways in which a god can be construed. Now, illuminated by Scripture in general and the Hebrews text in particular, there is most definitely a "this" to be affirmed. We have a vulnerable God, the God of the "Christic journey." Christ poured out himself for us, becoming flesh, suffering, and dying on the cross. Only then did he enter into his glory. The Christic journey is one of *kenosis*. Friend-Jones summarizes it:

It is a journey from wholeness into nothingness, and a return to wholeness. It is descent and ascent, from light to darkness into light, from life into death into authentic life.

In Jesus, the One poured out for us, we see the true identity of God. In place of worldly notions of power we see incredible love and self-giving, even to the extent of Christ suffering for us on the cross.

Now the sermon enters a final stage where the two elements—the Huntington's chorea patients, and the mystery of the Christic journey—are woven together. They belong together. Here is the core of their unity: "It was not enough that God became flesh so that flesh could become God. God had to become *this* flesh, this palsied, jerking, spastic flesh, so that *this* flesh could begin to realize its divinity." God was there, Friend-Jones concludes, in the worship at the unit. But God was enfleshed there just as God was enfleshed in Jesus. Here is God making the Christic journey once more, by way of that same *kenosis*, that same drama of becoming flesh, that same act of human suffering.

Once more, the preacher recalls for the hearers the song of praise at the unit, quoting again the first verse of "Oh, for a Thousand Tongues to Sing." Now the homiletic payoff is made. The patients, "well into their own Christic journeys," know something many of us only intuit dimly. "The life we enjoy or suffer is both much less and much more than we imagine." Worship in the chorea unit at the Good Samaritan Society's University Center (a name now profoundly more meaningful) has illuminated the human condition for the preacher and for listeners. Much more, this worship has revealed the very nature of God.

SUMMARY

"The Christic Journey" is a sermon whose structure is essentially a binary linking of the profound suffering found in a chorea hospital unit and the testimony to Incarnation proclaimed in the text from Hebrews. It is not that the preacher and the congregation have to flee from that suffering to find the deepest truths about themselves and about God. Rather, in the worship of those patients and in their suffering is to be found the very truth of God. The chorea patients are making their own Christic journeys as did Christ, "the pioneer and perfecter of our faith." The word to the hearers is that all of us are in some way or another on that same cross-shaped journey.

There is much to learn from the rhetoric and method of Friend-Jones' sermon. Its strengths are evident and its impact remains powerful in the translation to a literary form. The sermon displays a number of effective homiletic virtues. First, the preacher displays a rich palette of rhetorical patterns. (Whether he was *taught* these moves or has *caught* them in his own homiletical formation is an interesting question!) The closure systems are a real strength throughout the sermon, and we can learn from their usage. Without these closures, the congregation continues to dwell in a previous location in the sermon even as the preacher tries to move on. Also, Friend-Jones has a real gift for terse and vivid descriptions of characters. The patients described in the sermon become "enfleshed" in our hearing. Moreover, while some congregations on this Lord's day were fed romantic pulpit tones and warm fuzzies, Friend-Jones was inviting his people to struggle with the most profound questions of human life and death, and of the very identity of God. Bravo, Dr. Friend-Jones!

A few cautions and questions also are in order relating to this sermon's performance. First, as noted above, at about one-third of the way into the sermon, we come upon a sequence of rapid shifts in point of view and content. It is like those home videos where the operator gives us a fast series of shots that tumble on top of each other until the whole effect is quite boggling. Fortunately, the power and clarity of the material beginning with the unit's worship gets us back on track and we stay there. We can all learn from this experience. Rapid shifts in tense, subject matter, or point of view (say, from first-person to third-person and back to first) are extremely troublesome for congregational consciousness. After a very few rapid shifts, hearers are simply incapable of following further. The material will delete from consciousness.

From this sermon we also gain another insight related to homiletic method. Every section of a sermon where a single meaning is at stake—such as in Friend-Jones's material on the *imago Dei*—needs to be imaged out of the lived experiences of the congregation. It would be pleasant for us preachers if conceptual discourse alone would take shape in hearers' minds. These days, such is not the case. In "The Christic Journey," we have seen the conceptual material most vividly in the description of the chorea unit and in the depiction of God's *kenosis* in Christ. Where the conceptual material is not imaged, it will not be retained by hearers. All of us who are servants of the Word are learning afresh in these days how communal language functions on behalf of a hearing of the Word.

Richard L. Eslinger

EASTER FEAR

MARK 16:1-8

REV. DR. DAVID C. FISHER
COLONIAL CHURCH
EDINA, MINNESOTA

REV. DR. DAVID C. FISHER

EASTER FEAR

MARK 16:1-8, NRSV

Very early this morning several hundred people drove through the darkness to Cornelia Park. There, huddled in the cold and dark, they waited for the dawn. For thirty-five years now, Colonial Church has sponsored that community sunrise service. And people come! Hundreds of them. There's something about Easter that provokes unusual behavior!

In fact, even earlier, at 3:00 this morning, the church volunteers who make that service happen met at Perkins restaurant for breakfast before they headed for the park to set up for the service. Now the amazing thing is, they tell me they enjoy it! Easter drives some people toward extraordinary behavior!

We're not alone. Across the world today Christians gathered, millions of them, in the predawn darkness to wait for sunrise and celebrate the resurrection.

Through the morning, as the sun makes its way from east to west, Easter worshipers are gathering. In cathedrals and in country churches, under trees and in storefronts, in the cities and suburbs, too, we've come to celebrate the dawn of Easter day. Easter morning is the climax and center of the Christian year and, at the same time, the core reality of the Christian faith.

Churches are packed, we add extra services to hold the crowds, the music is grand and powerful, anticipation fills the air, and Easter joy pours into and out of our souls. Easter certainly does prompt extraordinary behavior!

Why? What is it about Easter that brings us here, that prompts this unusual behavior? I suppose all of us have come hoping to hear a word that will assure us we will cheat death. Some come longing for a word or an Easter experience that will confirm their faith. Others come hoping to make more sense of their lives. Others hope for strength for the journey. And, of course, some of us just sense some "ought." This is where we should be on Easter morning.

Beneath all those reasons lies a deeper one, a powerful human instinct that longs for something more—something more than our ordinary mortal lives. We long for a touch of eternity. We wish God would make things right, fix our lives, and do something in this world too.

It seems the whole world shares this instinct for eternity. Each Easter, it seems, God makes the headlines. This year is no exception. The cover story of a recent issue of a national magazine is about prayer. Despite modern America's secular face, our nation still has a soul. According to the magazine's poll, 87 percent of Americans believe God answers prayer. Perhaps even more amazing, 82 percent do not turn away from God when their prayers are unanswered. Isn't it amazing that even in our modern secular, technological times, people still display a deep hunger for God?

The Old Testament lesson for this Easter Sunday speaks powerfully to this deep and eternal longing for something more. The prophet Isaiah declared that a day is coming when God will make "a feast of rich food, a feast of well-aged wines." On that day, the prophet declares, "[God] will destroy...the shroud that is cast over all peoples.... [God] will swallow up death forever. Then the Lord God will wipe away the tears from all faces.... Lo, this is our God; we have waited for him" (Isa. 25:6–9).

We Christians believe, and the church declares, that the something more we long for came in Jesus Christ who, by his life, death, and resurrection, conquered death and sin and established the reign of eternity right here on earth. Those who believe that good news possess something more that makes sense of life and death.

No wonder Easter music speaks with extraordinary power. No wonder the pews are packed, the anthems ring, and good news is heard by all. Easter by its very nature prompts extraordinary behavior.

But then there's Mark's Gospel. Did you hear Mark's account of Easter morning? Mark's Easter story is remarkably brief, just one long paragraph, eight verses, one hundred and thirty-six words in Greek, Mark's language. That's less than one typewritten page in any language.

Mark could have made it longer. He wrote many years after the resurrection. He'd heard the longer version of Easter morning. But he kept it short. I wonder why? After all, this is the story on which the history of the world turned. Christians believe Easter morning is the most stupendous event in the history of the universe.

Yet, Mark's version of Easter morning seems so unspectacular, even stark. One commentator notes that Mark writes with remarkable restraint. No celestial spectaculars, no bright lights, no flutter of angel's wings, no special effects. I tell you, if I were writing the Easter story, I'd pull out all the stops. I'd tell the whole story and try to find even more.

Why, if I were in charge of Easter I'd make sure nobody missed that morning. I'd have Jesus march straight into Pilate's courtroom, point his finger at that cowardly governor, and say, "I'm baaaaaack!" I'd call a special session of the Sanhedrin and let Jesus tell those bad-news religious leaders the really good news, that he'd brought the reign of God to the earth. I'd send Jesus to Rome for an appearance at the Senate to announce they were history and a new day had just dawned. I'd put Jesus on CNN, all three networks and MTV too.

I think I'd arrange a special appearance for the soldiers who crucified Jesus, whom Jesus forgave and one of whom was so struck by Jesus' death he said, "Truly this man was the Son of God." Now, soldier, hear the rest of the story!

But I'm not in charge of Easter, and I'm not in charge of Mark's Gospel. Mark is. He wants us to know something about Easter. He wants us to know there's another side of Easter we might miss if we're not careful.

Easter morning is, of course, the end of a terrible weekend that began on Friday morning at an ugly place called Golgotha. The twelve apostles fled for their lives, but the Easter women—Mary Magdalene, Mary, James's mother and Salome—stood near the cross and watched their dearest friend die slowly and brutally. From a distance they watched Joseph, a follower of Jesus, take Jesus' body from the cross and wrap it in a burial shroud.

They followed Joseph to a garden where he placed the body in his own tomb carved out of a rock hillside. He was in a hurry—the sabbath began at dusk.

The women bought spices and scented oil and waited through the long sabbath for Sunday morning. They planned to go to the tomb and anoint Jesus' body with aromatic spices.

At dawn they arrived at the tomb and found the stone was rolled back from the door. Inside, to their astonishment, sat a young man. They were terrified. We would be too.

Then the young man spoke a word, a word from God: "Jesus has been raised. He is not here. Look and see. Go tell his disciples, especially Peter, to go to Galilee. Jesus will go before you."

The result, Mark tells us, was that the women fled from the tomb into the dawn, seized by terror and amazement. That's not too surprising given their empty tomb experience. But the way Mark ends his story is stunning. "And they said nothing to anyone, for they were afraid." End of story. End of book.

Is that any way to end a Gospel? After all, Mark begins his book with a powerful affirmation, "The beginning of the good news of Jesus Christ...." Mark's entire book is filled with more good news. And now, the best news of all, Jesus is risen from the dead! You'd expect a choir anthem or at least some resurrection appearances.

But not Mark. I don't know about some seminaries, but Mark would have flunked the course in Gospels at my seminary. This is not the end of the story. But Mark ends it here. No intimate suppers for three in the evening. No breakfast for the disciples on the beach. No special words for Mary, no instructions for the church. Just Easter fear.

Some well-meaning preachers in the second century thought they could improve on Mark's ending. Most translations of the Bible now put those improvements in brackets and note that they really don't belong to the Gospel.

If you want a technicolor Easter filled with flowers, choir anthems, and powerful, positive sermons, you have to go to another Gospel. If you want your faith tied up tight or nailed down well, you've got to travel next door to Matthew or Luke. If you want proofs, certainty, quick answers, everything all spelled out—"they lived happily ever after"—Mark just won't do. In Mark, Easter is the witness of women running silently through the morning chill, terrified, traumatized, and trembling. Mark's Easter good news is a young man who tells those terrified women, "He was here a minute ago; sorry, you just missed him!" Yes, Easter does prompt extraordinary behavior.

I'm not sure why Mark ends this good news book with Easter faith mixed with fear. It may just be that for Mark, Easter did not come easily then. And it doesn't come easily now either. In fact, Easter is the end of a long, grueling story that began in a wilderness where Jesus wrestled with God, his own destiny, demonic forces, and wild animals too. The story Mark tells is filled with Jesus' continual struggle against dark forces of evil and his constant awareness of the darker side of life. His ministry is to the sick and oppressed, the outsiders and the lonely, with a special interest in those tormented by demonic forces.

At the end, Jesus bade a tearful farewell to his disciples in a last supper. They went to Gethsemane where Jesus wrestled with God and his own destiny one last time, weeping and begging God for escape. The disciples abandoned him there and by morning he'd been condemned to death. Good Friday was the darkest day in human history as the Son of God died in agony.

Then came Easter. The power of Easter morning flows through and comes from Jesus' lifelong struggle and suffering, his abandonment and agony. Easter cannot be separated from the rest of the story, or its message and its power are reduced to something less than the real good news.

I think Mark wants us to know that Easter faith, then and now, is not, nor can it be, detached from the reality of our lives. The fact is, Easter morning dawned on a Good Friday world full of darkness, suffering, and death. Our world is little different. It's much more like Good Friday than Easter morning. And truth be told, we all dragged a bit of Good Friday darkness into church this Easter morning.

Our lives are not continual Easter. Our lives are more like Lent than Easter, at least most of the time. Easter faith provides neither quick fixes nor a pious detachment from the rest of life. Faith does not place us in a parallel universe exempt from the ordinary stuff of life. There is no escape from this Good Friday world nor from the reality of our Lenten lives. Christianity is no happily-ever-after life free of pain and cares.

No. Easter, the Christian faith, lives in and through all the realities of our very ordinary lives. Easter dawns now and then with all its brilliance, but most of life is just ordinary and difficult. Tomorrow Easter is over and it's back to work. Work isn't easy and certainly isn't at all like Easter, and being without work can be hell. Life isn't easy. Never has been. Marriage is not easy. Being single isn't easy either. Raising children is not easy. It can't be. Having parents isn't easy either. All of life is—well, it's life. Reality is not Easter every day. It can't be.

If you want faith and life nailed down tight, risk-free, predictable, without ambiguity, a pie-in-the-sky, happily-ever-after existence, Mark's Easter is not your story and, to be honest, the Christian faith is not for you.

But if you want the adventure of a lifetime filled with unknowns and wonderful risks of faith, if you want extraordinary lives in this Good Friday world, let the words of that young man in the tomb ring in your ears, "He is risen, go.... He goes before you." No matter what. No matter when. No matter where, "He goes before you."

In 1929, a young nun from Albania was sent to the streets of Calcutta. She didn't know what would happen there. She suspected she would die quickly from disease. Somewhere I read that in those early days, Teresa's evening prayer each day was, "If I die, let me die on these streets among these people with the name of your Son on my lips." Yes, Easter does prompt extraordinary behavior.

When Desmond Tutu was named a bishop in South Africa, he didn't know the depth of the struggle he faced. He couldn't know that one day he would sit on the council hearing the terrifying, bloodcurdling stories of the oppression, suffering, and death of his people. He didn't know he would be so overcome by those stories he'd put his head on the table and weep. He didn't know he'd lift his head and with the council forgive the sins, brutality, and murder of his oppressors. He couldn't know. But he knew the Risen One and he knew no matter what, when or where, Jesus went before him.

I don't suppose any of us will be called to the heroic faith of a Mother Teresa or Bishop Tutu. Let's bring the story closer to home.

People have been listening to Clem Haskins lately.[1] It's about time. Did you hear him? At the beginning it wasn't easy for him to be a public figure in white Minnesota. The phone calls came, anonymous letters and death threats too. He thought about leaving. But he stayed. He said, "God brought me here, so I stayed." Clem knows the Risen One and he knows no matter what, no matter when, no matter where, Jesus goes before him.

I don't know the call of God on your life and I don't know the life circumstances most of you face. Downtown office, classroom, home, retirement, looking for work, sick, dying, children, relationships. But I do know this: Jesus is risen and he goes before you. No matter where. No matter when. No matter what.

Mark ends his story right here. Easter faith is open-ended and unpredictable. Now, you write the rest of the story. And remember, "He goes before you."

Note
1. Clem Haskins was the head coach of the University of Minnesota Golden Gopher basketball team. An African-American and a Christian, he had just led his team to the NCAA Final Four basketball tournament the year this sermon was preached.

Comment

The Homiletical Plot and the Congregation as "Audience"

If the congregation has to listen to us think out loud every week, what we say had better be interesting. A sermon is meant to engage the audience as an event, not merely as the presentation of content. Eric Routley says that if we think of a continuum between a phone book on one end and a poem on the other, a sermon is much nearer a poem.[1] A sermon is not a scientific treatise. It is a work of art. That is the essence of a book by Eugene Lowry called *The Homiletical Plot: The Sermon as Narrative Art Form.*[2]

David Fisher's sermon, "Easter Fear," is a splendid example of Lowry's method. Lowry says that we tend to think of the sermon as a wall with bricks. We see the bricks and not the mortar. We might build a traditional sermon by assembling individual parts until they form a whole. However, this is not how most sermons are birthed. Nor should they be!

The "bricks" of a sermon are the problem(s) we illuminate and the solution or solutions we offer from the gospel. We can begin with one and move to the other, but it is the tension between these—the "mortar"—that makes the sermon happen. This tension, Lowry says, comprises "a premeditated plot which has as its key ingredient a sensed discrepancy, a homiletical bind."

A good sermon, therefore, begins by engaging listeners at a point of tension. The sermon portrays some human dilemma or sets forth a problem, the resolution of which captures the hearer's interest. The stages of such a sermon move us from upsetting our equilibrium, through analysis of the problem/tension, to a disclosure of the key to resolution of the tension. Here, in the disclosure of resolution, we experience the gospel. The "gospel" in such a sermon lies in the identification of where God is at work, in the world, in the church, or in our lives. Lowry warns that "the gospel" lies not in *our response* (which puts us too close to works righteousness), but in God's nature, character, and activity. Our response comes only after the climactic moment—the recognition of the acts of God.

Fisher's sermon title itself captures the ambiguity and tension of the sermon: "Easter Fear." Most of us thought Easter was only about unrestrained joy until we read carefully the Gospel narrative—and especially Mark's Gospel. Easter provokes strange responses. Listen again to how Fisher begins this sermon:

> Very early this morning several hundred people drove through the darkness to Cornelia Park. There, huddled in the cold and dark, they waited for the dawn.... There's something about Easter that provokes unusual behavior!

Here Fisher begins laying the groundwork for the "plot" of the sermon. Easter evokes "extraordinary behavior." People huddled in the cold and dark at unspeakable hours. Churches are packed. But why? Ultimately, Fisher says, because of a "powerful human instinct that longs for something more....We long for a touch of eternity." The opening paragraphs of the sermon immediately begin building a tension between the first Easter and this Easter, between the pages of Scripture and our lives, between time and eternity, between hope and fear, between faith and empirical knowledge. This tension, or ambiguity, Lowry contends, is a critical dynamic of a good sermon.

Tension alone does not a sermon make, however, and Lowry believes that a preacher must explore and analyze the tensions between problem and answer. We must live with the tension, experience it fully, and resist the temptation to give answers prematurely. Analysis is often the great failing of sermons, says Lowry, for we do not move to a level of depth about why things happen as they do. This gets to the issue of motives. Fisher's descriptive analysis of why people behave as they do on Easter pushes us. We begin to encounter the tension between our hope for "something more" and our realization that life is often "somewhat less" than we hoped. Yes, Easter is joyous, triumphant, and powerful. "No wonder the pews are packed"—there's a hunger in our souls. It's a great day! "But then there's Mark's Gospel…Mark's version of Easter morning seems so unspectacular, even stark…[Mark] wants us to know there's another side of Easter we might miss if we're not careful."

Notice how Fisher continues to build the tension and ambiguity. Now he shows that tension to us in the biblical text itself—the abrupt ending of Mark's Gospel in which Easter faith is mixed with Easter fear.

CRITICAL QUESTIONS AND HONEST ANSWERS

In the best manuscripts of Mark, the Gospel ends at 16:8—"So they went out and fled from the tomb, for terror and amazement had seized them; and they said nothing to anyone, for they were afraid." Verses 6 and 7 announce the resurrection, but this ending leaves the matter unresolved. Scholars have debated as to why this is so.

Some speculate that Mark may have died before finishing the Gospel. Others conjecture that a longer ending was once attached but was separated, for three alternative endings to Mark all show up in later manuscripts. Whatever we think of these theories, there is little question among textual scholars today that vv. 9–20 as we have them in our Bibles are not original to the Gospel. Eusebius, a fourth-century Christian historian, mentions that in the oldest and best manuscripts, Mark ends at verse 8.

A third alternative, and one that fits better with the truth about the manuscripts, is that Mark chose to end the Gospel just as we have it. But why? Why leave us with such a jarring ending as verse 8? Fisher quite skillfully weaves this critical question itself into the tension of the sermon and allows his exegesis of Mark 16:8 to become central to the homiletical plot.

Mark's ending is not easy, Fisher asserts, because life is not that way. Mark wants us to grapple with the ambiguity of life and faith. Christ is risen, but we also must experience Easter within the uncertainty of life. "Easter faith is open-ended and unpredictable. Now, you write the rest of the story." That is what Fisher believes Mark is saying in his perplexing ending. You decide. God has spoken—do you believe it?

One of the important things Fisher does is to trust his congregation to face the problem of "Easter fear" and the ending of Mark's Gospel with him. He does not prematurely resolve the issue ("of course, this can be easily explained") or hide it from his hearers. He trusts their judgment with the facts. Just as importantly, he does not simply preach his questions. He allows the congregation to explore the text with him even as he moves toward his own answers and tells us why.

PROCLAMATION

So where is the gospel here? "I think Mark wants us to know that Easter faith, then and now, is not, nor can it be, detached from the reality of our lives." Easter is not "nailed down" (what a wonderful irony for a post-Good Friday homily!).

But, we may ask, what kind of "good news" is that? Well, that is precisely the point. The Christian faith is not disconnected from suffering, from the real world, from life. It transcends it. It will finally triumph over it. But it goes through real life and human suffering, not around them. This is good news. It means that Easter faith is real. It is honest. It is true to the tensions and ambiguities of real life. And it is therefore believable. Here, the tension has finally found resolution. The good news is that "Easter faith is open-ended and unpredictable," but the risen Christ goes before us—no matter what, no matter where.

Every worshiper comes to church on Easter full of hope but also aware of the suffering of the world and tinged by personal experiences of suffering that say, "It isn't that easy." Fisher's sermon meets them precisely at that point and proclaims that the Christian life is cruciform in character. In all ages of the church, those with insight into this life have told us the same thing—the way to glory leads through the darkness of night. That night is not defeat, but the way of purgation, of testing, of persistence and faith. Christ is there in the midst of that life.

Some accounts of the Christian life leave us feeling depleted and overwhelmed. We walk out thinking, "If only I could live such a life!" or "It's up to me; how can I ever do it?" The gospel declares something different: "He is living this life with me! He goes before me offering the grace and strength I need." That is gospel.

Fisher helps us to affirm Christ "in the midst" of life, not in spite of it. That is gospel.

SUGGESTIONS

- Read Eugene Lowry, *The Homiletical Plot.* Examine some old sermon outlines and rethink them in light of Lowry's approach. What would you do differently? What did you do well?
- Lowry suggests that we express the tensions of a plot in our titles. Look back over a dozen or so of your sermons. Did the titles captivate the listener? Did it make you wonder what the sermon was about? How could you have done it differently? What about the opening sentences or paragraphs of the sermon? Did they introduce the ambiguity or tension of faith or of the human situation which you later addressed in the sermon?

Gary A. Furr

Notes
1. Eric Routley, *The Divine Formula* (Princeton: Prestige Publications, 1986), p. 130.
2. Eugene L. Lowry, *The Homiletical Plot: The Sermon as Narrative Art Form* (Atlanta: John Knox Press, 1980).

DEALING WITH NEGATIVE ATTITUDES

JONAH 1–2

REV. DR. GARY A. FURR
VESTAVIA HILLS BAPTIST CHURCH
BIRMINGHAM, ALABAMA

REV. DR. GARY A. FURR

DEALING WITH NEGATIVE ATTITUDES[1]

JONAH 1-2

Most of the discussion about the Book of Jonah in this century, unfortunately, has been about Jonah's adventure with the great fish. "Great fish" is the best translation of the Hebrew, so it is not possible to say with accuracy whether it was a whale or some other great fish that swallowed Jonah.

Fishermen the world over, of course, have a natural suspicion of any story involving men and fish. Fish tend to grow in size in the retelling. The first liberal Bible scholar was most likely also a fisherman who knew his own tendency to expand a story. Like the little boy who went to ask his pastor father, "Daddy, is that the truth or is it just preaching?"

I said "unfortunately" about all this fish-analysis on purpose. The story of Jonah has suffered at the hands of both liberals and fundamentalists as they have argued about history and myths.

Could a whale actually swallow a man and live? That focus, important as it is, misses the whole point of the story! I have no trouble swallowing this idea. My problem is not whether a man could really survive it…it is whether the whale could. As Frederick Buechner put it, "Jonah's relief at being delivered from the whale can hardly have been any greater than the whale's at being delivered from Jonah."[2] Imagine swallowing anyone with such an attitude! No Tums could dissolve him.

The story of Jonah is about a stubborn prophet whose heart is resistant to God. God calls Jonah to go to Nineveh and preach that the city's Assyrian inhabitants must repent, for judgment is at hand. But the Assyrians are Israel's enemies—a cruel, vindictive, idolatrous people. How can he preach to them that God will forgive them if they repent? Jonah refuses the assignment and runs away. He hops aboard a ship bound for Tarshish, a destination as far from Nineveh as the people of that time knew about.

God sends a storm upon the ship. The sailors discover that Jonah is the cause and that he is running from God. He begs them to throw him overboard. At first they refuse, but finally, seeing no other course, they relent and toss him into the deep. There he is swallowed by a great fish, where he resides for three days.

While Jonah is in the fish's belly, God deals with his heart. Jonah calls out to God and God hears him and causes the fish to vomit Jonah out upon the dry land. And a pleasant moment that must have been!

Many of us are like Jonah. Like him, we may harbor harsh attitudes toward others, attitudes that can cause us to run away from opportunities to meet and know those who may be different from us. When those attitudes are revealed by the light of God, we see them for what they are—self-centered, immature, or even wicked. Who are we, indeed, to tell the God of the universe whom he may love, whom he may redeem, or whom we should love?

Unfortunately, these attitudes are hidden deep within. We must plunge into the depths, just as Jonah had to descend into the sea, to uncover them. Often our culture confirms these negative attitudes. After I got to know some Arab friends, I began to notice how many vicious portrayals of Arab people often occur in the American media. I have noticed many other such portrayals that confirm or play up to popular stereotypes of other groups.

These hateful attitudes originate in the human heart. Often we do not wish to face them or to admit that we have them. It is far easier to run from the whole problem. We run in many ways, but one of the most familiar is to attribute our own deepest failings to someone else. What we feel most guilty about we project onto our "enemies."

We must be careful of where our anger goes, of what we listen to, what we are willing to believe. When we say, "Those people...," separating ourselves from them, we are not far from the sin of Jonah, the sin of creating a too small world. God loves his entire creation.

To build friendships across cultural lines, we must be willing to confront our own long-held attitudes. Some of these attitudes are part of our culture. Some are misunderstandings that have come from unfortunate contacts we may have had or from bad relationships with someone from another group of people. Some are simply based on irrational ideas that we have always held without even knowing where they come from. Because these beliefs can be so deep, it will take "surgery of the soul" to overcome them. Often it takes a spiritual crisis to force us to see these truths. We might wish that we did not have to make such a journey. For many of us, though, there is no other way. We must face the truth that such attitudes are in utter contradiction to the purposes of the great God of heaven and earth. We are running in a direction opposed to God's loving purposes when we despise others.

The careful ways in which we have arranged our lives, the filters of our experiences that help us to avoid repeating past mistakes, can make us blind to the truth. So changing our attitudes is a tricky thing. It takes God's help.

There are two truths that Jonah's story can teach us. One is that God loves the world, the whole world, even the part of the world that Jonah hates with all his heart. It may be just a well-hidden condescension toward others that keeps us from ever knowing another's heart. It may be a stubborn determination to make things come out the way we think they should, so that no other way is allowed. More about that later.

But back to the whale's belly. Jonah has run as far as he can from God's direction in his life. God wants Jonah to stop resisting his will and learn that God loves the Ninevites. But there's a second point here, and it is that God loves Jonah too.

I. God Loves Jonah

Why did God go to so much trouble to hunt Jonah down, toss him into the sea, and force some poor whale to upchuck? God had thousands of potential prophets, hundreds as capable as Jonah. What's the point? Why does this God of ours go to so much trouble to reach us?

I can think of no other reason than that God loves us. Our suspicion of others, our hatred, our selfishness, our condescension, are not only destructive to others, they cripple us. God loves us. It is not love but indifference that permits us to go on in our destructive way. Love doesn't turn away from evil. Love has to deal with it. Love gets in your face, hunts you down, hangs in there, and doesn't quit. Love pursues you to the belly of a whale in the deep blue sea.

"This generation will be given the sign of Jonah," Jesus told the Pharisees. By that he meant that just as Jonah was in the belly of the whale for three days and nights, so he would descend into the dark and terrible depths of the tomb of death. In that darkness all hope is abandoned and sin has its day. And in the darkness, in the inmost caverns of our nature, our deepest hatreds and most primal fears are formed.

By entering the darkness, God confronts us with the truth about ourselves and pursues us to show his love. He breaks through the façades we have so carefully constructed to convince all those around that we are good folks indeed, façades that depend so much on affluence and image and trickery. Only God knows the truth and still loves us to the bottom of all our ambiguity. God, you see, cares not only about the people of Nineveh, but also about Jonah.

James McClendon tells the story of Dorothy Day, a bright young woman who arrived in New York in 1916 to find her fortune and fame. She became involved in socialist politics and ran with the fast crowd in Greenwich Village, hobnobbing with famous people. One of those was Eugene O'Neill, the playwright, whom she would often help into bed after late-night drinking bouts at a bar called the Hell Hole. O'Neill would drunkenly recite to her Francis Thompson's poem, "The Hound of Heaven," about a God who pursues human beings until they are his. Day never told him how deeply that drunken recitation affected her. Later, she converted to Christianity and became the leader of the Catholic Workers' Movement.[3] Listen to Francis Thompson's words:

> I fled Him, down the nights and down the days:
> > I fled Him, down the arches of the years;
> I fled Him down the labyrinthine ways
> > Of my own mind; and in the mist of tears
> I hid from Him, and under running laughter.

Finally the poet returns to God, who says,

> "Whom wilt thou find to love ignoble thee,
> > Save Me, save only Me?
> All which I took from thee I did but take,
> > Not only for thy harms,
> But just that thou might'st seek it in My arms.
> > All which thy child's mistake
> Fancies as lost, I have stored for thee at home:
> > Rise, clasp My hand, and come!"[4]

God pursued Jonah—for God's purposes in Nineveh, and because he loved Jonah. God's purposes pursue us too. Not simply for God's kingdom, but also for our own good.

II. GOD LOVES THE WHOLE WORLD

Jonah hated the Assyrians in Nineveh. But what he really could not stand was God's all-inclusive love! He feared that God would spare Nineveh. Jonah's deep hatred stood in the way of his ever loving the Ninevites. So Jonah needed to be healed of his hatred. Often, we too need to be healed of our hatreds.

One of the hateful attitudes we often harbor is racism. When we talk about racism in the Christian community, we sometimes talk about it as though it is an optional issue for us. Nothing could be further from the truth. Several years ago I was involved in some efforts at racial reconciliation in the little community where I lived. It attracted some attention, not all of it positive. One day I received a letter from a Ku Klux Klansman who spewed hatred toward African-Americans that was so horrible I would not repeat its contents to you.

Beyond the sadness and danger of such attitudes is a spiritual question: What has happened to the soul of such a man, raised in the South where the story of Jesus is so well known? What keeps us from seeing the obvious connections between the love of God for all and our own attitudes? I care about justice, but I also worry about the poisonous wells in so many hearts, about deeply held attitudes that cannot be legislated away.

Like Jonah, we must go deep into the depths of the sea, to be healed. It is what the Bible calls repentance, *metanoia*, change. In the depths, we can find new life that is unafraid to love others.

You see, our hatreds and selfishness are not necessarily the result of self-conscious evil. Often they exist simply because we are so busy keeping ourselves in a position of advantage over others or reacting to our wounds or protecting our own vulnerability. So God's kingdom cannot enter us. We find it too risky.

Louis Evely put it this way in his book, *That Man Is You*:

> Since people don't have the courage to mature unless someone has faith in them, we have to reach those we meet at the level where they stopped developing, where they were given up as hopeless, and so withdrew into themselves and began to secrete a protective shell because they thought they were alone and no one cared. They have to feel they're loved very deeply and very boldly before they dare appear humble and kind, affectionate, sincere and vulnerable.[5]

We wait for a sign before we'll turn loose and live out this kingdom thing of God's. Like Jonah, in our fear and hatred, we run away and try to hide from God. We descend into the depths. But God comes looking for us. In fact, Jesus has gone into the ocean depths of death for you and for me. What are we waiting for? We are free to trust, free to follow, free to love.

There in that whale's belly, God was dealing with a hard-hearted man. "Have it your way or have it mine, Jonah. But I will not leave you alone. Because I love you too much." So he loves each one of us too!

Notes
1. This sermon is adapted from an essay by Gary Furr previously published in *Many Nations Under God: Ministering to Culture Groups in America* (Birmingham: New Hope/Woman's Missionary Union, 1997). Used by permission.
2. Frederick Buechner, *Peculiar Treasures: A Biblical Who's Who* (San Francisco: Harper & Row Publishers, 1979), p. 171.
3. James Wm. McClendon, Jr., *Systematic Theology: Ethics, Vol. 1* (Nashville: Abingdon Press, 1986), p. 284.
4. Francis Thompson, *The Hound of Heaven* (Portland, ME: Thomas B. Mosher, 1911).
5. Louis Evely, *That Man Is You*, trans. Edmund Bonin (Ramsey, NJ: Paulist Press, 1964), pp. 102–3.

Comment

First Impressions

When I first looked at Gary Furr's sermon, I had two thoughts. My first thought was: "Jonah! What a terrific sermon to use as a teaching tool for other preachers!" This is ideal subject matter for learning homiletics. It's one of the few biblical stories known by most Christians and a good number of nonchurchgoers, as well. It's always interesting to see how a preacher handles a well-worn passage by putting his or her own spin on it. I was immediately eager to see what angle Furr would take.

Second, I was curious if or how Furr would deal with the conservative-liberal debate over Jonah. Would he side with the fundamentalists and defend the literalness of the text and the possibility that a human could, indeed, survive being ingested by a big fish? Or would he skirt the issue in favor of the metaphorical meaning of the story? How competent an acrobat is this preacher? Can he preach an engaging sermon about an all-too-familiar and controversial text, while at the same time making it theologically viable and avoiding the temptation to neuter the text? I had to know.

Style & Structure

In the sermon, Furr demonstrates a winning combination of hermeneutical responsibility and audience accessibility. He doesn't allow Jonah's important theological agenda to be sidetracked by popular fascination with "the fish." Preachers too often underestimate both the intelligence and theological appetite of their listeners. How do we preachers get off thinking competent exegesis and lively presentation are mutually exclusive? Furr proves they are not. He preaches in everyday language: "Tums," "upchuck," "Ku Klux Klansman," "Love gets in your face." He makes the vernacular work without distracting from the seriousness of the textual message. There is a refreshing naturalness to his style, as if he is talking to us over a cup of coffee. Not only is he unimpressed with his own "professional" insights into the text, but he doesn't expect us to be impressed either. This makes for a good preacher—one who communicates depth and content without becoming intoxicated with his or her own delivery.

Look at the sermon's introduction. Here we have a page or so of open access into Jonah's story. There is humor. "Fish tend to grow in size in the retelling." "Daddy, is that the truth or is it just preaching?" There is also an immediate acknowledgment of the fundamentalist-liberal debates surrounding Jonah. As proof of how well Furr handles this controversy, let me ask you—after reading the entire sermon, did you know for sure which camp he himself occupies? Probably not. This is a sign that the preacher is majoring on the majors. Furr doesn't ignore these debates, but he defuses them with a wry comment: "My problem is not whether a man could really survive it [being eaten by a whale]—it is whether the whale could." Not only is this clever, it is wise. It rescues us from petty squabbles and frees us up to hear what God might have for us in Jonah's adventure.

Furr's primary agenda is not the historicity of the story nor its various elements but the universal mandate woven into the narrative. As quickly as possible, the preacher guides us into the moral of the story—a moral generally agreed upon by fundamentalist and liberal scholars alike. It is this: Jonah is a prototype for breaking down prejudice. Given this as the thrust of the text, Furr readies us to apply that mandate to our own lives. And he does this without becoming "preachy." He doesn't beat us up or lay a guilt trip on us. Instead, he quietly ushers us through Jonah's misadventures and enlightens us to the lessons along the way. Furr obviously knows how receptive a congregation can be when they don't feel shamed or humiliated. The sermon is delivered in a soft but authoritative tone.

Problem & Solution

For Furr, what life situation does the Jonah story address? We see it first in the face of the preacher's Arab friends, persons who have felt the sting of America's bias against Semitic nationalities (yes, Arabs are Semites). We see it again in the person of a Ku Klux Klansman, and this time it's the ugly specter of white America's bigotry against black America. Jonah's call to go to the Ninevites is representative of God's call to all his people to embrace those we consider pagan or unclean, and to reexamine our own self-righteousness.

Jonah's hatred of foreigners is no different than our own hatred of those different from us. This is the problem. In Furr's words, we ourselves "are not far from the sin of Jonah, the sin of creating a too small world." Further on in the sermon, he puts it like this: "We are so busy keeping ourselves in a position of advantage over others or reacting to our wounds or protecting our own vulnerability. So God's kingdom cannot enter us." If we, as listeners, are honest with ourselves, this is a charge that is hard for us to evade.

If this is the problem, what is the solution? In a word, the solution is Jonah or, to be more precise, God's handling of Jonah. The reluctant prophet proves that escape is not an option when God addresses our biases. God is relentless in calling us to love all persons genuinely. No matter how far or how fast we may run, God will find us. And God will use whatever means available to bring us in line with his will…even a man-eating fish. The preacher drives the moral home, identifies our problem, and offers God's solution. A complete sermon.

Using the Text & Applying Its Message

Furr is faithful to the text in announcing that God's love is not only for those who have been marginalized but also for those who do the marginalizing. God loves "them," and God loves "us," stubborn as we may be. On both a personal and a corporate level, God desires for us to do his bidding. God longs to have us as partners in his kingdom work. This is the modern application of the ancient mandate.

Jonah is seen by biblical scholars as an Old Testament precursor to the Great Commission at the end of Matthew's Gospel. Centuries before Jesus, the story of Jonah declared God's compassion for all the peoples of the earth. The Ninevites represent all the "everyone elses" from all other eras—those who are alienated from mainline society or discriminated against in any way. Furr grabs on to this universal truth and brings it home to his congregation. (Do you get the feeling racism is a real problem in their community?) He does so without compromising the original text or reconfiguring the current realities to make them fit awkwardly into an archaic mode. Furr empowers us to discover our own Ninevites. He pivots the spotlight away from a stubborn Jonah and squarely onto us.

One of the great challenges in preaching is to make the gospel "hurt so good." In other words, we must faithfully proclaim a kerygma which may be laden with correctives and chastisements. But we must proclaim it in such a way that it doesn't leave our listeners feeling beaten down or beaten up. We must get them to listen to words they may not want to hear. We must leave them convicted but invigorated, convinced of their own sin, but not ashamed. Furr's sermon accomplishes this task very well. He exposes the hardness in our own hearts via Jonah, but he mixes it with a powerful reassurance of God's relentless love for us.

Response

The story of Jonah lends itself well to a call for response. It's a nice slow pitch thrown right over the middle of the plate. Even a rookie preacher should be able to drive this message deep into the center-field bleachers. Furr—who is anything but a rookie—doesn't disappoint. He uses the words of Louis Evely to hit the homer, imploring us to escort others to maturity by having faith in them, caring for them, loving them. Then he adds his own words of challenge to "turn loose and live out this kingdom thing of God's...free to trust, free to follow, free to love." It comes down to this: Either we continue to run away with Jonah, or we obey the prophetic call and bring the good news to Nineveh. If we choose the former route, we might well find ourselves looking a "big fish" in the mouth. If we choose the latter, we become a player in God's redemptive work in the world. Given these choices, Furr asks, "What are we waiting for?"

SUGGESTIONS

- Learn from this sermon how to avoid the "land mines" buried within certain biblical texts. It is a waste of time for preachers to get hung up on the incessant arguments over historicity, rationality, credibility, and every other "-ity" conservatives and liberals bicker about. The average person in the pew could care less. In the end, what the preacher needs to center on is the truth of the text, not merely the facts. Without dismissing the questions regarding the viability of a man's surviving in a fish's belly, Furr puts them aside in order to get us to the kerygma of the text.
- Here we have a laudable example of accessible preaching. In his language and style, Furr talks clearly to us regular folks, without insulting our intelligence or underestimating our ability to make our own connections with the text. The sermon is blessedly bereft of platitudes and preachy padding. It is conversational and relevant to the modern listener. Bye-bye, religious jargon—hello, clarity! Nothing fishy here, just good, solid preaching.

Richard A. Davis

STEPPING OFF
THE CURB

MATTHEW 21:1-11

REV. DR. MICHAEL P. HALCOMB
LAKE COUNTRY CONGREGATIONAL CHURCH
HARTLAND, WISCONSIN

Rev. Dr. Michael P. Halcomb

Stepping Off the Curb

MATTHEW 21:1-11

Joe Tucker was a third grader in my wife's Sunday school class sometime ago. Joe's parents didn't bring him to Sunday school, they sent him. He was a gregarious child, and some thought his parents sent him to have an hour without Joe. When my wife asked the class what Jesus did on Palm Sunday, several in the class knew that this was the day when Jesus made his entrance into Jerusalem. But when she continued by asking what Jesus went to Jerusalem to do, little Joe, always quick to have an answer, blurted out, "He went to set up the Red Cross and stuff like that"!

In some respects Palm Sunday is a puzzling day, not only for Joe, but for anyone who reads the biblical account carefully. First, there are the contrasting emotions of the day: Jesus weeping over the city just before the delirious shouts of "Hosanna" welcomed him into Jerusalem. And then there is the ambiguity of the crowds surrounding Jesus.

Actually, there was not one crowd but several that awaited Jesus in Jerusalem. There was the emotional crowd which shouted, "Blessed is he who comes in the name of the Lord." Most of the people in that crowd were probably from Galilee, and Scripture tells us that they were enamored of the miracles of Jesus. Most likely they expected Jesus to use his miraculous powers to overthrow the Roman government and give them the freedom they so long had desired.

A second crowd consisted of the curious bystanders who watched all of the fuss and asked "Who is this?" Yet another crowd was made up of the critics of Jesus, people such as the Pharisees and the Sadducees. These critics were afraid of Jesus' popularity and knew that he had the ability to challenge the religious establishment. You will note that they were the ones who warned Jesus to silence the crowds and later questioned his authority.

As we watch these conflicting emotions and powerful forces whirl around Jesus, we can't help but ask ourselves "What is happening here?" In answer to that question, we should note that Palm Sunday is the first time Jesus allowed his identity as the Son of God to be publicly proclaimed. Early in the Gospels, Jesus seemed to hide his identity as the one sent from God and he bound his disciples to secrecy. Now he allows it to be publicly proclaimed. This would suggest that Jesus intended Palm Sunday to be a day of decision about his Lordship, his Messiahship. If nothing else, his entrance into Jerusalem made it clear that he was coming in the name and power of the Lord God so that men and women could choose to follow him if they wished. It is almost as though Jesus wanted there to be no mistake about why he was coming to Jerusalem and eventually to the cross. He was not going to be crucified because of any tragic misunderstanding or confusion over his claims. Men and women would either follow him as the One sent from God or fade away into the confusion of the marketplace. They would either deny him as the Christ or accept him as Lord of their lives.

That is the decision that lies before each of us today.

The fact that Christianity requires a decision sometimes makes us uncomfortable. We are like the donkey who stood between two large haystacks, starving to death because it was unable to decide which haystack was better! Important decisions can cause us to suffer "the paralysis of analysis." Perhaps you have come right up to the point of decision to take a new job, to go on a trip, to propose marriage, or to take a strong stand to do what is right. But then your heart beats, your mind races, anxiety mounts, and you pause rather than act. Sometimes when we fail to act, circumstances change and the opportunity never quite comes again in the same way. How many of us have failed to act and then later thought "I nearly decided...but nearly was not enough!"

Great leaders are those who define the decisive issues of life and demand that a choice be made. The Bible is a book of decision. "Choose for yourselves this day whom you will serve," Joshua said to the Israelites. "But as for me and my household, we will serve the Lord" (Josh. 24:15, NIV). Jesus said simply, "Follow me." Many whom he called did take the step of faith and follow him. Matthew left his tax table; Peter, James, and John left their fishing boats. But others were like the rich young man who could not make that decision because he was attached to possessions and family. He was curious about Jesus, but he knew that commitment would be a life-changing event, and he couldn't make it. That's the way it is with the decision to accept Jesus Christ as Lord. Someone has said "Christ is either Lord of all, or he is not Lord at all."

Elton Trueblood, a philosopher of religion, said that the strength of Christianity is that it accepts the scandal of particularity. By this he meant that the Christian faith goes beyond just believing in general concepts; it calls us to live out our faith in the particular details of our lives. That is why the New Testament is filled with challenges such as that of Paul in 1 Corinthians 13: "If I speak in the tongues of men and of angels, but have not love, I am a noisy gong or a clanging cymbal" (v. 1, RSV). James calls us to apply our faith to the particulars of our lives when he writes, "Faith without works is dead" (2:26, KJV). It is not enough to believe in general that God is out there. We are called to invite the Lord into the particulars of our daily lives: into our homes, our marriages, our work, and our play. It is one thing to believe in general that God forgives, but another thing altogether to ask God to forgive us for a particular sin. It means nothing to believe that God can be trusted if we do not have the faith to trust God in a particularly difficult situation. The gospel's scandal of particularity is that it demands a decision. Either our faith in God is enough to make a difference in the daily details of our life, or we are forced to admit that we really have no faith at all.

Frank Gaebelein, one of the great Christian intellects of this century, understood this fact better than most. Educated at Harvard and Oxford, Gaebelein was well-known as a writer, a theologian, and an educator. In addition to founding a prestigious preparatory school in New York State and writing Bible commentaries, he was a concert pianist and a mountain climber. Later in his career, Dr. Gaebelein became the editor of *Christianity Today*. In the 1960s he traveled to Alabama to cover the civil rights march from Selma to Montgomery. Standing on the sidewalk, with all kinds of emotions swirling around him, he tried to keep his journalistic objectivity. As he watched the marchers with their signs demanding justice and equality under the constitution, he also heard the voices of hatred around him cursing, hurling obscenities and all kinds of invective at the demonstrators. Later, he described the moral crisis that engulfed him as he witnessed people spitting upon the marchers and even assaulting them while the police refused to intervene. Surrounded by such hatred and seeing the marchers continue courageously and yet nonviolently, Gaebelein said he knew that his Christian faith demanded a decision. He stepped off the curb and joined the march.

If Christ is to be Lord of our lives, there will be moments in our lives also when we need to make a decision, to step off the curb, to act upon our beliefs, to give witness to our commitment, to put feet under our faith. At school it may mean speaking the truth when it is unpopular. At work it may mean doing what is fair and just, rather than playing "go along to get along." In business dealings it may mean being guided by Christian principles rather than profit. But our choices will seldom be made in the heat of the moment. Most likely they will be determined by a more basic life decision—a faith decision or Palm Sunday decision—when we decide in our hearts whether or not we are willing to step off the curb and follow Jesus Christ as Lord.

When our son Jonathan, just out of college, accepted a sales position, he was thrown quickly into the crucible of the Chicago business world.

He told us of suddenly being faced with many difficult decisions and even some ethical dilemmas. Early on he was faced with the temptation to say whatever would help make the sale, but he determined to stick by his principles. He told of going to one appointment, where the president of the company was a brusque, outspoken man. He looked Jonathan over from head to toe and said somewhat sarcastically, "New suit, new shoes; you're new to this business, aren't you?"

Sensing he was in for something of a hard time, Jonathan responded, "Yes sir, just out of college and hoping to make it in sales."

Sensing his uneasiness, the man pushed further. "What makes you think you're going to make it in sales? Tell me, what are your goals? What is most important in your life?"

Jonathan swallowed hard. This was an impossible situation, he thought, and he felt like walking out. But he decided to answer, "My faith is the most important thing in my life, and then my family, but I also think my hard work will help me do well at my job."

The man responded in a surly way, "Your faith! I suppose you're one of those people who calls yourself a Christian. You don't believe that stuff in the Bible, do you?"

Wetting his dry lips, our son answered, "Yes sir, I do."

There was a pause before the man suddenly broke into a smile. "Well, I'm pleased to hear that, young man, because I believe it too! I was just testing you to see what kind of character you have."

For Jonathan, that was a decisive moment, when he stepped off the curb to follow Christ. He had been forced to decide whether Christ was going to be a part of his daily business life or not. Later he said to me, "Dad, I'm so glad I had decided earlier to stand by my beliefs."

But it is not easy to step off the curb and follow Christ. If you have truly struggled with the issues of what Christ's Lordship means in your daily life, you probably have a good deal of sympathy for those in the crowds on that first Palm Sunday. Some find it easy to scoff at the fickleness of the emotional crowds who expected Jesus to start a revolution and then abandoned him at the first sign of opposition. Or to feel self-righteous, looking down upon the curious crowds who have trouble making that step to commitment. Most of us certainly judge ourselves to be better than the critics of Jesus. But before we scoff or make our self-righteous judgments, we need to be reminded that we are much like the people in those crowds. We have the same struggles, the same temptations, the same rationalizations for taking the easy way, for saying that now is not the right time to step off the curb and follow Christ, not the time to take up our cross and follow him.

Each of us started our journey of faith from a different place. Some of us had critical questions. Others came with a naive curiosity. Perhaps we had some emotional need which we wanted Christ to meet. Whatever our starting point, the important thing is that at some time we made a decision. We took that decisive step of commitment to follow Christ for who he is and not for what he gives.

Read the Gospels carefully and you will find that these Palm Sunday crowds in Jerusalem should not be considered the enemies of Christ. Jesus had compassion on the crowds. He knew that the emotional crowd, the curious crowd, and the critical crowd, could each be starting points for growing a vital faith.

In the crowds were people like the women who were later at the cross. People like Peter, Thomas, and Nicodemus were in the crowd. They and others may have struggled for a time, but eventually they came to faith in Christ. Then there is what we might call the hidden crowd. There may have been much they did not understand, they may have had questions and serious doubts, but deep within their hearts they wanted to follow Christ.

Many in that first Palm Sunday crowd did step off the curb, making that important act of commitment. This hidden crowd didn't understand everything, but they had faith. They weren't sure where Christ would lead them, but they wanted to follow him. There were the women who followed Christ to the cross—and then discovered the empty tomb. Peter had been one of the emotional zealots, even trying to start a violent revolution in the Garden of Gethsemane. At the end of the Gospels we see

Peter, not just stepping off the curb, but jumping over the side of the boat to splash ashore and come to Christ. Nicodemus, the Pharisee, first came to question Jesus by night, but he left again when he learned that commitment really means starting a whole new life. We hear of Nicodemus again when he spoke up in the Sanhedrin, though rather feebly, when Jesus' fate was being discussed. And then there is silence. We are left in suspense about Nicodemus until the end of John's Gospel when we find him coming to provide for Jesus' burial. The man who had come with questions in the darkness, finally in the daylight took an open step of commitment.

Perhaps some of us are like some of those people in the crowd. We may have questions or doubts. Perhaps you came this morning because of some emotional need that is unmet. Or you may simply be among the curious. Those are good reasons for coming to church on Palm Sunday morning. Any of them can be the starting point for growing your Christian faith.

Now the challenge is to step off the curb and truly follow Christ, to make him Lord of every aspect of your life. Someone has said that all that is required to make Christ Lord of your life is to entrust as much of yourself as you understand to as much of Christ as you know. And it is important to do it now. If you wait, you may not have the resolve to act in the midst of a difficult situation. But if you take that important step today, it will influence how you act and think at crucial moments in the future. When you step off the curb to follow Christ, that small step can become the beginning of a wonderful journey of faith.

COMMENT

I once worked for a man whose greatest weakness in business was his inability to make a decision. He was bright, talented, creative, and persuasive. But he put off making decisions until matters reached "critical mass." By not deciding, he created a crisis that forced a decision.

Fence-sitting. Ambivalence. Creative neglect. Whatever we call it, we all know the impact of not making a decision. But *not* making a decision *is* making a decision—the two actions differ only in methodology. One is passive, the other active. One is by default, the other by design. Too often our lives aren't determined by what we decide, but by what we fail to decide.

This is the spiritual reality Michael Halcomb addresses in "Stepping off the Curb." This sermon offers listeners a spiritual looking glass with a mirrored reflection of the anatomy of choice: our choice—a personal choice each of us must make in the journey of faith.

Because of the many freedoms we enjoy in America, we can easily live our lives as "comfortable Christians." Our faith can be virtually invisible to those around us. We are rarely challenged to confront the cost of commitment. Yet challenging the complacency of comfortable Christianity is exactly what Halcomb does in "Stepping off the Curb."

Let's face it. Palm Sunday can be a difficult Sunday to preach. In seven short days the church calendar moves from the jubilant crowds of Palm Sunday to the darkness of Good Friday, then turns on a dime to the resurrection of Easter. What can you say that's fresh, stimulating, challenging? What can you say that doesn't diminish the spiritual depth of the coming week? Palm Sunday isn't an easy Sunday to stand in the pulpit.

Halcomb uses the Palm Sunday dilemma to get back to the basics. He asks the questions, What does it mean to follow Christ? What does it mean to declare him Lord? And for those who think they've "been there, done that," how do you break through the complacency? "Stepping off the Curb" is about making a decision, being clear about our decision, and following through with our decision. These are no small spiritual matters. These questions are the heart and soul of Christian commitment.

A Parabola of Decision

John Vannorsdall, for many years chaplain at Yale University, once preached a sermon in which he spoke of "the parabola of grace." By that phrase he spoke of the unlikely intersection of God's grace from eternity into our lives and the ensuing "grand reversal" that grace brings about. In "Stepping off the Curb" the parabola of grace is also an occasion of decision and commitment.

This sermon is one that is "littered" with illustrations of one person after another who encountered Christ and had to decide what that meant in the context of their own lives. From Joshua and the Israelites to contemporary theologian Elton Trueblood to evangelical intellectual Frank Gaebelein and the civil rights movement, Halcomb walks the listener through moments when simple decisions became defining moments.

The story of Gaebelein embodies the parabola of grace in this sermon—the point at which the arc of eternity intersects time and human experience and the grand reversal occurs. One moment Gaebelein is the observer, the uninvolved spectator in life's drama playing out before him. The next moment he is the participant in that drama, stepping off the curb. It is a moment of decision which forever changes the direction of his life.

Proclamation & Response

Every good sermon has at its center a parabola of grace, a grand reversal, for that is at the heart of all Christian proclamation. Christ enters our lives and the holy happens. In the sermon Halcomb confronts us with the necessity of decision while reassuring us that when we do step off the curb, Christ meets us in that moment.

Halcomb structures the sermon with a seesaw rhythm, a back and forth between story and proclamation, gradually moving the sermon in a stairstep pattern to the conclusion:

Now the challenge is to step off the curb and truly follow Christ, to make him Lord of every aspect of your life. Someone has said that all that is required to make Christ Lord of your life is to entrust as much of yourself as you understand to as much of Christ as you know. And it is important to do it now.

Do it now. These are words of action. Words of clarity. Words that leave no doubt about what is expected. This sermon clearly concludes with a call to commitment. The preacher challenges the congregation to be definitive about where they stand in relationship to the Palm Sunday Jesus. Halcomb asks us to identify who we are in the crowd. Are we critics? Skeptics? Hopeful followers? Faithful believers? Have we made our faith decision by design or by default?

When it comes to the ambivalence and complacency of comfortable Christianity, Halcomb pricks the comfort zone—a role every preacher must assume if he or she is to be faithful to the gospel. He has the boldness to preach a sermon that makes the decision to follow Christ one of black and white, yes or no, now or never. Halcomb models boldness combined with gentleness, confrontation with affirmation. He makes it clear that when it comes to matters of faith and questions of ethics, we can't afford to allow ourselves the luxury of "creative neglect." For Christians, there's no in-between.

SUGGESTIONS

- Halcomb uses several illustrations, any one of which can provide a springboard for a sermon by itself: the Elton Trueblood quote, the Frank Gaebelein story, the story of Halcomb's son, Jonathan. Reflect on these stories and consider how you might use them in a sermon.
- Have you preached a sermon on the Palm Sunday crowd? Halcomb draws word pictures of the crowds who stood at the roadside leading into Jerusalem. We are all there—the critic, the believer, the curious. What parallels can you make to your congregation?

- What have been the defining moments in your faith journey? And what do those moments tell you about the nature and character of God? Do you draw upon your faith autobiography to illustrate your preaching?

Debra K. Klingsporn

Religious Closed-Mindedness

JOHN 5:1–18, 39–47

Rev. John G. Hargis
Chapel Hill United Methodist Church
San Antonio, Texas

Rev. John G. Hargis

Religious Closed-Mindedness

JOHN 5:1–18, 39–47

I may be the first preacher you've ever heard tell you this, but Scripture reading or Bible study might not do you any good! Did you hear me? Bible reading and study will not automatically make you a better Christian.

I'll be the first to admit that Bible study is important to spiritual health. The Bible, we commonly say and hear, is the Word of God. While in divinity school, of eight possible subject areas, I chose to major in Bible. So of all people, I'm going to be the last to discourage you from reading your Bibles.

But according to the text we just read—and according to the Bible itself—it's possible to be a student of the Bible and still miss the point. "You pore over the Scriptures," Jesus told some of his Bible-studying detractors, "believing that in them you can find eternal life; it is these Scriptures that testify to me, and yet you refuse to come to me to receive life" (John 5:39–40).

Did you catch that? Scripture reading won't necessarily do you any spiritual good. Bible study won't automatically give you life.

The title of my sermon is "Religious Closed-Mindedness." We've all known people whom we would characterize as closed-minded. Some people, for whatever reason, just seem to be utterly closed off to new insights in a whole variety of areas.

I grew up on a ranch in southern Oklahoma at a time when most ranchers raised white-faced or Hereford cattle. My father, though, started raising a different kind of cattle—Beefmasters. The result was that though the calves were no bigger when they were born and there was no increase in calving difficulty (an important consideration), by the time a calf was weaned and ready to go to market, it was some one hundred fifty to two hundred pounds larger than a Hereford calf of the same age.

One day at the sale barn, Dad was talking to a neighbor about the calves he had just sold. He was talking about his increased weaning weights and how proud he was of his calves. The neighbor said, "But with the Hereford calves you get paid more per pound, and so it comes out the same in the end."

Dad said, "Well, look, here are my sales tickets. Look what I got paid per pound. What'd you get on yours?"

The other man looked at the sales tickets, then looked at his own, chewed his lower lip a minute, and then said, "Well, I don't care if they do make more money, I still like them white-face." In other words, don't confuse me with the facts; my mind's already made up!

There's religious closed-mindedness too. John's Gospel says that earlier Jesus had healed a man of a disease that he'd had for thirty-eight years (John 5:1–18). Obviously only a very gifted individual could do something like that, someone whom God was with. This was a person to pay some heed to, a person to learn from. But—Jesus had done the deed on the sabbath, and that was a no-no. It only made the religious authorities, the people who were the avid Bible students, that much more anxious to do away with him.

"He healed a man who had been sick for thirty-eight years?" they might have thought. "He showed a power we normally attribute only to God himself. Well, don't confuse me with any more facts. We already know that a good, religious man doesn't work on the sabbath. My mind is made up."

Some people are closed-minded. Their minds are closed off to any new insights, any new way of seeing things. If you already know what the

Bible says before you read it, your chances of seeing something new or insightful are considerably lessened. Scripture reading, Bible study, even listening to sermons, will tend to make no difference in your life if you already think you know what is there.

What are the advantages of being closed-minded? We choose to do it so often, there must be some advantages to it. Why is it that people close themselves off to new insights? The text from John's Gospel seems to indicate that human pride has a lot to do with it. "Human glory means nothing to me" (v. 41), Jesus said, as if to say that was their problem. "You look to each other for glory and are not concerned with the glory that comes from the one God" (v. 44).

Human pride. That's what seems to lead to the loss of real guiding purpose that should be behind one's study. Let me be more specific and tell of a couple of more particular ways in which I think this happens.

People have a tendency to give loyalty to a particular way of seeing and explaining things that subsequently inhibits alternative ways of seeing and explaining the same data. In other words, we tend to like the old and comfortable explanations.

In the popular media these days we hear a lot about "paradigm shifts." A paradigm is a particular way or model of viewing and explaining data. People have a tendency to cling to old paradigms, to the systems in which they have been able to make sense of things in the past. A person shifts paradigms or goes to a completely different system for explaining a particular set of data, only at great personal cost.

This whole notion of paradigm shifts has come, I think, from a book by Thomas Kuhn called *The Structure of Scientific Revolutions*.[1] That being the case, let me go to the world of science to try to show what happens when an old paradigm runs into new data it can't explain.

Ignaz Semmelweis was a Hungarian obstetrician who worked at a hospital in Vienna in the first half of the last century. He practiced at a time when, on the average, some 10 to 35 percent of the women who had babies died from something called childbed fever. At the time, of course, there were no antibiotics. They didn't even have a germ theory.

Semmelweis discovered that if he washed his hands thoroughly, until his hands were slippery, in a chlorine-lime solution (something like Clorox), before delivering a child, then the incidence of childbed fever dropped markedly in his patients. He published his results showing that whereas other doctors and midwives lost 10 to 35 percent of their patients, in his Viennese hospital one year he lost only 1 percent, and the next year he lost none.

Unfortunately, Dr. Semmelweis did not know why this procedure worked. He had no intellectual framework, no paradigm, within which to explain his results. Louis Pasteur would not convince the world of the pernicious effects of germs until some thirty years later, and so the other practitioners had no plausible way of understanding the whys and wherefores of Semmelweis's success. They had no paradigm, no conceptual framework, in which to explain it, so they kept their minds closed to his suggestions.

If Semmelweis was right, then that meant that their own unwashed hands, with which they had intended to do so much good over the years, had instead been agents of destruction to some 10 to 35 percent of the women they had sought to help. Who could bear to hear that? To admit that Semmelweis was correct was concurrently to acknowledge that much of what they had given their lives to was misspent. Pride in their lives' work was at stake. The result was that Semmelweis could get no one to believe him. His articles and letters became even more desperate and hysterical in tone. Finally, friends lured him one day into a sanitarium, where they left him. Semmelweis was subdued, straitjacketed, and confined. Two weeks later he died, just one day after Joseph Lister had begun his experiments on antisepsis, and about thirty years before Louis Pasteur gave the theoretical framework that explained, among other things, Semmelweis's success. But in the meantime, doctors continued to lose 10 to 35 percent of their obstetrical patients.[2]

"Don't confuse me with any more facts," we say, "when I have just now got my world figured out."

Jesus' detractors here in the text from John's Gospel hated him. Either he was right with God, or they were. So they couldn't be confused or convicted in their hearts by the evidence before them. This healing of a man sick for thirty-eight years just could not be a good thing. Having occurred as it did on a sabbath (and they had always known that no godly person works on the sabbath), the healing had to be construed in some way other than good and holy. The sabbath was the excuse they needed to dismiss Jesus. The gift of healing and its Giver were rejected. They couldn't have been wrong all these years about what God really values, could they?

Our pride in how we have understood the world, our pride in the intellectual framework we have constructed, sometimes does not allow us to be open to new, contradictory data. We shift paradigms only at great emotional cost. Only with courage!

There's another reason for closed-mindedness. Not only do we have pride in ourselves and our intellectual constructions, but we have loyalty to our group. We give loyalty to a group of people with a shared vision. To see things differently is to be disloyal to our group.

Out of our human pride, we tend to divide the world into "us" and "them." Pharisees will be loyal to Pharisees. Upper-middle-class professionals tend to be loyal to upper-middle-class professionals. Politically correct liberal arts professors tend to be loyal to their group. Rush Limbaugh fans in their shirts and ties tend to be loyal to their group. Groups have their own culture. They tend to have their typical ways of speaking. They have their own styles. These things are cues as to whether or not someone is in or out, accepted or rejected.

A person from the wrong style or group tends to have opinions that we discount. The result is that it's often the young or the very old, the outsiders and the nobodies or the marginalized who are capable of entertaining a new outlook.

I'm a graduate of the Vanderbilt University Divinity School. There are certain disadvantages to that. In fact, there are certain disadvantages to graduating from any "prestigious" institution. Here you are, you're a new graduate, and you're presented with a new idea from someone who is not of your background. You think in the imagination of your heart: "I'm a graduate of Floocie U., and if this is such a great idea, how come I haven't heard of it before? If this is such a great idea, why isn't it *my* idea?"

The group we are a part of, the group that gives us our identity and pride, may lead us to discount ideas and persons who are not of our social or intellectual set. Jesus was too much of an outsider to be taken seriously by the Jerusalem establishment, no matter what his qualities and accomplishments were.

Simply reading and studying the Bible (or listening to sermons for that matter) are not necessarily helpful to your spiritual health. (Of course, not reading at all is certainly no way to make progress either!) Sometimes we can be so closed-minded, we can already be so sure of what the Bible is going to tell us, that we don't hear anything different. What a shame!

How can we read the Bible to our advantage? How can we read it for life? Here are a few suggestions:

First, before you begin your reading, pray that God will help you in it. Acknowledge to God even before you begin that you're a sinful, pride-filled person who has a tendency to be self-serving in all things, but who, even so, wants to grow in grace and knowledge. First, pray.

Second, read a good modern translation so that you have at least a fighting chance of understanding. Vary the translation you use from time to time to get a new sound in your head.

Third, make an intentional effort to read what's there and not to fill in the gaps out of the folklore you've inherited. Face up to the fact that no number of wise men who came to Bethlehem is given in the text. We don't know if there were three, six, or a hundred. Nor are they called kings in spite of what the song says. In the other nativity story, though there is a manger, no stable is mentioned, and certainly no innkeeper is ever mentioned. Apparently Luke had no intention of getting us focused on some unmentioned innkeeper. The daughter of Herodias who asked for John the Baptist's head in last week's Gospel lesson, is not named, and there's no statement, in the text anyway, that her dance was lascivious, no matter what the movies might do with it. In the Genesis flood narrative, not one word is said about the faith of Noah, nor is there a single line about his neighbors laughing at him for building the ark on dry land.

Try to read what is actually there in the text and not just what you've always thought was there!

Fourth, find the one thing in the text that is most uncomfortable to you and bore in on that. Figure out why it makes you uncomfortable. This may be the point where you can actually learn something. If you read about Jesus cursing the fig tree for not having figs, and then you read further and learn that it's not even the season for figs, and that bothers you, well, bore in on it. Try to figure out why Jesus did what he did in the text. Find the thing in a given text that most bothers you and dwell on it a while.

Fifth, take it personally, but at the same time realize it wasn't written originally to you. The other day I was reading 1 Corinthians, and I wasn't paying as much attention as I might. I began to insert my name occasionally in the text. Paul was letting the Corinthians have it, and when I imagined him saying those things directly to me, it woke me up, and I started paying attention.

Still, Paul didn't write that letter to me. My situation is not exactly like theirs was then, and it is the height of impudence to think that every single text in the whole Bible should be of immediate relevance to my current situation. Take the Bible seriously. Take it personally. But remember, it wasn't first written to you. We're eavesdropping.

Sixth, look for Christ in the text, even in the Old Testament. Look for hints of his crucifixion and resurrection especially being prefigured there.

Abel, the younger brother in a world that valued older brothers, seems to be the preferred one of God. Yet he's killed by his brother Cain. Can one, in the slightest way, see prefigured there the cross of Jesus?

Abraham and Sarah are past the point of child-bearing. Sarah's womb cannot bring forth life. Then, miraculously, as from a grave, comes a child. Is this analogous to resurrection?

Jacob was to be a blessing to the whole world, but he's not! He's a shyster and a con-man—at least until he becomes wounded in a wrestling match with God. Does this prefigure Jesus, our wounded healer?

Moses was placed among the bulrushes out of fear of Pharaoh. Does this prefigure the slaughter of the innocents and the flight to Egypt by Joseph, Mary, and the baby Jesus out of fear of Herod?

David was the youngest son of Jesse, the youngest and the least, but he, the unexpected one, is the anointed king of Israel.

Then there are the Suffering Servant songs of Isaiah, where the Servant, whoever he is, is "wounded for our transgressions, and bruised for our iniquities."

There is a ton of material in the Old Testament. There's violence and intrigue and power grabbing, and much of it by some of the heroes! Still, through it all, look for Jesus. Look for the long-suffering patience and love of God that results finally in Jesus on the cross.

Finally, my last bit of advice is to read. Read and don't give up. Read daily. Read weekly. Read in season and out of season. Read when you want to read and love it. And read in the dry times when the pages seem like dead, lifeless leaves. Read.

Remember, we don't have eternal life simply because we read the Bible a lot. But we can be changed. If we're open to the Spirit of God, we can grow in the knowledge of God and deepen our faith. Come to the Bible with an open mind. Come to God with an open heart. God will honor it, and you will have true life.

Remember Ignaz Semmelweis, that Hungarian obstetrician condemned to a sanitarium to die among the lunatics? He was a man with an open mind. He was willing to embrace a different view of reality. Today a hospital in Budapest, Hungary—the main research hospital in that country—is called the Ignaz Semmelweis Hospital.

Notes
1. Thomas S. Kuhn, *The Structure of Scientific Revolutions,* 2nd edition (Chicago: University of Chicago Press, 1970).
2. William Broad and Nicolas Wade, *Betrayers of the Truth: Fraud and Deceit in the Halls of Science* (New York: Simon & Schuster, 1982).

COMMENT

John Hargis's sermon addresses two problems: closed-mindedness and misconceptions about reading the Bible. Both are important issues and could be developed into separate sermons.

The introduction to the sermon is strong, perhaps even startling to some who couldn't imagine a minister saying such a thing. Contrary to what many would think—that the last thing we hear in a sermon has the greatest effect—what we hear first is actually remembered longest. The risk in such an opening is that it's hard to live up to in the remainder of the sermon. Yet this sermon does continue to hold our attention throughout.

TEXT

During the sermon Hargis continually relates the text to his thesis and finds in the text reasons people didn't understand or recognize Jesus for who he was. These are the same reasons we still do not understand Jesus today.

At one point, by suggesting the advantages of keeping a closed mind, Hargis piques our curiosity and makes us wonder what's coming next. "What are the advantages of being closed-minded?" he asks. Even though we may see ourselves here and recognize that such "advantages" have no virtue, we keep listening because the sermon has our attention.

PROCLAMATION

Just as Jesus in the first-century challenged rigid, old ways of thinking, based on rules and formulas, he still challenges us today. The good news does not always come in "old and comfortable explanations" but in experiences which require new ways of looking at truth. Hargis illustrates this with the intriguing story of Ignaz Semmelweis, showing how devastating it is not to follow where truth leads. He also reminds us of the beneficence of God. God often offers solutions to our problems and opportunities to advance the science of healing, even though we are unable to see them. When we do see such solutions, they are so different from what we expected that we find it difficult to believe they came from God.

"Paradigm shift" is today a very popular phrase frequently used with the assumption that everyone knows what it means. Hargis is wise in explaining it in such a simple and straightforward way. Anyone in the congregation could understand this key point because of the explanation given. In doing this, Hargis reminds us that often the most profound things can be made simple.

Just as Jesus recognized the poor and undistinguished as children of the kingdom, Hargis offers a poignant insight when he says, "It's often the young or the very old, the outsiders and the nobodies or the marginalized who are capable of entertaining a new outlook." Is it because they have the least to lose by being open to new truths? Are they least in debt to systems? How often do we see such persons as those who are most open to truth and to change?

In preaching, a question is often stronger than a declarative statement. For example, at one point Hargis asks concerning Jesus' detractors, "They couldn't have been wrong all these years about what God really values, could they?" This question engages us by giving us something to ponder. As we reflect on it in the larger context of the sermon we begin to reflect on our own lives—whether we are wrong in many of the assumptions we make about God. This question in the sermon reminds us of the values Jesus proclaimed.

Notice how Hargis ties the John 5 text to stories in the Old Testament illustrating the long-suffering patience and love of God which found final expression in Jesus on the cross. By citing these Old Testament stories, the preacher helps us see the unfolding of the gospel of redemption throughout our faith history. Setting the John 5 story in the larger context of the biblical story strengthens the sermon and teaches redemptive history.

Concluding the sermon by briefly returning to the story of Semmelweis's having a research hospital named after him, Hargis offers hope for all who recognize truths that others are not willing to consider.

The sermon challenges us to live on the frontiers of faith, open to seeing realities to which others are blind or which they are unprepared to accept.

Response

The response the preacher urges is for his listeners to read the Bible more openly and deliberately. He suggests some very practical ways of doing this. I find three of these suggestions especially helpful.

1) In reading the Bible, Hargis says that we are "not to fill in the gaps" in the story out of the folklore we've inherited. Hopefully, listeners will be jolted at the reminder that many things we thought were part of the story are not in the Bible at all! What a powerful way to make us more careful in reading the Bible and in looking at details. We may be surprised by the absence of many things we could have sworn were there. If this were the only point hearers got from the sermon, it would be a helpful sermon.

2) A second good suggestion for reading the Bible is to notice what makes us most uncomfortable. This can really open us to new insights if we are sensitive enough to recognize what we don't like or what we resist. Just as God often speaks to us through failure instead of success, God also speaks in what disturbs as well as what comforts us. By mentioning the story of the cursing of the fig tree, a difficult story to understand, Hargis reminds us that we have to live with questions as well as with answers. Questions may keep us more alert and open than when we think we have all the answers.

3) A third suggestion, to read the Bible personally, can bring a new perspective to our spiritual understanding. We may get a better feel for what people in the early church felt. And remembering that Paul's letters were not written specifically for us should help us avoid the pitfall of trying to make everything in them relevant to our time. We do not live in the first century.

Suggestions

- This sermon is a good example of the effective use of illustrations. The stories, especially the Semmelweis illustration, are well suited to the sermon and easily remembered. That's the best kind of preaching. Jesus, of course, used many stories in his teaching. How do you use stories in your preaching? In sermon preparation, ask yourself, Why am I using this story? or Would a story help illustrate my point?

- While the sermon topic is relevant to any congregation, it might be even more engaging to arouse the hearer's curiosity with another sermon on "The Advantages (or Disadvantages) of a Closed Mind," a sentence used in the sermon. What would such a sermon look like?
- Look back at the sermon. After the story about Semmelweis, could there be a smoother transition linking the story to the John 5 text and to Jesus' detractors? What do you think? Try this: "Just as the doctors in Semmelweis's day wouldn't risk changing their rigid view of reality, neither would Jesus' detractors. They both had the world figured out." Transitions from illustrations to sermon text or ideas should be clear for listeners to follow. Be conscious of all your transitions.
- It would be interesting for a ministers' study group to discuss whether this sermon would have been strengthened or weakened by more explicit, contemporary illustrations of religious closed-mindedness. What do you think?
- Christians are divided today on so many issues: styles of worship (which one writer calls "worship wars"), lifestyles, ecclesiastical structures, ordination of women, and others. At times we all think the person who disagrees with us is closed-minded! In what areas are we closed-minded? Is God still hoping we'll recognize and confront these issues in ourselves? Think about developing one or more sermons on this theme drawing upon issues important in your church and community.

Paul D. Lowder

Led by a Lamb

REVELATION 7:9–17

Rev. Dr. C. David Matthews
Good Samaritan Church
Orlando, Florida

REV. DR. C. DAVID MATTHEWS

LED BY A LAMB

REVELATION 7:9–17

In our culture, the name of the game is winning, and we want all the advantage we can get. One of the first steps to winning is to look like a winner, and so we want to project winning images.

I love sports, and I love for my teams to win. We are in that time of year that is ideal for sports fans. The World Series is still on our minds. Football is only at midseason. This weekend basketball season started.

Sports teams choose names and mascots that project a winning attitude or image—at least most of them do. When we are naming a team, we draw on strong images. We may speak of threatening images from nature: Cyclones, Hurricanes, Blizzards. We may choose menacing or combative human types: Pirates and Vikings, Warriors and Cavaliers. Or we pick various kinds of Indian names and create unfortunate stereotypes like Redskins, Braves, Seminoles. Then there are the Cowboys. Of course, there are exceptions, like the New Orleans Saints. On the other hand, if you've ever tried living with a saint you may not think it's an exception.

If the names do not speak of fighters, they picture strong, invincible human types: Steelers, Oilers, Mariners, Whalers. For me Wake Forest has the best team name: the Demon Deacons.

But our favorite source of intimidating nicknames is the animal kingdom: Broncos and Rams; Lions and Tigers; Wildcats, Wolverines, Razor-backs, Bears, and Gators. How much more successful might Miami's professional football team have been if they had chosen the terrifying shark instead of the friendly dolphin?

We like tough, intimidating names. We want winners' names.

When my son Kyle and I were in the YMCA Indian Guides, we were allowed to choose our Indian names. We didn't name ourselves after bunnies or puppies or duckies. We became Big Thunder Hawk and Little Thunder Hawk. Don't dare ask me which was which!

There is biblical precedent for these images. When the Bible reaches its triumphant conclusion in the Book of Revelation, the kingdom of God is identified with an animal. What creature from the animal kingdom could possibly suffice to represent the eternal kingdom of God in Christ? A lion, perhaps, as in the lion of Judah? Or an eagle, as in "You shall mount up with wings like eagles"?

Neither. In the kingdom of God the name of the game is not competition or winning by overpowering. There is a great reversal in God's kingdom, where the point is winning by losing. We see this most clearly in Jesus Christ. The image of Christ's team is a lamb.

The bizarre imagery and strange symbolism of the Book of Revelation have left generations of readers wondering what this perplexing book is about. The book itself contains clues. For one thing, there are clear references to persecution and to emperor worship in chapter 13. Most scholars today place the composition of Revelation in Asia Minor during a time when Christians were persecuted by the Roman government, probably around A.D. 95, during the reign of the Roman emperor Domitian.

Read from this perspective, much of the strange symbolism in the book becomes understandable. Bizarre creatures, such as the seven-headed beast from the sea in chapter 13, can be understood as the writer's way of describing Rome (built on seven hills) and Roman officials.

Understanding the historical context of Revelation helps us see that it is not so much a book containing predictions of events in some distant future, as a writing for first-century Christians, offering them words of comfort and consolation in their current predicament, and reinforcing the promise of an ultimate victory that all believers have in Jesus Christ.

Our reading today is from Revelation 7. When we read verses 9–17, did you hear that truly ironic statement? The Lamb will be the Shepherd. What an unlikely people we are called to be: people led by a Lamb. True followers of Christ belong to Someone who transcends all winning and power plays and aggression, all Super Bowls and World Series and Olympic triumphs.

On this All Saints' Sunday we honor those of Christ's flock who have gone before us. Who are they? A mother here, a father there. A Sunday school teacher from our childhood who communicated the love of God in words and in spirit. An older friend who imparted a piece of simple wisdom that has not failed us yet. Someone who believed in us through a season when we were not sure we even believed in ourselves. Someone from the community who always blessed us by simply making eye contact and smiling and knowing our name. A preacher or two, perhaps. All people we knew ourselves.

There are also those saints we only learned about from history or from someone else. Those who rose to some dangerous task and saw it through in the name of God. Those who sacrificed lives of comfort to step down into some ditch or to venture out into some foreign place to minister to the forgotten of God's children. Those who reflected long and deeply on the word of God so as to increase our understanding and devotion. Those who died in the service of Christ because for them to live was Christ and to die was gain. Heroes all. Heroes of the faith.

There are others. The silent, now forgotten, saints, who in small ways and with no glory prepared the way for the Lord, who is always coming into our world.

What do these saints, this great host of witnesses, share in common? Not a place or a time: some are ancient and biblical, some as contemporary as those we ourselves have known. Not some cultural identity, or national unity, or political persuasion, or even ideological commitment. They were as diverse as humanity itself. Some might not like to think of others of them as even being Christians!

What do they all share in common, these saints? One thing. They were all led by the Lamb. They all moved upstream in a world rushing downstream. For them the call of Christ was a priority that diminished the importance of everything for which most people live. They did not seek their own fulfillment but found themselves in self-giving love. They reflected in their individual and myriad ways the awareness that real power lies not in wealth, not in strength, not in fame, not in control, but in a cross, in a child, in a Lamb.

They dared to live by this truth in a world that rejects it on a daily basis. That is why they are saints and why they are honored today. To be a saint can be a dangerous thing, but it is the finest use of a life.

I know a few living saints. (By the way, it's a lot easier to be a dead saint!) There are some people still in this world who inspire me with friendship and wisdom and love. I am grateful for them, especially as their number becomes fewer as I grow older. I need them. One of them is Marion Bascom.

Marion Bascom retired a few years ago from the Douglas Memorial Community Church in Baltimore, one of the largest black congregations in that city. Dr. Bascom was on a nickname basis with both Martin Luther Kings, Senior and Junior. Many times he has gone to the front line for his people as well as for his faith. Such courage and such a dear man.

A couple of years ago he signed off on a letter to me: "Peace, power and love, Marion." Not "Sincerely," but "Peace, power and love."

I wondered how he came to put those three words together as he did. I don't think I had ever heard them used in just that way. The benediction stuck in my mind. I thought about it often. Finally the insight came and bubbled over into a slightly elaborated benediction of my own:

> Peace, power and love,
> God, grant from above.
> In Your peace alone is power;
> And Your power is suffering love.

This is what the saints know, and we must learn. That God's peace, the peace "that passes all understanding," is the only source of enduring power; and that the highest expression of God's power is a cross.

The saints know this because they are led by the Lamb.

Most Sovereign and most Holy God, you could have overwhelmed us with power and ruled us as the strongest of kings, yet you came to us as a little child.

You could have roared through our world like a lion and brought all nations to their knees at your feet, but your love for us led you to become the Lamb that was slain.

We have gathered as your church, grateful that the One who leads us is the One who died for us.

We hear your call to the table set before us. Help us to hear your call to move beyond the table, carrying light and bread into a world of darkness and hunger, until that day when tribulations are behind us and we gather around your eternal throne to worship you and the Lamb, in whose name we pray. Amen.

Comment

For centuries, the standard guide for preaching throughout Christendom was the lectionary, a rotating schedule of assigned readings followed by most of the traditional churches. Generally, this lectionary included an Old Testament reading, a reading from one of the Gospels, an epistle lesson, and in most cases, a psalm. Preachers were schooled to adhere faithfully to the lectionary texts in the preparation of their weekly messages. If the preacher did so, over the course of one to three years the congregation was given a comprehensive overview of the whole of Scripture. The lectionary also guided the preacher through the shifting emphasis of the Christian calendar, highlighting particular passages for each appropriate holy day or season.

It can be argued whether more recent de-emphasis or neglect of the lectionary in some quarters of the church is good or bad. This much is certain: When a preacher is given a weekly assignment of texts to preach, there is a reduced chance the congregation will be subjected to recurring soapbox issues-of-preference. More than that, the preacher will be challenged, and hopefully stretched, in having to expound on unfamiliar (even undesirable) biblical passages. Many of those who have stuck with the lectionary for a year or two admit to being surprised how doing so expanded their preaching repertoire and improved their pastoral scholarship and the congregation's worship.

At a time when modern sermons are characterized by topical and relational styles (Did someone say "sugarcoated"?), it is both unusual and refreshing to find in many churches lectionary-inspired sermons. David Matthews presents us with just such a message which also commemorates one of the lesser known holy days on the church calendar. All Saints' Sunday. One wonders how many of the megachurches across America would deem All Saints' Day important enough even to give it so much as a passing nod, not to mention basing an entire sermon on it. In this sense, what we have here is, by some American Protestant standards, an anomaly.

STYLE

By the time we're into the first few sentences of this sermon, we become aware that lectionary-based preaching need not be stale or stuffy. While Matthews has taken his text straight from an ancient list of assigned readings, that's where the semblance to antiquity ends. He immediately asks his listeners to consider our society's obsession with "winning images." How better to do this than by taking a lighthearted inventory of the names and mascots we choose for our sports teams? In a culture obsessed with sports while inconvenienced by religion, the preacher decides to utilize his competition to make his point. He draws from secular sources to score sacred points, using the very subject that occupies the minds of many of those who sit in pews trying to listen to sermons. This makes for an engaging introduction to the message which serves to validate a deeper truth: We as Americans are more drawn to images of power, violence, and intimidation than we are to the softer and gentler things of life. This, in turn, sets the table for the paradox to follow: that God has chosen as his mascot a lamb rather than a lion. Christians are called to rally round a symbol of sacrifice rather than domination. Here is the wonder of Christianity's success in recruiting saints both past and present.

Matthews successfully integrates age-old structures (the lectionary, All Saints' Sunday, the Roman context of the Book of Revelation) with the trends of the 90s (sports franchises and Y Indian Guides), demonstrating that such mixing can be done smoothly and effectively. He is not the least awkward at making the leap from the Miami Dolphins to the lion of Judah. Why should he be? He clearly understands that humanity's infatuation with power images hasn't waned in the last three thousand years. In fact, this is why God's choice of mascot was and is so startling. No one would ever expect much from a movement whose battle cry is the bleat of a sheep. Matthews wants us to wrestle with this incongruity in order to understand better the mind of God and to contemplate his call on our lives.

TEXT

Anyone who has preached much knows how awkward it is to preach from the Book of Revelation. For one thing, no other biblical document carries so much baggage. Liberals and conservatives alike wince at the notion that they might be forced to take a doctrinal stand regarding this mysterious book. As a result, sermons from Revelation are few and far between, especially in mainline churches. Preachers simply don't want to get hung up—or get their congregations hung up—between the historical and the hysterical. Fortunately, to his credit, Matthews isn't intimidated by this provocative piece of the canon.

Whether you agree with his conclusions or not, you have to admire how adeptly Matthews tiptoes through the land mines of textual argument in order to get to the deeper message. And he does it without negating the importance of such discussions. The sermon makes it clear Matthews is of the opinion that Revelation is more historically descriptive than it is prophetically predictive. But he is much more interested in the image of the Lamb in Revelation than he is curious about the second coming of that Lamb, and he hopes we will join him in this interest. While he chooses not to dredge too deeply into the text, Matthews remains true to the text by focusing clearly on the Lamb of God as the ironic symbol of God's ultimate victory.

WHAT IS THE POINT OF THE SERMON?

Okay. So God chooses a lamb as his mascot. So what? How does that impact our lives? For one thing, as Matthews says, that seemingly docile image has inspired some of the most courageous women and men the world has ever known…even unto death. The saints of the church down through the ages—those who have directly impacted our own lives—have all shared the commitment to conquer the world with "self-giving love," with poverty and submission rather than wealth and tyranny…

"not in strength, not in fame, not in control, but in a cross, in a child, in a Lamb."

Compared to the power images with which we are bombarded daily, how peculiar it is that the symbol of a lamb can inspire such heroism. And yet, not only does the Lamb of God motivate persons to go against the odds, the Lamb's followers gain ground while moving "upstream in a world rushing downstream." The Lamb convinces would-be intimidators to convert to a methodology of peace and supplication. That's some amazing Lamb there!

In a nutshell, the sermon calls us to abandon the pursuit of winning through the aggressive ways of the world in favor of adopting an attitude of "peace, power and love." As Matthews puts it, "God's peace, the peace 'that passes all understanding,' is the only source of enduring power." To be sure, this is the gospel of Jesus Christ.

SUGGESTIONS

- Matthews has a style of preaching which incorporates the frequent use of word sets, or rhythmic series of phrases. For some preachers, this works. For others it can backfire. Go through the sermon again and notice the times Matthews uses back-to-back groupings of illustrative examples. He does it often. But is it too often? Does he risk falling into a sing-song style that detracts more than it enhances? Does it feel like overkill? While it may work for Matthews, there are many preachers who smother their point under layers of over-extended examples. Be careful not to run on…and on…and on in your use of series. One word often says more than many.

- We are fortunate to have attached to this sermon the prayer Matthews wrote to conclude his thoughts. Quite often, a prayer is useful to draw together and reiterate the main point of what has gone before. Such is the case here. It is not an improper use of prayer to summarize a sermon. In fact, it often adds emphasis and brings closure to a message, leaving the congregation with a keener sense of their responsibility to live out what they have just heard.

- Thankfully, this preacher was not put off by the lectionary reading or the liturgical calendar. All Saints' Day might be imposing to preachers who would wonder how to incorporate such a theme into a modern message. Matthews does so with great skill and without sacrificing his gift of relevancy. The sermon is neither long nor cumbersome. It is engaging while also faithful to the liturgical tradition. Can modern preachers adhere to traditional guidelines and still preach effective contemporary sermons? This one certainly did.
- Note Matthews's ability to incorporate the interpretational issues surrounding the text without making them the central concern of his message. Some preachers spend so much time and effort laying the hermeneutical groundwork that their audience is distracted and never ushered to the higher ground of the text. The primary emphasis of the biblical passage must never be drowned out by technical, historical or doctrinal issues and jargon. Few people are interested in such things. They are much more curious to know what the Bible has to say about everyday life.

Richard A. Davis

WHEN THE WINE GIVES OUT

JOHN 2:1–11

REV. DR. WILLIAM J. IRELAND, JR.
BRIARCLIFF BAPTIST CHURCH
ATLANTA, GEORGIA

Rev. Dr. William J. Ireland, Jr.

WHEN THE WINE GIVES OUT

JOHN 2:1-11

Things seem to go wrong at weddings. Plan to have a wedding, and all the gremlins of the world hear about it and plan to attend—even though they're not invited. Bring together two different people and their families, add in all the stuff necessary to put on a wedding (flowers, invitations, pictures, music, caterers and receptions) and you have the makings for a major disaster. No wonder the witty and popular writer Robert Fulghum observed that "weddings are rarely dull."[1] Things just naturally go awry.

At the first three weddings I ever did, people in the wedding party passed out cold. Then there was the time the parents of the bride were divorced and not on good terms. Unfortunately, they used the occasion of their daughter's wedding to get back at each other in an ugly way. I really thought we were going to have to call the police. Then, there have been all those times when the flower girl absolutely refused to walk down the aisle or when someone dropped the ring. Things just seem to go wrong at weddings.

John tells us that something had gone terribly wrong at the wedding attended by Jesus and his disciples in Cana. The wine for the wedding celebration gave out. Now, in those days, wine was the lifeblood of any celebration, particularly a wedding. A wedding without wine for them would be like a wedding without a cake for us. This meant that the wedding feast itself was in danger of being disrupted. It also meant embarrassment and dishonor for the hosts, branding them forever with the failure to provide adequate hospitality.[2]

How could such a thing happen? Perhaps they were poor folks and could only afford X amount. Or it could be that they failed to estimate adequately how much they would need. No matter what the reason, the wine gave out, and a joyous wedding was on the verge of turning into a disaster. And that's what we should expect, shouldn't we? After all, things just go wrong at weddings.

What's true of weddings is also true of life. Things just go wrong. The wine gives out for all of us. What we have on hand proves inadequate. Whatever we count on to live joyously, whatever we look to for vitality and hope, just won't stretch far enough. We are in danger of running out. We are in danger of bringing the party to a premature end.

About midway through the Civil War, Abraham Lincoln made an extended tour to review the troops in the Union Army and to confer with his commanders. It was one of the few occasions in the course of the war when Lincoln was able to shed some of the pressures and responsibilities of his office. He returned to Washington after this tour, and a friend commented that he looked rested and more healthy. Lincoln replied that it had been "a great relief to get away from Washington and the politicians." Then he added, "But nothing touches the tired spot."[3]

That's the way it is when the wine gives out. Nothing touches the tired spot. Nothing really renews us. We give out and we run out.

It's that way for the family whose loved one is in the hospital. They huddle around the monitors, anxiously watching their displays, looking and willing the vital signs to remain stable. Their hope rises only to slide back down into despair. They ride the roller coaster up and down. They treat one problem only to have another develop. What else can go wrong? The wine has given out for them.

Talk to the young person who was brimming with dreams and aspirations. Eyes bright with possibilities. Now, even though she's smart and has a degree, she can't find a job. She's sent out dozens and dozens of resumes but has received no offers. She has to move back in with her parents. College-educated and forced to work in a burger joint. There are no dreams now, only cynicism. Her voice sounds much less enthusiastic. The wine has given out for her.

And what about the person who reaches middle age, whatever that is. He or she begins to realize that life no longer offers an endless stream of opportunities. There are fewer chances that doors will open. Instead of being able to make that desired change in life, they are stuck right where they are. Life is narrowing down. The wine is giving out.

It happens to all of us. The wine gives out, and what is meant to be a joyous celebration soon turns quiet, anxious, and empty. Whatever we have relied on to lend order, significance, and joy to our days suddenly runs out or proves woefully inadequate.

That's why we need to pay attention to what Jesus did here. He commanded the servants to take the six stone water pots used for the cleansing of utensils and the washing of hands, and to fill the jars with water, right up to the brim. He then commanded that some be drawn out and taken to the steward or headwaiter. When this man took a sip, it was not water, but fine wine. Water had become wine.

What's the significance of that? Jesus' turning water into wine is itself a picture of all that he came to do. Jesus took what is and said it has the possibility to become something else. What is can become something else. Just what you have on hand can be the main ingredient in the chemistry experiment he wants to work in your life. What is—whatever is tired, worn out, devoid of joy, empty, and lacking purpose—can be turned into something else. Something rich, fragrant, and ripe with the fullness of joy. What is, no matter how lifeless and stagnant, can be turned into something else by the power of Jesus. There's a lot of gospel in that for all of us. Jesus can bring new life. He can take whatever is stagnant and stale in your life, whatever has failed to live up to its potential, and renew it.

Where are you today? Are you out of wine? Are you drained of joy, hope, and delight? Do you feel the party may be on the verge of ending early? Jesus stands ready to transform and change your life. Believe. Commit your life to him and his way. Put your faith in him. And by his power, what is in your life can become something else.

Notes
1. Robert Fulghum, "All You Really Need to Know about Marriage You Learn at the Wedding," *Redbook*, June, 1989, p. 84.
2. Leon Morris, *The Gospel According to John* (Grand Rapids: Eerdmans, 1971), p. 179.
3. Shelby Foote, *The Civil War: Fredericksburg to Meridian* (New York: Vintage Books, 1963), p. 251.

COMMENT

"Things seem to go wrong at weddings." This is the opening sentence of William J. Ireland's sermon, "When the Wine Gives Out." It is a clever introduction to his text, Jesus at the wedding in Cana of Galilee (John 2:1–11). Who of us does not agree, even identify, with this statement? But more importantly, who of us does not agree with Ireland's main idea: "What's true of weddings is also true in life. Things just go wrong. The wine gives out for all of us"?

In succinct and pointed prose, Ireland tackles a question with which all people struggle. He capitalizes on one sure way of arousing an audience's attention, namely, preaching on a universal human problem. Ireland speaks to a very real and universally felt experience. All of us know what it feels like to "give out and run out."

Another distinctive quality of this sermon is its use of a provoking, intriguing, even controversial metaphor. Running through the sermon is the comparison between the wine at Cana and the wine of life. Just as the wine ran out at Cana, the wine of our lives can run dry too. I imagine this is not an image some preachers would readily embrace. Perhaps, it would even be inappropriate in some churches. Nevertheless, Ireland uses the word picture in a fresh, creative, and meaningful way.

THE OPENING

What better way to introduce the Cana wedding story than with a reflection on the problems often encountered at weddings? Ireland's opening introduces the context of Jesus' miracle of turning water to wine and helps bridge the historical/cultural gap of two thousand years. "Things just seem to go wrong at weddings," even weddings which Jesus attended two thousand years ago! We all understand and most of us can identify with Robert Fulghum's quote, "Weddings are rarely dull." Moreover, Ireland explains the importance of wine to a wedding in biblical times, an important and necessary point if the listener is to fully grasp the idea of the sermon.

Ireland's opening is good for another reason. It introduces the sermon's main point. Just like weddings, things in life go wrong. The comparison creates a concrete, tangible metaphor for listeners. Ireland is not interested in exploring the "why" question—why do things in life go awry? Instead, he focuses on the "what now" question. What do we do when our wine runs out, when we lose our ability to cope with life's difficulties?

TEXT & PROCLAMATION

Perhaps the greatest strength of this sermon is its creativity. It is built on an allegory of the biblical story. The wedding in Cana represents our lives and their inevitable problems: "Things just go wrong." The wine that gave out at the wedding represents our ability, or inability, to cope with life's problems: "The wine gives out for all of us." Jesus' turning the water into wine is the picture of what he does to our wineless lives. He takes the water of our life and makes it into something as rich, fragrant, and full as wine. "What is, no matter how lifeless and stagnant can be turned into something else by the power of Jesus."

One danger, of course, in allegorizing biblical stories is that there is a temptation to stray from the original author's intended message. We listen to ourselves rather than to the text. The biblical text can be sacrificed on the altar of creativity. We may end up with a highly creative, even God-centered sermon, but what we lose in the process is authenticity and integrity.

Ireland maintains the story's meaning and integrity in a fresh and lively way. Jesus performed the miracle at Cana to reveal his glory and to enable the disciples to put their faith in him (John 2:11). In other words, Jesus wanted to communicate who he was in order to bring people to faith. He continues to do this, and this is Ireland's point. "Jesus can bring new life…Jesus stands ready to transform and change your life." Like the disciples, we only need to believe. Ireland concludes, "Commit your life to him and his way. Put your faith in him. And by his power, what is in your life can become something else."

Another reason this sermon is effective is that it addresses a universal theme of human existence. At some point in life, every person comes to the realization that life is hard. It is tiring. It is disappointing. Who of us has not wrestled with these feelings? After all, "It happens to all of us." But what makes this idea come alive is Ireland's effort to make the abstract concrete. He dresses feelings in reality. He gives three real-life examples of the problem. The first is the emotional roller coaster of watching a loved one fight for life, when "hope rises only to slide back into despair." Next, a young person's dreams are smashed. The final example is at midlife when you realize life is narrowing. Each illustration builds on the other, creating tension, and begging for resolution.

In his conclusion, Ireland does not promise that a Christian's life is free of problems. He clearly asserts the opposite. "It happens to all of us. The wine gives out." What then is the solution? Jesus turns the water into wine. It is "a picture of all that he came to do." Just as wine consists mostly of water, and Jesus used the water to make wine, so in our lives Jesus uses what is already there and transforms it. Jesus gives us his grace that is sufficient for all circumstances.

RESPONSE

At the end of the sermon, Ireland asks several pointed questions. "Where are you today? Are you out of wine? Are you drained of joy, hope, and delight? Do you feel the party may be on the verge of ending early?" These questions challenge the listener to self-examination and honesty. The questions call for a change.

In the end we are reminded of the promises of God, the promises made real in Jesus Christ. "Jesus stands ready to transform and change your life.... And by his power, what is in your life can become something else." The sermon encourages us to remember Christ's promise made real through his miracle and the meaning of that promise in our own lives.

Suggestions

- Preach a sermon that utilizes allegory and metaphor.
- Think about the theme of this sermon. What other biblical texts speak of the change and renewal God brings in our lives? Identify some of these texts, explore them, and out of your exegesis, preach one or more sermons on them.
- Be concrete and specific. Always ask, How can this abstract idea become concrete in the imaginations and souls of my listeners? What stories of real people will make the abstract become concrete?
- Be realistic and relevant. We preach to real people, with real needs and problems, who need real solutions.

Karen F. Younger

Topical Index

Adversity
  When the Night Is Darkest 111
  When the Wine Gives Out 279
Age to Come
  Jesus' Final Exam 13
All Saints' Day
  Led by a Lamb 267
Angels
  Angels We Have Heard Nearby 79
Assumptions
  Jesus' Final Exam 13
Bargaining with God
  How Much More? 27
Beginnings
  Becoming What We Are 39
Bible
  Religious Closed-Mindedness 253
Calling
  The Text You Live By 67
Christian Faith
  A Letter to Harold 55
Church
  A Letter to Harold 55
Closed-Mindedness
  Religious Closed-Mindedness 253
Comfort
  A Comfort, Deep and Lasting 167
Commitment
  Stepping off the Curb 239
  Jesus the Rabbi? 95

Death
    All That Lives Must Die 137
Decision
    Stepping off the Curb 239
Denial
    All That Lives Must Die 137
    Becoming What We Are 39
Discipleship
    Jesus the Rabbi? 95
Easter
    Easter Fear 209
Failure
    Coming Up Short 123
Faith
    Easter Fear 209
    Stepping off the Curb 239
Fear
    Easter Fear 209
Freedom
    Freedom! 181
God, Goodness of
    Becoming What We Are 39
God, Identity of
    The Christic Journey 189
God, Love of
    A Crazy, Holy Grace 153
    Dealing with Negative Attitudes 225
    The Text You Live By 67
God, Presence of
    A Comfort, Deep and Lasting 167
    Angels We Have Heard Nearby 79
    Becoming What We Are 39
    The Christic Journey 189

TOPICAL INDEX

When the Night Is Darkest 111
God, Sovereignty of
    Jesus' Final Exam 13
Grace
    A Crazy, Holy Grace 153
    Coming Up Short 123
    How Much More? 27
Hatred
    Dealing with Negative Attitudes 225
Hope
    The Text You Live By 67
    When the Night Is Darkest 111
    When the Wine Gives Out 279
Incarnation
    The Christic Journey 189
Jesus
    A Letter to Harold 55
    Jesus the Rabbi? 95
Jonah
    Dealing with Negative Attitudes 225
Joseph
    All That Lives Must Die 137
Mystery
    Angels We Have Heard Nearby 79
Naaman
    How Much More? 27
Obligation
    Freedom! 181
Open-Mindedness
    Religious Closed-Mindedness 253
Palm Sunday
    Stepping off the Curb 239

Power
    Led by a Lamb 267
Pride
    Religious Closed-Mindedness 253
Questions
    Jesus' Final Exam 13
Racism
    Dealing with Negative Attitudes 225
Renewal
    When the Wine Gives Out 279
Responsibility
    Freedom! 181
Saints
    Led by a Lamb 267
Sin
    Coming Up Short 123
Suffering
    The Christic Journey 189
    Led by a Lamb 267
    When the Night Is Darkest 111
Transformation
    When the Wine Gives Out 279
Trust
    A Comfort, Deep and Lasting 167
    The Text You Live By 67
Vision
    The Text You Live By 67
Zacchaeus
    Coming Up Short 123

Scripture Index

Genesis 50:15–21 137
2 Kings 5:1–14 27
Psalm 103:1–14 39
Isaiah 40:1–2 167
Jonah 1–2 225
Matthew 16:13–28 137
Matthew 21:1–11 239
Mark 1:9–11 153
Mark 1:16–22 95
Mark 12:13–17 181
Mark 16:1–8 209
Luke 1:26–38 79
Luke 19:1–10 123
Luke 20:27–40 13
John 2:1–11 279
John 5:1–18, 39–47 253
Acts 16:16–26 111
Romans 3:23–24 123
Romans 8:28–30 67
2 Corinthians 4:6–12 39
2 Corinthians 5:17–18 39
Hebrews 11:29–12:2 189
1 John 5:1–5 55
Revelation 7:9–17 267